THE SOUTHERN ALBATROSS

THE SOUTHERN ALBATROSS

RACE AND ETHNICITY IN THE AMERICAN SOUTH

Edited by
Philip D. Dillard and Randal L. Hall

MERCER UNIVERSITY PRESS
1979 - 1999
TWENTY YEARS OF PUBLISHING EXCELLENCE

ISBN 0-86554-666-5   MUP/H200

Copyright ©1999
Mercer University Press, Macon, Georgia 31210-3960 USA
All rights reserved
Printed in the United States of America

Library of Congress Cataloging-in-Publication Data

The Southern Albatross: Race and Ethnicity in the American South/
edited by Philip D. Dillard and Randal L. Hall
    p. cm.
Includes bibliographical references and index.
ISBN 0-86554-666-5 (alk. paper)
    1. Southern States—Race relations—Congresses. 2. Southern
States—Ethnic   Relations—Congresses.   3.   Southern
States—Historiography—Congresses. I. Dillard, Philip D. II. Hall,
Randal L.

F220.A1 S68 1999
305.8'00975—dc21

                                                    99-043941

CONTENTS

INTRODUCTION

The albatross of race has long troubled the history of the American South. Like the Ancient Mariner described by Samuel Taylor Coleridge, the South also has to tell its many stories. Only as southerners explore the past and come to grips with racial and ethnic issues will the albatross begin to loosen its hold. At the Symposium on Southern History, held at Rice University in May 1997, fifteen graduate students and young faculty members presented their work. Many of the papers wrestled with these troubling and vital matters. Historians John B. Boles, Lacy Ford, Sylvia Frey, Howard Rabinowitz, and Emory Thomas provided valuable critical commentary that aided the participants in revising and sharpening their essays. This collection features the revised work of eight of these young scholars—all but one of whom were graduate students at the time of the symposium—and an epilogue by the eminent historian Donald G. Mathews.

The essays are grouped into four sections, each containing two articles, and will highlight the themes of race and ethnicity in the history of the American South. Some papers present these old topics from fresh perspectives, focusing on the region's cultural boundaries or on the recent past. Other essays offer new interpretations of perennially contested events in the South's troubled history. The epilogue evaluates these new findings in the context of the voluminous and important literature on the so-called central theme of southern history.

The first section, "Ethnic Conflict on the Southern Borderlands," analyzes the stormy relationship between Anglo settlers and American Indians during the mid-nineteenth century. " 'This Thankless . . . Unholy war': Army Officers and Civil-Military Relations in the Second Seminole War," by Samuel Watson, illuminates the views that Army officers and local settlers held of Seminole Indians and also the dissent within white groups. In the complex context of the professionalization of the American military, officers expressed respect for the Seminoles and disdain for the Florida settlers who eagerly anticipated the decimation of the Indians. Watson's paper relates well to Clayton E. Jewett's piece, "Establishing a Separate Identity: Texas's Offensive Struggle with the Indian Nations, 1861-1862." Jewett finds that Texans and Indians engaged in a series of heated encounters early in the Civil War despite a treaty of alliance between the Confederacy and the Five Organized Tribes. He details the bloody nature of the exchanges and shows that although Texans regarded the Indian tactics as savage, the Anglos employed similar brutal measures. Jewett concludes that the willingness of the Confederacy to ally with the Indians stood in sharp contrast to the ethnic conceptions of most Texans and significantly weakened the commitment of Texans to their new Confederate government. The irony of Texans and Native Americans facing a changing world, both groups feeling that they must fight against long odds to retain their way of life, provides a compelling example of the complexity of the Civil War.

The second section, "Development of African American Identity in the Reconstruction South," examines social and political struggles by blacks in two diverse regions of the South. David H. McGee's " 'I Have Never Been Free and I Am Goin' to Try It': The Development of Black Families in Wake County, North Carolina, 1865-1870," looks at blacks' search for stable family lives by examining their efforts to establish legal marriages and their attempts to construct homes. Wake County mixes urban and rural areas, and McGee takes historiographical arguments in a new direction by showing that black families in the rural districts had stronger nuclear families than the blacks in Raleigh. James D. Wilson Jr. looks at a very different area of the South in " 'A Bitterness of Feelings': Black Intra-Race Relations in Civil War and Early Reconstruction Louisiana." After summarizing the three-tiered social structure uniquely prevalent in antebellum Louisiana, Wilson details the changing historical understanding of the stormy relationship between freed slaves and elitist, former free persons of color who after emancipation were left without clear distinction from the mass of freedpeople. The article climaxes with the campaign for governor in 1868 in which former free persons of color lost control of the Republican party to a coalition of carpetbaggers and former slaves, ending the traditional power and leadership of the free people of color. Analyzing two disparate regions, the two articles together reveal the urgency with which black southerners seized freedom.

The next section, "Ethnicity, Gender, and Violence in the South," similarly uses intensive mining of fresh sources to cast new light on old debates. Angela Boswell's essay, "The Social Acceptability of Nineteenth-Century Domestic Violence," focuses on the unique ethnic blend of women with African American, Anglo, and German identities in Colorado County, Texas, between 1837 and 1873. She canvasses court records to demonstrate the progressively greater relief that juries granted to abused women through the cruelty clause of the state's divorce law. However, Boswell perceptively notes that German women and black women were less likely than Anglo women to receive favorable court action. Her fresh analysis posits that nativist judges and jurors linked alcohol and violence to the German community, viewing a higher level of violence as natural among Germans who consistently opposed Anglo advocacy of temperance. In " 'A Thing So Illogical' in Georgia: Reconsidering Race, Myth, and the Lynching of Leo Frank," Stephen A. Brown also explores the role of ethnicity in questions of legal justice. He shifts the emphasis in the study of the Leo Frank case away from the courtroom drama and onto the broader question of the myths about Jews that circulated among white Protestants in Georgia. Within the southern culture of honor, Brown argues, beliefs about Jewish sexual appetite, monetary influence, and the alien nature of their "race" worked first to convict Frank, then to justify his death. These two essays reveal the ethnic complexities of a southern society too often depicted only in black and white.

The final section, "The Enduring Significance of Race and Ethnicity in the Modern South," contains two groundbreaking essays that intricately examine events of the recent past. In "The City It Always Wanted to Be: The Child Murders and the Coming of Age of Atlanta," Nancy Lopez uses oral interviews, trial records, and press reports to analyze the series of murders of black children in Atlanta between 1979 and 1981. She investigates the racial mistrust surrounding the murders and the conviction of a black suspect in the context of race relations, black political office holding, and the city's boosterism during the 1970s. Jeff Roche's "Asa/Forrest Carter and Regional/Political Identity" probes Carter's deft transformation of ethnic identity from white Ku Klux Klan organizer and speech writer for George Wallace to American Indian and author of the best-selling, supposedly autobiographical story of a Cherokee child. Roche's article presents this story in full for the first time by utilizing oral interviews, files from the Federal Bureau of Investigation, and editorial correspondence. The resulting portrait of the modern South suggests that the albatross still clings firmly around the neck of the modern South (and of the entire nation).

Despite analyzing a wide variety of times, groups, and areas within the South, the essays of this collection work together to broaden in many directions the discussion of racial and ethnic turmoil and subtleties. Uniting the different viewpoints is the burgeoning realization by historians that constant negotiation and renegotiation determine the protean boundaries of race and ethnicity at any particular time and place. Only at the level of detailed case studies is this fact most fully apparent. Soldiers, Seminoles, and farmers in Florida in the 1830s inhabited a world that differed greatly from that of Asa/Forrest Carter, but in both instances, racial and ethnic sympathies and identities varied and evolved as the cultural and social settings changed.

These essays contribute to several fields, including legal, cultural, military, and women's history, while exploring important questions of race and ethnicity in a variety of times and places within the South. Together they are an important addition to the ongoing discussion in the South and the nation about the importance of race and ethnic identity, a story that must be told and retold if the South is ever to overcome the legacy of hatred and mistrust among its diverse groups that has been its albatross from its beginning.

I.

ETHNIC CONFLICT ON THE SOUTHERN BORDERLANDS

1

"THIS THANKLESS . . . UNHOLY WAR": ARMY OFFICERS AND CIVIL-MILITARY RELATIONS IN THE SECOND SEMINOLE WAR

Samuel Watson

The scene was Florida, the year 1838, the author a career soldier, his medium the army's only professional journal. The army had just won its largest battlefield victory of the war, but something continued to trouble this veteran:

> The present state of affairs cannot exist much longer; the army is becoming daily more dissatisfied, and justly so; and if some hope of receiving justice . . . is not shortly held out to them, the country will find . . . that it must look elsewhere for the courage, energy, and devotion, heretofore so repeatedly displayed in contending against a foe, whose defeat brings with it neither honor nor reward.[1]

The southern borderlands were an arena for conflicts not only between whites and Indians, but between whites with different interests and values. Modern scholarship warns us to be conscious of the ethnicity of dominant as well as marginalized groups; this essay attempts to complicate our visions of interethnic relations in the

---

[1]"Sheer Justice," "Battle of the Okee-Chobee—The Army," in the *Army and Navy Chronicle* (hereafter ANC) 6 (March 8, 1838): 154. This privately published weekly was the army's only professional journal between 1836 and 1842; contributors normally wrote pseudonymously.

southern borderlands by assessing army officers' attitudes toward other whites, whose interests they supposedly served and to whom they were politically accountable, as well as Indians. This essay explores the sources and extent of officers' discontent during the Second Seminole War, the forms and circumstances in which it was expressed, and the significance for American civil-military relations. Monolithic stereotypes about federal officials and Jacksonian Indian policy quickly become suspect when viewed through the prism of the regular army officer corps in Florida: no army officers joined the Seminoles in their resistance to American aggression, but many questioned the war's motivation, and virtually all of those who wrote on the conflict questioned its desirability and the effectiveness of the means used to fight it. The onset of war in 1835 proved the catalyst for an unprecedented wave of resignations from the army: over two hundred officers resigned between 1835 and 1837, 117 in 1836 alone—nearly eighteen percent of the entire officer corps, in an era when an average of only twenty officers (less than four percent of the corps) resigned per annum. Throughout the war commanders constantly pursued leaves of absence to avoid service in Florida, quarreling with civilians, politicians, and citizen-soldiers to the point that many seemed to prefer the Seminoles to the white citizens they were charged with "defending."[2]

Indeed, the army officer corps ultimately became a force for peace in Florida, though this came too late for hundreds of dead combatants and thousands of deported Seminoles. Faced with the Seminoles' unyielding determination, by 1838 few officers believed that the war was worth its cost in lives, political capital, or, perhaps most importantly for individual soldiers, personal inconvenience. The collision between the corps' quest for occupational security, its search for social and political order, and the frustrating circumstances of its service in Florida led many commanders to question where their duties and

---

[2]Edward M. Coffman, *The Old Army: A Portrait of the American Army in Peacetime, 1784-1898* (New York, 1986), 52, and William B. Skelton, *An American Profession of Arms: The Army Officer Corps, 1784-1861* (Lawrence, 1992), 216. The number of resignations exceeded forty in only one other year between 1820 and 1860.

responsibilities as public servants lay—to ask to whom they were primarily accountable in their professional practice. These doubts recurred throughout the conflict, while the army's professional journal mirrored officers' disgruntlement in the most extensive debates ever published in its pages. In the end, the war was halted before a complete victory had been won, largely because the military commanders in charge of negotiations convinced the government that the chance of success was not worth the cost of continued fighting. Until that point was reached, a compound of political neutrality (the product of an ethos of disinterested professional subordination to the civilian political authority that represented the national interest), group cohesion, and self-interested careerism sustained the officer corps' allegiance to the policy and practice of Seminole removal.

It would be grossly inaccurate to portray the officer corps as a countercultural force resisting American aggression, but neither were the regulars the mercenary automatons feared by civilian critics of standing armies. Indeed, some readers might see a principled group driven to oppose the dominant Jacksonian ideology of ethnic chauvinism and racist expansion, and might then interpret Jacksonian critiques of the regular officer corps as evidence that civilian expansionists distrusted the army's eagerness to serve their ends, a much more valid conclusion than the predicate. Individual officers felt moral qualms about their duties, and many thought that the nation's honor had been tarnished by the faithlessness of its Indian policies, but the officer corps' interest in peace was complex and ambiguous in motive and expression. Officers' antagonism toward white settlers preceded and outweighed any antipathy they developed for the Seminoles, and the former sentiment appeared in many soldiers who felt nothing but hatred and contempt for the "savage" foe: the officer corps' attitudes toward frontier whites were much more uniform, and uniformly negative, than those toward its designated opponents. The point of this essay is not that army officers were moral paragons ahead of their time, but that the specific situation in which their mission placed them produced a remarkable degree of alienation from the government and society they were paid to serve. The Seminole war brought repressed grievances to the forefront of American civil-military relations by casting a spotlight on the contested meanings of public service and the officer corps' distinctive values as an professionalizing group. Ultimately, however, the experience strengthened the corps' commitment to serving the national government, and these tensions would not recur with equal intensity until 1861.[3]

The men who resigned did so for essentially personal reasons, be they health, isolation from wife and family, or more attractive opportunities outside the army. The timing of the Second Seminole War gave added impetus to all these traditional motives for resignation, for the conflict began amidst an economic boom and a sustained political assault on the army, but neither partisan nor ideological dissent were primary factors influencing any of the resignations for which information is available. Demoralization and discontent became pervasive as the war ground on into 1838 and 1839, but the wave of resignations peaked in 1836 and receded to normal levels by 1838, as civilian opportunities dried up amid economic depression. Rather than emphasizing the anger soldiers felt toward the Seminoles, a reaction we expect, my essay concentrates on exploring their mixed feelings toward their civilian employers and "clients," especially the local citizenry, and the policies the army was ordered to carry out.

---

[3]See Thomas C. Leonard, "Red, White, and the Army Blue: Empathy and Anger in the American West," *American Quarterly* 26 (May 1974): 176-90, for a superb depiction of these tensions (especially the psychological ones) in the post-Civil War era. Leonard notes that he was unable to find an officer who had resigned because of moral qualms. See Skelton, *An American Profession of Arms*, ch. 16, and idem., "Army Officers' Attitudes towards Indians, 1830-1860," *Pacific Northwest Quarterly* 67 (July 1976): 113-24, concerning army officers' attitudes toward Amerindians and "Indian warfare" before the Civil War; Sherry L. Smith's attention to the nuances of postbellum attitudes in *The View from Officers' Row: Army Perceptions of Western Indians* (Tucson, 1990) has no parallel for the antebellum era. See Michael Paul Rogin, *Fathers and Children: Andrew Jackson and the Subjugation of the American Indian* (New York, 1975) and Ronald N. Satz, *American Indian Policy in the Jacksonian Era* (Lincoln, 1974) for context, and James W. Covington, *The Seminoles of Florida* (Gainesville, 1993); Edwin C. McReynolds, *The Seminoles* (Norman, 1957); and J. Leitch Wright Jr., *Creeks and Seminoles: Destruction and Regeneration of the Muscogulge People* (Lincoln, 1986) for narratives of "Seminole" history.

What were the sources and limitations of officers' disenchantment with war and removal? What sort of conflicts fostered officers' antagonism toward civilian settlers and citizen-soldiers, so often in contrast to their admiration for the Seminoles? How much of their discontent was with the circumstances, how much with the methods, and how much with the ends for which the war was fought? How did embittered regulars balance their feelings of alienation with subordination to civilian political authority, and why was this unrest virtually absent during the Mexican War several years later? In other words, what did the officer corps learn from the Seminole conflict, not in the realm of tactics or strategy, but in that of civil-military relations: what role did their experience play in the development of their accountability to civilian authority?

The Second Seminole War was the longest continual "Indian war" in U.S. history. Over nearly seven years (from December 1835 to June 1842), the army suffered 1,466 deaths, 328 of them in combat, a fourteen percent mortality rate among the regular forces stationed there. The situation was all the more frustrating because the army's commanders knew from the outset that the war would be a difficult one—after his unsuccessful campaign in 1836, Brigadier General Winfield Scott warned the public that "it [will] continue . . . to be the policy of the enemy to remain scattered in small parties and to avoid a general battle—thereby protracting the war almost indefinitely." This pattern was clear to officers of all ranks and experience, and a much more junior soldier expressed the growing consensus that chasing after the Indians "to capture or give them battle [is] useless and absurd."[4] In February 1838, six weeks after the battle at Lake Okeechobee (the largest since early in 1836), surgeon Thomas Henderson observed that "should [the Indians stand and]

---

[4]Statistics in John K. Mahon, *History of the Second Seminole War, 1835-1842* (Gainesville, 1967), 325; Brigadier General Scott to Capt. F. M. Robertson of the Augusta (Ga.) Volunteers, May 26, 1836, published in *ANC* 2 (June 16, 1836): 380; "Florida War," *ANC* 8 (March 10, 1839): 155. Mahon provides the standard modern narrative on the war; the only full-length contemporary account was army captain John T. Sprague's *The Origins, Progress, and Conclusion of the Florida War* (1848, reprinted Gainesville, 1964).

fight the result cannot be doubted," but the Seminoles continued to disperse into small bands, avoiding the army unless conditions seemed favorable for an ambush or surprise attack. Some of his comrades estimated that fewer than 200 hostile warriors remained in Florida, but Henderson believed that the Seminoles were unbeaten, lamenting that "no human mind can discern the probable termination of this war." Theater commander Thomas Sidney Jesup shared these doubts and declared a truce while he asked the War Department to allow the Indians to remain in southern Florida. The truce failed, however, and in 1839 another surgeon estimated the war would take five or ten more years.[5]

Repeating a seemingly endless cycle of advances and pursuits, occasionally catching a Seminole or two while seizing their cattle and burning their villages and crops, each operation came to seem much like the others, spurring frustration, disillusionment, and discontent. In 1841 Captain John Clark asserted that the war would go on "so long as there [are] one hundred warriors in this country"; nearly a year later Captain Michael Clark feared "there [would] be no end to it." Indeed, the army never completed its assigned task in Florida, for despite the efforts of seven different theater commanders (including such luminaries of the army as Jesup, William Worth, and Zachary Taylor) and the adoption of several strategic plans, the conflict did not end until the War Department allowed the army to cease operations, with several hundred Seminoles still remaining, in June 1842. Several theater commanders, and from all available evidence the majority of the officer corps as a whole, had sought such an armistice since 1838, when one weary veteran had concluded that

---

[5]Assistant Surgeon Thomas Henderson to Assistant Surgeon Benjamin King, February 6 and 13, 1838, Benjamin King Papers, Library of Congress Manuscript Division (hereafter given as LC); Jesup to Secretary of War Poinsett, February 11, 1838, in Sprague, *The Origin, Progress, and Conclusion of the Florida War*, 199-201; "On the Florida War," ANC 9 (November 7, 1839): 291. I will refer to the senior commander in Florida as the "theater commander," although this was an ad hoc post created by the president's choice rather than a permanent position in the army hierarchy. There were less than 5000 "Seminoles," including allied Indian ethnicities and blacks of varied ethnicities and sociolegal status, throughout Florida.

"We are . . . really 'licked' and that's the long and short of it. . . . God and nature have interposed such obstacles as man cannot surmount. I for one feel humiliated at this confession and would rather have perished than live to make it—but it is true—we cannot [beat] these Indians." The war's duration prompted Captain George Pegram to joke uneasily with Robert Anderson: "Think not, my dear Capt[ain], that we shall leave nothing undone for you. There will be plenty of game left to hunt up, for years yet to come . . . and the bones of many will yet bleach upon these unhealthy shores, before it is ended."[6]

The danger and discomfort were not ameliorated by the consolations of family to which most officers had been accustomed in the static posts they occupied before the war. Between the Seminoles, the heat, and the malaria, few officers would bring their wives to Florida, so many regarded their service as "banishment." Unmarried officers also felt this isolation: even before the war Lieutenant Morris Smith Miller wrote to his sister Sarah that "I would prefer any other post, as far as society is concerned," for he considered himself "entirely out of the world." Not much changed during the six years that followed: Florida seemed the embodiment of "a howling wilderness, the proper abode of Owls and bats and Snakes . . . savage things all, in a savage land"—one hardly worthy of the sacrifices of gentlemen eager to serve their country. As 1841 drew to a close Captain Nathaniel Hunter sounded a doleful refrain: "Here we are on Christmas night twenty-six miles from Tampa with the eternal forest around us and nothing but Indians and wolves . . . what a holiday it has been. I doubt that I will ever forget it."[7]

---

[6]Captains J[ohn B.] Clark and M[ichael] M. Clark to Benjamin King, May 18, 1841 and February 17, 1842, King Papers, LC; "On the Florida War," ANC 9 (November 7, 1839): 291; letter to Benjamin King, February 10, 1838, King Papers, LC (author's name illegible); Pegram to Anderson, February 3, 1841, Robert Anderson Papers, LC.

[7]Lt. Charles E. Woodruff (who was unmarried) to James Banks, June 25, 1839, Charles E. Woodruff Papers, U.S. Army Military Historical Institute, Carlisle Barracks, Pa. (hereafter given as USAMHI) ("banishment"); Morris Miller to Sarah Miller, April 29, 1835, Morris M. Miller Papers, United States Military Academy Library, Special Archives (hereafter given as USMA); Assistant Surgeon Lewis Birdsall to Benjamin King, July 17, 1841, King Papers, LC; Hunter, Diary, I, p. 126, in Reynold M. Wik, "Captain Nathaniel Wyche Hunter and

Under these circumstances postings to Florida were a subject of constant conflict between officers and their civil and military superiors, one in which junior officers often had the upper hand because of the shortage of men willing and qualified to take their places if they resigned. (The size of the officer corps actually declined some ten percent due to the resignations in 1836, an unprecedented event for a year in which its authorized size was not reduced.) Field commanders routinely planned to avoid summer duty by securing leaves of absence, and a number of officers threatened to resign if not given leave. This aggressive pursuit of self-interest, so far removed from the career officer's avowed ethos of public service and duty, forced the government to adjust its personnel policies. In one such compromise, Lieutenant Joseph R. Smith gained relief by appealing directly to the commanding general (bypassing his company, regimental, and theater commanders). He received leave and was then posted on recruiting duty in New York state, gaining a total of nearly twenty months to rest and recuperate before being sent back to Florida.[8]

The most important spur to officers' frustration was potentially more "political," the "ignominy" of what several soldiers publicly labeled "this inglorious war." Such discontent proceeded from two sources: the officer corps' distaste for the "drudgery" of Indian-fighting and their realization that there was little public acclaim to be won in return for their sacrifices. Jungle skirmishes did not fit the conventional image of Napoleonic battle that permeated officers' socialization and civilian ideas of warfare; patrols and convoy escorts were unlikely scenes for winning reputation and fame. Veteran soldiers quickly came to respect the Seminoles as determined fighters, but they remained disenchanted with their work because ethnocentric civilians refused to recognize the Seminoles' valor (or, on the part of many northerners and Whigs, to accept removal and war as morally

---

the Florida Indian Campaigns, 1837-1841," *Florida Historical Quarterly* (hereafter cited as *FHQ*) 39 (July 1960): 69 (n. 30).

[8]Skelton, *An American Profession of Arms*, 136 (Figure 7.1); Lt. Joseph R. Smith to his wife Juliet, March 6, 1838, in "Letters from the Second Seminole War," ed. John K. Mahon, *FHQ* 36 (April 1958): 338-42.

legitimate endeavors), or by extension that of the officer corps. Officers socialized in Napoleonic visions of grandeur reacted by belittling their tasks: "Very little [glory] could have been gained in the best possible issue of the war, against so small and miserable a race of Indians." Watching sweating troops swing pick and shovel to build roads and forts for the 1839 campaign, another veteran looked ahead to tending the sick that summer and sarcastically observed that "this is warfare! glorious, noble, chivalrous warfare!"[9]

Glory and reputation were rewards that could only come from civilian society. Officers praised each others' gallantry at every turn, but it was public recognition they were looking for, and this was hard to come by in a guerrilla war against Indians in Jacksonian America. The army officer corps faced constant criticism from opponents of West Point and supporters of the volunteers and militia during the 1830s and 1840s. In addition, the rash of resignations in 1836 reinforced popular Democratic beliefs that career officers were lazy place-seekers. At the same time, the army in Florida frequently came into conflict with local settlers who sought military protection without accepting the need for any sort of discipline or constraint, which they labeled "unrepublican." In turn, the regulars considered most white Floridians greedy cowards unworthy of officers' sacrifices. This attitude reflected views which had developed long before the war, and they quickly became evident at the very top of the army hierarchy: after the panic that followed the Dade Massacre at the outbreak of the war, Winfield Scott publicly excoriated the planters of Florida for

---

[9]Hunter, Diary, I, p. 130, in "Captain Nathaniel Wyche Hunter and the Florida Indian Campaigns," 69 ("ignominy"); "Florida War," ANC 7 (August 16, 1838): 105; "Quasi Major," "The Seminole War" [a public letter addressed to the Secretary of War], ANC 7 (October 18, 1838): 249; "A Subaltern of the 7th," "The Seventh Infantry," ANC 9 (August 22, 1839): 116; Lt. Thomas Boylston Adams to Major Rufus Lathrop Baker, April 12, 1836, Rufus Lathrop Baker Papers, USMA ("drudgery"); "Agricola," "The Army," ANC 5 (October 26, 1837): 267; "A Subaltern," "Florida War—No. 3," ANC 8 (February 21, 1839): 124. The first three citations from the ANC all use the term "inglorious." See Skelton, An American Profession of Arms, 255-56, 318-25, and 346-47, regarding the officer corps' lack of interest in Indian-fighting. The lack of attention to this subject was the greatest practical weakness of the West Point curriculum.

their "infinitely humiliating" exodus to the neighboring towns and states. "The inhabitants could see nothing but an Indian under every bush," he claimed, contrasting their behavior with that of the army and warning that "no General . . . can cure a disease in the public mind, so general and so degrading, without some little effort on the part of the people themselves." Rather than adopting the "manly course" of self-defense, they had unjustly vilified "the general [Scott] who has the misfortune to command a handful of brave troops in the midst of such a population."[10]

Civil-military strife had always been common in frontier regions, where soldiers were often charged with restraining squatters and enforcing regulations against selling liquor to the Indians, and there had been friction between soldiers and settlers since the acquisition of Florida in 1821. Civilians considered the army's enlisted men scum, its officers effete aristocrats or petty tyrants. Soldiers and officers returned the civilians' contempt in full measure, and the duration of the war intensified this acrimony. One officer wrote that "the iniquity of the people in this country is a frightful thing and . . . their code of morals is sunk [extremely] low," and officers up to and including General Jesup began to complain that whites were supplying the Seminoles and fomenting or taking advantage of the chaos in order to enrich themselves: in 1841 a captain asserted that whites "are doing more to keep [the war] up than the Indians. . . . I believe that two-thirds of the recent murders have [been] committed by the whites themselves." An anonymous veteran wrote to the *Army and Navy Chronicle* with an astoundingly tactless solution:

> The war can never be ended until the savages are cut off from supplies; they will be joined by whites, and I only wonder that more do not join the marauders. There never was a better theatre for land piracy than Florida is now. . . . I would advise that an appropriation be made for hemp, to hang a squad of

---

[10]Scott, Order No. 48, May 17, 1836, in ANC 2 (June 16, 1836): 379.

pale-faces, who infest the country much more to its detriment
than [any] troop of red-skins.

He concluded with a telling reference to Andrew Jackson's drumhead
court-martials in 1818: "It would have a good effect to Ambristerize
a few of them." But in 1837 the supposed traitors were U.S. citizens
whose interests the army was charged with advancing, not foreign
infiltrators stirring up resistance to American expansion.[11]

Some junior commanders took matters into their own hands and
had civilians imprisoned or whipped, while others looked on with tacit
approval when soldiers under their command retaliated against
civilian attackers. Florida grand juries constantly brought in "findings"
of military "incompetence," and theater commanders Jesup and
Taylor both sought but were refused relief from their posts due to
civilian criticism. Such antagonism came to a perversely logical
conclusion in September 1842, when Lieutenant Colonel Josiah Vose,
the acting theater commander, refused to execute War Department
orders to resume operations against the Seminoles, blaming "vagabond classes" among the whites for any ongoing unrest. (It should be
noted that Zachary Taylor displayed similar doubts about civilian
rumors of Cherokee aggression in the Indian Territory that winter.)
The War Department ultimately tended to sympathize with the army
in these disputes, because it had to perform the same sort of balancing
acts between local and national considerations, and reprimanding the
army would have brought discredit on the national government.
Indeed, the department not only agreed with Vose—who had warned
four years before that whites were always the aggressors in conflicts

---

[11]"Allen" (probably Capt. George W. Allen) to Capt. Samuel P. Heintzelman, August
9, 1840, Samuel P. Heintzelman Papers, Box 6, LC; Mahon, *History of the Second Seminole
War*, 298 and 203; Capt. J[ohn B.] Clark to Benjamin King, May 18, 1841, King Papers, LC;
letter, ANC 11 (August 27, 1840): 137.

with Indians—but ordered him to defend the Seminoles against white attack.[12]

The conflict between local settlers and the army was mirrored by that between professional and citizen soldiers. Large numbers of volunteers from throughout the southeast were called up to supplement the regulars, and there was constant conflict between them. White Floridians continually sought to embody new militia companies, whether for protection or employment (the federal government paid in scarce specie, a motive professional officers were quick to point out, and of course to share), while regular commanders argued that amateurs were a hindrance to military operations and an unjustifiable expense to the Treasury. Controversies over the conduct of the volunteers arose after every battle or campaign, as both sides criticized one another for indecisiveness or lack of courage. Colonel Duncan Clinch, the senior army officer in Florida at the outbreak of the war, initially praised territorial governor Call and the volunteers but almost immediately became embroiled in a dispute with the governor over their performance at the Withlacochee River on December 31, 1835 (the first major engagement after the Dade Massacre), where Clinch believed that they had hesitated to aid the regulars. Call responded with militarily sound arguments that Clinch had exercised insufficient caution by placing his troops in an isolated position, but the professionals found this explanation unsatisfying after a battle in which fifty-two of the fifty-nine wounded and all four of the dead soldiers had been regulars. These tensions persisted as

---

[12]James M. Denham, " 'Some Prefer the Seminoles': Violence and Disorder Among Soldiers and Settlers in the Second Seminole War, 1835-1842," *FHQ* 70 (July 1991): 43 and 45-47; Mahon, *History of the Second Seminole War*, 259 and 316-17; Vose to Adjutant General Roger Jones, April 13, 1838, House Executive Document 434, 25th Congress, 2nd session, 3. The War Department issued frequent, albeit largely ineffectual, orders that the army protect the Seminoles during periods of truce; see e.g. Chester L. Kieffer, *Maligned General: The Biography of Thomas Sidney Jesup* (San Rafael, Ca., 1979), 169. See Lt. Col. Ethan Allen Hitchcock to Secretary of War John C. Spencer, March 20, 1842, Ethan Allen Hitchcock Papers, LC, and Taylor to Adjutant General Jones, December 23, 1842 and March 28, 1843, cited in Brainerd Dyer, *Zachary Taylor* (Baton Rouge, 1946), pp. 138-40, for their skeptical responses to rumors of Cherokee uprisings.

long as the volunteers were employed on a large scale: discussing the battle of Wahoo Swamp two years later, Lieutenant John W. Phelps told his father that General Armstrong of the volunteers "refused to charge the hummock with his command because it embraced a large number of young men of the choicest families of Tennessee." The greatest of these controversies came when Colonel Zachary Taylor drew the ire of Missouri senators Thomas Hart Benton and Lewis Linn for his letter damning the apathy of the Missouri volunteers at the Battle of Okeechobee.[13]

Professional officers felt that the volunteers routinely left the regulars to do the actual fighting and dying, showing "a decided preference [for] the post of safety, rather than the path of honor," yet, knowing their culture, many feared that the volunteers would still receive whatever credit could be gained. One anonymous correspondent to the *Army and Navy Chronicle* contrasted the "manful" stand of the regulars with the volunteers' "base" retreat at Okeechobee, while another veteran told a friend that "it is said that the Genl [Taylor, the future president] put his pistol to the head of an officer of the Missipians [sic] and told him he would blow his brains out if he did not force his men over" a creek in support of the regulars. Thomas Henderson summed up this critique in a letter to his comrade Benjamin King: "in all [the battles] the regulars have done the fighting—in all the irregulars have been false—leaving the honor and the loss chiefly to the army."[14]

---

[13]Mahon, *History of the Second Seminole War*, 109-111, 184-85, and 227-29; Rembert W. Patrick, *Aristocrat in Uniform: General Duncan L. Clinch* (Gainesville, 1963), 97; Phelps to his father John, July 10, 1837, in "Letters of Lieutenant John W. Phelps, U.S.A., 1837-1838," *FHQ* 6 (October 1927): 75. See also George C. Bittle, "The Florida Militia's Role in the Battle of Withlacoochee," *FHQ* 44 (April 1966): 303-311. Clinch owned a plantation in Florida, where he had been stationed continuously since 1816, and he seems to have absorbed some of the attitudes of the local settlers: on the eve of the war he criticized their motives but declared that removal was both inevitable and a general good (Patrick, 73-74).

[14]"Sheer Justice," "Battle of the Okee-Chobee—The Army," *ANC* 6 (March 8, 1838): 154; "The Army," *ANC* 6 (February 15, 1838): 108-109; letter to Benjamin King, February 10, 1838, King Papers, LC (author's name illegible; presumably he meant "Missourians"); Henderson to King, February 13, 1838, King Papers, LC.

The nation's admiration for the citizen-soldier ideal also threatened the officer corps' occupational monopoly over the direction of American military force. The larger political dimensions of the regulars' uneasy relations with the volunteers were evident in their repeated calls for an enlargement of the army (which would also produce faster promotions and higher pay), in order to dispense with the volunteers and militia altogether. "Sheer Justice" carried this logic farther than most officers by publicly blaming Congress's failure to expand the army for the dire consequences supposedly produced by mixing regulars and volunteers, arguing that "the blood that has flowed so freely is to be charged to their account" (rather, apparently, than to that of the officers in command). Another correspondent to the *Army and Navy Chronicle* sneered that the Seminoles could never be subdued by "volunteers, whose lives are so valuable," and he lambasted the citizen-soldiers as "fit [only] to take up arms for political effect, at the expense of the nation."[15]

More politically astute, Winfield Scott attempted to ease this bad blood by establishing a clear and common chain of command based on the principles of rank and seniority. His "Order No. 1" to the Army of Florida emphasized that "every junior will obey any senior . . . whether the parties belong to the militia, or to the Marines and Regular Army," but regular officers frequently refused orders from higher-ranking volunteers, implicitly denying the legitimacy of their locally and politically derived commissions. Indeed, Lieutenant Colonel William Foster threatened to resign if forced to serve a second time under volunteer Colonel Leigh Read, while Duncan Clinch failed to act on an order from Scott to relieve a besieged blockhouse containing fifty Florida militiamen, later citing a shortage of troops as justification. Clinch may have believed that the "siege" was a figment of jumpy civilian imaginations, or that they could break

---

[15]"Sheer Justice," 155; "Canard," "Florida War," ANC 11 (July 30, 1840): 67. See also "Gen. Taylor, and the Missouri Volunteers," ANC 8 (April 11, 1839): 236, and "Mentor" (untitled letter), ANC 9 (October 17, 1839): 246, whose extensive critique included the unjust accusation that the volunteers fled "at the commencement of the battle" of Okeechobee.

it on their own with a little initiative and aggressiveness rather than wearing down his men with a relief march, but the siege lasted for forty-eight days before Read led a volunteer force to its relief. (Clinch resigned that fall, though it is unclear whether he was passed over for or had refused theater command; he later served a term as congressman from Georgia.) Most disturbingly, an anonymous group proclaiming themselves "Many Officers of the Army" appealed publicly to the attorney general in opposition to Governor Call's appointment as theater commander in November 1836, on the legal grounds that Call was a civilian with neither army nor militia rank. These professionals questioned whether the president's appointment was "a lawful order," asking if Call could "be held amenable to any military tribunal" (i.e., a court-martial) if accused of misconduct. Surprisingly, Jackson relieved Call from command within the month, replacing him with Quartermaster General Thomas Jesup, to whom Call had offered the command in September. (Diplomatically, Jesup had chosen to serve under Call until the governor had had the chance to prove himself.) The friction between Call and the army over raising and commanding local militia units eventually became so great that President Van Buren dismissed the governor from his civil post in 1839. The following June the army command tried to diminish the new governor's influence by requesting that he be required to route his communications to officers through the War Department.[16]

Much of the antagonism between regulars, volunteers, and civilians originated in their stereotypes about each other and their beliefs about the proper character of American soldiers. Career

---

[16]Scott, "Order No. 1," ANC 2 (March 17, 1836): 168; Mahon, 113, 159-60, 171, 179, 264, and 279; "Many Officers of the Army," (reprinted from the *National Intelligencer*, without date therefrom) ANC 3 (November 3, 1836): 285. Scott's order to the Army of Florida also reminded the volunteers that "valor and patriotism alone, are not sufficient . . . . Some tactical instruction and an exact obedience to commands, are also necessary." See also Patrick, *Aristocrat in Uniform*, chapters. 7-8; Tom Knotts, "History of the Blockhouse on the Withlacoochee," *FHQ* 49 (January 1971): 245-55; and Herbert J. Doherty, *Richard Keith Call, Southern Unionist* (Gainesville, 1961), chapter 7. Regular officers made few distinctions between the volunteers and militia, and since this is a paper about officers' perceptions I have followed their practice.

officers found volunteers, like the settler population they came from, "mercenary" and self-centered, "rapacious men who come for plunder [and] negroes, and run as soon as an Indian fires a rifle at them." Citizen-soldiers lacked "military discipline and subordination"; they had "no confidence in each other or in themselves," in contrast to the cohesion, moral stamina, and esprit de corps that professional troops developed while serving together for long periods under strict discipline. The volunteers' weaknesses provided regular officers with their most felicitous explanation for the war's unexpected duration: after the battle of Okeechobee Thomas Henderson concluded that "if the Missouri men had done their duty, that battle . . . would have produced results." The regulars were not to blame.[17]

Winfield Scott was careful to praise the volunteers, but the professional officer's division of military labor lay implicit in his disingenuous disclaimer that "it would be unreasonable to call on the gallant and patriotic to volunteer . . . where nothing but hardship and suffering can be expected, unrelieved by the hope of battle and the glory consequent upon victory." More than one officer suggested a compromise, usually by enlisting backwoodsmen as light infantry under regular command, but this satisfied neither side and was never tried. Ultimately only fifty-five of the 30,000 volunteers and militia who served in the war were killed in action, as opposed to 328 out of 10,000 regulars, numbers that suggest both the effectiveness of the regular monopoly and the volunteers' willingness to grant the regulars their wish.[18]

---

[17]Henderson to Benjamin King, February 6 and 13, 1838, King Papers, LC (quotations in first and third sentences); "Mentor," ANC 9 (October 17, 1839): 246 (quotations in second sentence).

[18]Scott, letter to Capt. F.M. Robertson of the Augusta (Ga.) Volunteers, May 26, 1836, published in ANC 2 (June 16, 1836): 380; Mahon, History of the Second Seminole War, 325. For proposals to put woodsmen under regular command, see "Quasi-Major," "The Seminole War," ANC 7 (October 18, 1838): 249-50; "Justice," "Gen. Scott and the Volunteers," ANC 2 (June 16, 1836): 378; "Sheer Justice," "Battle of the Okee-Chobee—The Army," ANC 6 (March 8, 1838): 154-55; and "Florida War," ANC 9 (December 19, 1839): 394-95. "Florida War—Captain Thistle's Plan," ANC 8 (March 28, 1839): 201-202, derided a volunteer's idea for raising civilian woodsmen to supplant the army.

Officers paid little explicit attention to Seminole ethnicity. Instead, the Indians served officers chiefly as foils for comparison, often to the Seminoles' advantage, with their antagonists among whites. Regular commanders held many values that they also ascribed to the Seminoles, affinities that increased their respect for their opponents at the same time that their regard for white settlers was waning. Professional soldiers showed little inclination toward primitivism and said very little about "noble savages," but they appreciated and acknowledged the Seminoles' patriotism, bravery, and self-sacrifice, qualities they thought themselves exemplifying in Anglo-American society. Officers often labeled the Seminoles treacherous savages, but veterans also contrasted their opponents' "freedom and daring" with the greed and self-interest of "the vampyre-like pioneers of civilization who have been fast crowding upon them." "Agricola" numbered the Seminole's advantages "the justice of his cause, and his abiding consciousness of moral right," while "Subaltern" emphasized the value officers ascribed to patriotism by condemning the relentless pursuit of men who would "live on roots rather than . . . desert the home of their fathers." Professional soldiers found such determination both admirable and daunting. Lieutenant William Chapman, a supply officer initially eager to see combat, called the Seminole chief Jumper (Ote Emathla) "a brave, devoted patriot, and an injured, unhappy Indian," and spoke of Osceola as "a brave warrior and a patriot," concluding that "future generations will honor his memory." Another veteran maintained that the Seminoles "will never leave this land while there is a swamp or a palmetto in Florida. They are as devoted to die on the soil that gave them birth as ever a martyr was to die for his religion." Though probably exaggerated in order to sway civilian opinion, this praise bolstered images of the Seminoles as worthy opponents, explaining away the inconclusiveness of the war.[19]

---

[19]"Agricola," "The Army," ANC 5 (October 26, 1837): 268; "A Subaltern," "Florida War, No. 4," ANC 8 (April 4, 1838): 220; Chapman to Blair, November 19, 1837 and February 28, 1838, in "A West Point Graduate in the Second Seminole War: William Warren Chapman and the View from Fort Foster," FHQ 68 (April 1990): 458-59 and

Career officers frequently blamed white settlers and their representatives for the causes—greed and land hunger—as well as the duration of the conflict. "[T]he source . . . is to be attributed to the misrepresentations of the Governmental agents," asserted Vermont-born Lieutenant John Phelps, a critic of the removal policy who believed that the Seminoles were tricked into signing the treaty of emigration "by the fawning machinations of unprincipled agents." Army officers were well aware of the fraudulent claims commonly put forward against Indians by local civilians, but they could do little to stop such malfeasance under the divided structures of federal authority and military subordination. Nathaniel Hunter privately labeled the treaty of removal "a compact begot in fraud and brought forth in the blackest villainy" by "a government that incites [me] to the commission of a crime." (He was later suspected of authoring an anti-removal petition circulated in Georgia, but like other dissenters he remained in uniform.) Engineer Lieutenant J. K. F. Mansfield, son of a West Point professor and Inspector General of the Army during the 1850s, echoed Hunter in a letter to his brother Edward, an academy graduate and professor of constitutional law at the College of Cincinnati. "I hope they will require no engineers":

[I]t would be a satisfaction to risk my life where honor is to be gained [but] not in an unjust war on a few miserable savages, goaded to the fighting point with a view to drive them from soil no rational man would live upon. Alas! my country, I blush for your principles of freedom, your justice and your honor! Heaven will reward thee according to thy deserts.

470-71; anonymous letter published in the ANC 6 (April 5, 1838): 216-17. I have found no evidence that the officers who led the seizure of Florida during the "First Seminole War" in 1817 and 1818 felt any admiration for the Seminoles, but sympathy for their plight was common among officers stationed in Florida during the decade between 1825 and 1835. The support for harsher measures that gained strength in 1839 signaled their growing frustration as the Seminoles proved recalcitrant and (to military eyes) faithless, as several armistices collapsed.

Mansfield went on to condemn "this money making, money loving, hypocritical community," envisaging the consequences of its moral degeneracy in a nightmare of civil war, "the glitter of thousands of bayonets in deadly strife[—]Father against son & brother against brother."[20]

Writing to the *Army and Navy Chronicle*, "An Officer of the 4th Artillery," probably Phelps, praised the Seminoles' "integrity" and adherence to the treaties made in the 1820s. In one letter, he labeled the war "our great injustice," invoking Christianity and republicanism against it:

> Can any Christian in this Republic . . . still pray for the continuance of blessings[?] . . . Can a people who boast the freest institutions, so far forget themselves as to assume the blackest attributes of tyranny[?] . . . [N]ot with impunity. An equilibrium will ever be maintained in the moral world as well as in the physical—retribution will inevitably follow dereliction.

He then attacked the removal policy in general, comparing the "crowding and condensing [of] disaffected Indian tribes" in the West to "congesting thunderous clouds" that would "[lavish] their fury on the earth" and bring desolation to the frontier.[21]

---

[20]John W. Phelps to his father, July 10, 1837, in "Letters of Lieutenant John W. Phelps, U.S.A., 1837-1838," 67-68 and 73; Hunter, Diary, I, p. 28, in "Captain Nathaniel Wyche Hunter and the Florida Indian Campaigns," 74; Lt. John King Fenno Mansfield to Edward Deering Mansfield, September 18, 1836, J. K. F. Mansfield Papers, USMA. See the quotations from Colonel Richard I. Dodge, in Leonard, "Red, White, and Army Blue," 181, for similar sentiments from the post-Civil War era.

[21]"An Officer of the 4th Artillery," (originally in the *Charleston Courier*) ANC 6 (January 25, 1838): 55. Phelps refused a brevet promotion to captain for gallantry at Contreras and Churubusco during the war with Mexico, although I do not know his motive. He then became an abolitionist and resigned his regular commission November 2, 1859, the day John Brown was convicted and sentenced to death. (I do not know if there is a direct connection, but officers' resignations were usually dated on the thirtieth or thirty-first of a month, indicating their submission several months in advance, so the timing is suggestive.) He received a commission as brigadier general of volunteers during the Civil War, but

Such apocalyptic imagery was rare among the pragmatists of the army officer corps. Products of an extensive socialization in a personal style modeled on the image of the English gentleman, most career officers were unreflective, unimaginative, and nonideological in temperament. Lieutenant William Wall agreed that the expropriation of the Seminoles "will be injustice in our view of it, and will result from selfishness and depravity," but like many civilians he saw the removal policy through the lens of a cultural determinism that presumed the ultimate outcome of Indian-white conflict to be inevitable because of the superiority of white civilization. "Who will call to account the majestic oak because his lofty and extended limbs prevent the mature growth of other trees in the forest?" Wall asked, illustrating the ease with which officers could reconcile their doubts without stopping to ponder the ethical implications of their compromises.[22]

Very few officers displayed an overtly racial consciousness, but neither did they question basic tenets of white supremacy. Indeed, the essence of their ethnocentrism lay not in belligerent Indian-hating but in what they took for granted. Yet qualms about the war began to penetrate these blinders, leading the "Officer of the 4th" to call on "the people" to "crush" the war by instructing their representatives "not to make the necessary appropriation," while other writers called for Congress to investigate and force negotiations. This unease was not confined to company commanders in the field: Surgeon General Thomas Lawson, who had commanded volunteers against the Seminoles during Scott's 1836 campaign, called for "acknowledging their independence, and yielding up to them the country for which they have so gallantly and so successfully fought, and so nobly won. It [is] manifest . . . that the Almighty is in their favor, and God's will should be done." Stung by criticism and frustrated by the difficulties

---

resigned in August 1862 after being refused permission to enlist escaped slaves in Louisiana. See Joseph T. Glatthaar, *Forged in Battle: The Civil War Alliance of Black Soldiers and White Officers* (New York, 1990), 7-8, and James G. Hollandsworth Jr., *The Louisiana Native Guards: The Black Military Experience During the Civil War* (Baton Rouge, 1995), 12-14.

[22]Wall to Robert Anderson, August 19, 1836, Anderson Papers, LC.

of his command, Thomas Jesup asked to be relieved when he came to the conclusion that extermination was the only way the Seminoles could be forced from their homes. (His request was rejected on the grounds that the administration wanted to retain his experience, and no doubt to avoid opening a new front for Whig criticism.)[23]

Military commanders began recommending peace early in 1837, and their proposals usually called for restraining whites while permitting the Seminoles to remain. "[D]rop that feature in the arrangement that requires their emigration; that done they will instantly make a treaty, and abide by it," one veteran suggested. Two years later, as Congress debated a strategy of armed colonization, "Mentor" advised *Army and Navy Chronicle* readers that the war would end much sooner if white settlers left East Florida—the center of plantation agriculture in the territory—altogether. Indeed, officers proposed to reverse the targets of their constraint by applying martial law to remove white settlers and their property from areas that could not be defended from Indian raids. (The officer corps' quest to press law and order upon both parties was evident in claims that this would lead the Seminoles to refuse refuge to "the vagabond white man," a scapegoat officers blamed for much of the lawlessness and disorder in Florida.) Thomas Jesup warned the settlers and speculators that he would declare martial law and deport them from the territory if they tried to seize the Seminoles or their property (including slaves) during the truces he negotiated. Waiting for the Indians to appear for removal per his first peace agreement (in March 1837), he forbade white civilians from entering the southern third of Florida to keep

---

[23]"An Officer of the 4th Artillery," 56; letter in *ANC* ("not intended to be published," according to the editor) 6 (April 5, 1838): 216-17; Thomas Lawson to Benjamin King, August 18, 1837, King Papers, LC; Mahon, *History of the Second Seminole War*, 204. See "A Lieutenant of the 2d Artillery," "Seminole War—Treaty of Payne's Landing," *ANC* 6 (May 1, 1838): 344-46, for an answer to Phelps that invoked duty and the "inevitability" of "progress" and "destiny" in favor of prosecuting the war. Antislavery forces in Congress made numerous attempts to cut military appropriations during the war years; northern opposition to the removal of the Seminoles is best represented by Joshua Giddings, *The Exiles of Florida* (Columbus, 1858), published in the aftermath of the Third (and final) Seminole War.

them from doing so, but their political influence led him to modify the order, effectively rescinding it.[24]

Convinced that removal was not worth the cost where so few whites were attempting to settle, Jesup sought peace beginning in February 1837, but the tenuous peace agreement he fashioned fell through because of the concerns of Seminole hardliners, particularly the Afro-Indians and maroons, who feared reenslavement if they surrendered. A year later, pressed by his senior officers after the major battles of Okeechobee and Lockahatchee (in which the Seminole force was about equally divided between Indians and blacks), Jesup declared another truce and wrote directly to the president (bypassing the secretary of war, through whom communications were supposed to be routed), recommending that the Seminoles be allowed to remain in Florida and asserting that "we exhibit in our present contest, the first instance, perhaps since the commencement of authentic history, of a nation employing an army to explore a country (for we can do little more than explore it), or attempting to remove a band of savages from one unexplored wilderness to another." Concluding the war without carrying out removal was also Major General Alexander Macomb's plan in 1839, undertaken at the recommendation of Zachary Taylor (then the theater field commander) and his council of officers. Artillery Colonel Walker Armistead, the least experienced of the theater commanders, deviated from this norm by planning an aggressive campaign in 1841, but William Worth (Armistead's senior field officer) seems to have avoided acting in earnest. Major Ethan Allen Hitchcock wrote directly to the secretary of war to counsel peace, maintaining that "sooner or later the government would be compelled" to agree, and found that "several officers rejoiced in the prospect of my being able to convince the Secretary . . . that a pacific policy was the only one that could succeed." Indeed, veteran Captain William McClintock

---

[24]"Seminole War," ANC 5 (August 3, 1837): 72-74; "Mentor," ANC 9 (October 17, 1839): 246; Kieffer, *Maligned General*, 163.

maintained that "the white flag" was "the most successful . . . commander" the army could have.[25]

These reactions proceeded from a pervasive sense of unappreciated sacrifice and isolation: "How little the country knows of the army when they prate about the danger of increasing our force. The intelligence, patriotism, and valour of our officers is not exceeded by any class of citizens in the republic—and this war tries those qualities severely." "When [we] gain a victory it is over a gang of negroes and savages, the whole of whom are not worth a finger of such a man as Thompson" (a lieutenant colonel killed at Lake Okeechobee). Surgeon Jacob Motte condemned "the abusive comments of some civilians, who reclining on cushioned chairs in their comfortable and secure homes vomited forth reproaches, sneers, and condemnation, wantonly assailing the characters of those who, alienated from home and kindred and all the comforts of life, were compelled to remain in this inglorious war." "They give us but little credit at the north for our sufferings and privations here; no one, out of Florida, knows what they are," lamented another veteran, calling for his regiment's removal from the swamps: "We are worn out and disheartened . . . a regiment of victims." A third surgeon rebuked "citizens who sit at home and smoke their cigars in the quiet enjoyment of ease and luxury, who have never seen the Territory of Florida, and are perfectly

---

[25]Mahon, *History of the Second Seminole War*, 199-202, 207, 235, and 257; Grant Foreman, Indian Removal:The Emigration of the Five Civilized Tribes of Indians (Norman, OK, 1932), 359 (who cites colonels Abraham Eustis and David Twiggs as advocates of peace); Jesup to Poinsett, February 11, 1838, quoted from Sprague, *The Origin, Progress, and Conclusion of the Florida War*, 200; Major Ethan Allen Hitchcock to his brother Samuel, August 22, 1842, Hitchcock Papers, LC (all quotations save the last); Capt. William L. McClintock to Robert Anderson, May 1, 1841, Anderson Papers, LC. See Frank F. White Jr., "Macomb's Mission to the Seminoles: John T. Sprague's Journal Kept during April and May, 1839," *FHQ* 35 (October 1956): 130-93, for a thorough account by Macomb's aide-de-camp. Jesup tried and was refused a second time in February 1838 (Mahon, 235 and 237). Hitchcock's letter recounts his efforts to persuade the War Department to adopt a pacific policy, contrary to Armistead's wishes. Hitchcock sent his letter to the Secretary of War after receiving Worth's approval; Worth initially switched to a policy of aggressive reconnaissance and pursuit when he assumed the theater command, then reverted to his earlier inaction and declaring victory.

ignorant of the difficulties which embarrass our military operations." He concluded that "the army does not need the advice of citizens to teach it how to do this duty."[26]

Junior officers directed their bile at politicians and superiors as well as ordinary civilians. Nathaniel Hunter thought that chasing the Indians in large bodies was "damned foolishness," and he confided in his diary that "General Armistead assumes command . . . to the surprise of all, the mortification of many, and the distrust of not a few. What does the grey-bearded and imbecile dotard [Armistead was about sixty] imagine he can do?" Elsewhere, an anonymous missive to the *Army and Navy Chronicle* labeled Senator Louis Linn "an intoxicated man or a falsifier" for his speeches against Zachary Taylor, while "Sheer Justice" reproached "those [civilians] who have not possessed the courage to face boldly and openly the enemies of their common country." "Canard" faulted the inertia of the government structure, which had "followed on, step by step, its own views until lives after lives have been lost, and the country disgraced." He concluded that the army was being "sacrificed by bad management. . . . This war has, with all its tragic scenes, been a farce from the beginning."[27]

Disenchanted veterans identified their sullied honor with that of the United States as a whole in their rhetorical appeals for peace. One supporter of Macomb's peace plan asked readers of the *Army and*

---

[26]Henderson to Benjamin King, February 6, 1838, King Papers, LC; assistant surgeon Jacob Rhett Motte, *Journey Into the Wilderness: An Army Surgeon's Account of life in Camp and Field During the Creek and Seminole Wars, 1836-1838*, ed. James F. Sunderman (reprint ed., Gainesville, 1963), 144; letter to ANC 11 (August 27, 1840): 137-38; "On the Florida War," ANC 9 (November 7, 1839): 290.

[27]Hunter, Diary, I, pp. 80 and 19, in "Captain Nathaniel Wyche Hunter and the Florida Indian Campaigns," 68 and 73 (n. 47); Mahon, *History of the Second Seminole War*, 315; "Gen. Taylor, and the Missouri Volunteers," ANC 8 (April 11, 1839): 236; "Sheer Justice," "Battle of the Okee-Chobee—The Army," ANC 6 (March 8, 1838): 154; "Canard," "Florida War," ANC 11 (July 23, 1840): 62. Though Hunter was exceptional in many ways, his persistence was highly representative of the career officer corps. The army does not seem to have been his first choice of career, for he resigned shortly after graduating from West Point in 1833, but he was reappointed in the Second Dragoons when it was formed three years later, and served throughout the Seminole conflict. He died a captain in 1849.

Navy Chronicle "what honor is there to be gained by the extermina-tion of a nation of aboriginal inhabitants, a brave but simple people, who, if they had been treated with less cruelty and injustice by their immediate neighbors, might before this, have ceased to be their deadly foes, and would probably have left the country of their forefathers . . . peaceably yielding [it] to the harpies [white settlers]." Another complained that his comrades felt "alienated from home, kindred, and friends . . . defending a domain which can never be densely populated, and protecting some . . . who would suffer much in comparison with the savages." "A Subaltern" exemplified this sentiment by proclaiming that "the war is a humbug. . . . there is but one thing in which it at all resembles a war . . . its loathsomeness. In a regular war, there is something noble, something inspiring. . . . It makes me sick to read the accounts. . . . No wonder the army should have become disgusted with this thankless . . . unholy war."[28]

Given these emotions it comes as little surprise that so many officers sought to avoid service in Florida. The army lacked any system for rotating units in and out of the territory, so disgruntled veterans continually wrote to the *Army and Navy Chronicle* to decry perceived favoritism and to press their regiments' case for relief. These arguments led to controversy within the officer corps by highlighting the ambiguities of professional duty and responsibility: Quartermaster General Jesup, a hero wounded four times in a single battle during the War of 1812, whose glasses were shot off while leading a charge at Lockahatchee, provoked cries of outrage from junior officers when he criticized their efforts to escape Florida by contending that "the spirit of the service is gone . . . when officers of respectable standing can be found ready to abandon the high and honorable duties of their profession to become schoolmasters at West Point." William Wall's sarcasm was more representative of the sentiments felt by the army's junior officers: "How happy I would be to surrender the command of

---

[28]"Gen. Macomb's Arrangement," ANC 9 (July 11, 1839): 25; "Florida War," ANC 7 (August 16, 1838): 105; "A Subaltern," "Florida War, No. 4," ANC 8 (April 4, 1839): 220. Note the latter officer's use of the word "regular," implying both orderliness and professional command, to describe a war he would consider noble and inspiring.

Company D 3d Artillery to some friend on such a glorious campaign," he wrote, after narrowly missing service under Jesup's command in the Creek War the previous summer. He added that an alert was "the nearest approximation that I have made towards being involved in an Indian battle—may I never be more near!"[29]

The desire to escape Florida spurred officers' eagerness for an end to the war. "I trust that the war will soon be closed, for I am heartily sick of this country," wrote Lieutenant Robert Auchmuty Wainwright, who was embroiled in a dispute with local officials over the murder of one of his men in Alabama. (Wainwright was detailed to teach at the military academy shortly thereafter, defusing that controversy, but his reassignment was the case that aroused General Jesup's ire over the spirit of the officer corps.) Like many of his comrades, Major Sylvester Churchill was "cheered with the favorable prospects of speedy peace" during the negotiations in early 1837, but he could do little more than give earnest thanks for "life, health and . . . exit from Florida" when granted leave two years later. None of these men were green lieutenants or mavericks: indeed, Churchill was appointed Inspector General of the entire army in 1841. That spring, the sixth of the war, George Pegram speculated that most of the veteran officers would "calculate on getting out in the summer. There

---

[29]Thomas Jesup to Colonel (and adjutant general) Roger Jones, August 13, 1837, quoted in Kieffer, *Maligned General*, 180; William Wall to Robert Anderson, August 19, 1836, Anderson Papers, LC. The August 22, 1839, issue of the *ANC* contained three letters defending units and their officers or appealing for regimental relief, from soldiers of the 2nd and 7th Infantry and the 3rd Artillery. Attacks on Jesup, who was not an academy graduate, can be found in "West Point," "Gen. Jesup and the Military Academy," *ANC* 6 (February 8, 1838): 93, and in three letters in *ANC* 6 (March 1, 1838). Jesup had been a line officer before his appointment as quartermaster general in 1818, and two decades of paper pushing had stirred him to seek field command whenever possible. Such commands ordinarily went to Winfield Scott and Edmund Gaines, the commanders of the army's geographic departments; Jesup got his chance when their Florida campaigns failed and they blamed one another. Supplying the war was the Quartermaster Department's chief problem, and as the army's fourth-ranking officer and a Democrat neutral in the feud between Scott and Gaines, Jesup was the natural choice for theater command. Few of the officers from the War of 1812 generation, who held the army's field and general ranks, were West Pointers, and many graduates felt that Jesup was aiding and abetting (however unconsciously) attacks on the institution they considered the core of the army.

will be [much] scrambling for leaves of absence." The army command reacted to this prospect by prohibiting furloughs from Florida, a measure that filled Captain William McClintock with foreboding: "This prohibition . . . seems to squint at a summer campaign. . . . The experience of the last five years is lost . . . much use is made of the words vigour and energy, in a manner that convinces me they don't know the meaning of those words as applied to Florida. . . . Our sick list next fall, will be sure to furnish them a definition."[30]

The officer corps' alienation was most obvious in the occasional, but by no means rare, use or advocacy of what scholars today might call symbolic inversion or appropriation—assuming Seminole dress or persona in order to attack opponents, be they white or Indian, more effectively. Officers had sometimes joined the Seminoles at dances and other festivities before the war, and they continued to do so during wartime truces. Lieutenant Morris Miller was one of several soldiers who wrote about the affection he developed for a Seminole child, and he found at least one Seminole woman "fascinating." More significantly, several satirists and critics signed their letters to the *Army and Navy Chronicle* with the names of Seminole leaders or used Indian characters to express their bemusement and disgust with the army's methods: in one seven-part series (one of the longest in the *Chronicle's* history) "Junius" pretended to visit the camp of "Sam Jones'" (the English name used by the Mikasuki chief Arpeika, one of the staunchest Indian hold-outs), only to be told that the chief's speech was "as long as a white President's message, except mine . . . has some sense in it." "Junius" then daydreamed about a "Miss Jones (the General's Daughter by a former wife), between whom and myself there had sprung up a sort of sentimental friendship." Other officers used "Jones" to defend the Military Academy against General Jesup. In the ultimate instance of inversion, Nathaniel Hunter compared himself to Lady Macbeth and asked whether "every act of the Indians

---

[30]Wainwright to William Chapman, March 17, 1837, William Warren Chapman Papers, USMA; Sylvester Churchill, journal entries, February 23, 1837 and May 7, 1839, Journals 1 and 3, Sylvester Churchill Papers, LC; Pegram and McClintock to Robert Anderson, January 18 and May 1, 1841, Anderson Papers, LC.

[is not] sanctioned by the practice of civilized nations? Are they not sanctioned [like ours] by expediency and revenge?"[31]

---

[31]Miller to his mother Maria and his sister Sarah, ? and April 29, 1835, Miller Papers, USMA; "Sam Jones," "United States Military Academy," ANC 8 (January 24 and February 21, 1838): 50-51 and 122-24; "Junius," "A Visit to Sam Jones's Camp, Part II," ANC 10 (May 7, 1840): 301, and "Part VII," ANC 11 (July 23, 1840): 59; Hunter, Diary, I, p. 28, in "Captain Nathaniel Wyche Hunter and the Florida Indian Campaigns," 74. See Sylvester Churchill, journal entry, March 8, 1837, Journal 1, Churchill Papers, LC, and "Mentor," ANC 9 (October 17, 1839): 245, for other examples of officers' sentimental attitudes towards Seminole families and children. Mahon, 303-304, notes a humorous bit of doggerel retailing the army's efforts to catch Arpeika.

The appropriation of Indian dress by whites dated back to the colonial period; besides the Boston Tea Party examples include the "White Indians" of Maine and among the Anti-Rent forces in New York during the early 1840s. See Alan Taylor, Liberty Men and Great Proprietors: The Revolutionary Settlement on the Maine Frontier, 1760-1820 (Chapel Hill, 1990), pp. 189-94 and 205, for a thoughtful analysis of the underlying dynamics of this phenomenon. The practice also bears some resemblance to the appropriation and reconfiguration of African-American cultural styles analyzed in works on blackface minstrelsy; see Eric F. Lott, Love and Theft: Blackface Minstrelsy and the American Working Class (New York, 1995), Alexander Saxton, The Rise and Fall of the White Republic: Class Politics and Mass Culture in Nineteenth-Century America (London, 1990), and Saxton, "Blackface Minstrelsy and Jacksonian Ideology," American Quarterly 27 (March 1975): 3-28. The case of officers is significantly different, however, in that a national elite was using Indian symbols to express antagonism toward local whites as well as disenchantment with national policy, an inversion of the usual relationships. These officers were not expressing humanitarian sympathy for the Indians, however: sentimental feelings toward Seminole women and children did not preclude the adoption of Indian dress to deceive and more effectively ambush and pursue refugees, and the letters to the Army and Navy Chronicle were written in tones of irony rather than empathy. The officer's use of Indian tactics did not represent a moral or ethical "counterculture" in formation, as Taylor suggests of the Maine settlers, but a practical adaptation to circumstances along with an inkling of regret overlaid by the employment of irony. Psychologically, however, it seems likely that (to quote Taylor, with alterations as appropriate) "by donning Indian costumes, [officers] doffed their inhibitions; as Indians they could engage in violence ["savagery"] inappropriate to white men; taking off their costumes, [officers] became [civilized gentlemen] once again, shorn, in their minds, of responsibility for what they had done as Indians" (189). Taylor notes that "there was more than a little . . . hypocrisy in this mock identity" (190), yet the tensions inherent in this sort of self-invention revealed the nuances of the officer's role and the complexities of his relationships with different "clients" and antagonists in the borderlands. Taylor observes a similar dualism in "the tension between the two faces" presented by the Maine settlers: "as 'white men' negotiating with outside authorities, they presented an alternative face: quiet, humble, obedient, and industrious citizens burdened . . . and deserving legislative redress" (205).

Tactically, this unorganized effort to understand the enemy underlay repeated proposals that the army dress like the Seminoles, a change that would help to ease the tortures of sawgrass, heat, and damp. Indeed, the *Army and Navy Chronicle* author "Canard" believed that only "when the whites will consent to live as the Indians . . . may these ruthless bands of savages be [defeated]." Such measures posed threats to the army's carefully cultivated discipline, and senior officers knew it. When Lieutenant Colonel William Harney of the Second Dragoons first asked permission to dress his force as Seminoles he was refused, and when he finally gained the authority to do so he promptly hunted down an Indian band and hung five of its members, shooting another as he tried to surrender. This was the most notorious of a number of atrocities perpetrated by the army in Florida, and Harney was also reported to have interrogated Seminole women by threatening to hang their children. The incident brought the army its only sustained applause from white Floridians, but northern civilians condemned the action and other officers were divided in their responses. The majority who put their opinions on paper seem to have found Harney's actions expedient, but they had to repress their occupational socialization in dispassionate gentility, discipline, and self-restraint in order to do so, a sure sign of their disenchantment.[32]

---

[32]"Canard," "Florida War," ANC 11 (July 30, 1840): 67; Mahon, *History of the Second Seminole War*, 278 and 283-84. Skelton, *An American Profession of Arms*, 318-22, points to an increasing hardening of officers' attitudes during the antebellum period, beginning with the later stages of the Florida war and accelerating (as exterminationist sentiment did among civilian frontiersmen) during the 1850s. I would hesitate to endorse Reginald Horsman's suggestion in *Race and Manifest Destiny: The Origins of American Racial Anglo-Saxonism* (Cambridge, Mass., 1981), 205 (citing Thomas Hart Benton), that the Seminole conflict became racialized, however: army officers continued to use the rhetoric of savagery and civilization rather than the idiom of racial differentiation (allied to the new "scientific racism") to which Horsman averts.

Harney repeatedly displayed psychopathic tendencies while forging a reputation that followed him throughout his controversial career—his brutality toward the Seminoles seems to have been a reflection of a brutal man and a true Indian-hater, and officers' opinions of him split depending on whether they stressed decorum or decisiveness. Harney seems to have had a cruel streak which he displayed toward anyone who came within his power: he had narrowly escaped civil conviction in St. Louis for the murder of a slave woman in 1834; he forced enlisted soldiers and slaves to fight one another for his amusement and to resolve

Yet it was hardly necessary for officers to adopt disguises to carry out practices they would otherwise have labeled barbarous. These could easily be sanctioned by the assumption that the "savage" Indians—whose presumed racial and cultural inferiority and putative statelessness denied them the protection of European laws of war—deserved no better. Departures from the norms of "civilized" warfare began as early as the spring of 1836, when Major Francis Belton had pits with stakes in them dug and concealed outside Fort Brooke to trap and maim attacking warriors. Fort Alabama was booby-trapped to explode when it was abandoned in April that year, and Thomas Sidney Jesup began a highly mixed record early in 1837, when he ordered blacks hung if taken prisoner in combat. Jesup soon rescinded the order—and it does not appear to have been carried out, since active operations had come to a halt in the summer heat—but he gave Harney a free hand and later threatened to hang prisoners if they refused to give him information. Jesup also extended his practice of seizing Indians under flags of truce to hostage-taking and threatening the hostages with death if other Seminoles did not surrender.[33]

---

disputes; and in 1855 he refused to take male prisoners among the Brule Sioux and allowed his troops to kill their women and children. I think it worth noting that Harney was one of the half-dozen officers commissioned without West Point training between 1821 and 1832, and that when initially formed in 1836 only four of his regiment's officers were academy graduates (though several had withdrawn or been dismissed from the school). The 2nd suffered under a high rate of officer attrition, and by 1841 only nine of its twenty-six original company officers remained, meaning that few of the 2nd's junior officers had much experience to ameliorate the friction and stress fostered by active service and poor leadership from their superiors. The officers of this unit soon gained a widespread reputation for mistreating enlisted men. It is therefore notable that Nathaniel Wyche Hunter, whose dissenting views and concern for enlisted soldiers have already been mentioned, was one of the few West Pointers in the regiment during its early years. See Skelton, *An American Profession of Arms*, 321-22; George R. Adams, "General William Selby Harney: Frontier Soldier, 1800-1889" (Ph.D. dissertation, University of Arizona, 1983), pp. 74-78, 130-32, and passim; Felix P. McGaughy Jr., "The Squaw Kissing War: Bartholomew M. Lynch's Journal of the Second Seminole War, 1836-1839" (M.A. thesis, Florida State University, 1965), 98, 101, and 179.

[33]Mahon, *History of the Second Seminole War*, 135, 160, 209, 204, 209, and 225. Repeated proposals were made to employ bloodhounds and offer bounties to catch the Seminoles. The first idea garnered great opprobrium in the North, largely due to the obvious parallel with the techniques of slave-catchers. In 1837 Jesup sought War Department advice

William Worth briefly tried similar tactics in 1841, but none of the theater commanders appear to have carried out their threats. The contrast with Harney's behavior may have lain in his personality and lack of West Point socialization, or in the fact that he was actually in the field and had just chased the Seminoles down after a month of heated pursuit, whereas Jesup and Worth were sitting at headquarters and talking about Indians who had come into U.S. camps and surrendered. Harney's actions aside, the officer corps' sympathy for the Seminoles had a very direct humanitarian effect, for the army did not resort to the massacres that characterized so many of the army's encounters (including Harney's against the Sioux in the 1850s) with the western Indians between 1848 and 1890, nor to the routine use of torture that characterized many counterinsurgency operations during the Philippine War for Independence (the army's next experience with tropical guerrilla warfare). To whatever extent officers may have sought to resolve the psychic tensions of their duty by punishing or eliminating the intractable enemy whose persistence brought civilian criticism,[34] they continued to fight the war in a remarkably Europeanized way. This illustrated their personal, institutional, and occupational commitment to ideals of gentility, decorum, and order. Indeed, harsh measures could only have raised further qualms among the disenchanted by undermining their carefully cultivated sense of identity as regular officers practicing a civilized profession. It therefore stands to reason that they ultimately

---

on the probable public reaction to the use of bloodhounds; he seems to have doubted that it would be favorable. With the Seminoles dispersed and refusing battle the following year, both Jesup and Zachary Taylor suggested their use, and in 1839 thirty-three were imported from Cuba by the state of Florida. In response to congressional critics the War Department ordered that they be leashed and muzzled. Only two saw duty and only two Indians were captured as a result. Most pecuniary incentives were directed toward citizen-soldiers and Indian allies like the Lower Creeks; regular soldiers were not offered a bounty for Seminole warriors (of $100 apiece) until 1842. See Kieffer, *Maligned General*, 172; K. Jack Bauer, *Zachary Taylor: Soldier, Planter, and Statesman of the Old Southwest* (Baton Rouge, 1985), 87; Mahon, 204, 239, 265-67, and 307; and James W. Covington, "Cuban Bloodhounds and the Seminoles," *FHQ* 33 (October 1954): 111-19.

[34]This is a prominent argument in Leonard, "Red, White, and the Army Blue," concerning the army after the Civil War.

found it necessary to stay the course in order to retain the genteel status and respectability they sought. Today we almost take it for granted that officers would have committed atrocities because we know that they shared the racism of other contemporary Anglo-Americans, but in doing so we fail to see the ameliorative effects of their socialization in class- and occupationally-based norms of gentility and honor.

A letter from "Omicron" to the *Army and Navy Chronicle* denouncing Jesup's seizure of Osceola during a truce illustrates the social and cultural origins of this uneasiness in genteel visions of warfare that drew on the eighteenth-century heritage of European limited war as well as Eurocentric concepts of savagery and civility. The author maintained that "it is impossible that the army can improve while officers can employ themselves in introducing such novel and barbarian methods of warfare," and he avowed that "the old-fashioned and civilized . . . forms of intercourse, which should obtain [even] with a savage foe, are the only ones which can be upheld by good policy, propriety, or the voice of the people"—by pragmatism, honor, and accountability to national (including northern, rather than merely local or southern) opinion. Out in the field, Nathaniel Hunter referred to such policies as "the vilest machinations man or demon could invent," and noted that he had decided to ignore an order to stop taking prisoners, which he termed "wringing [my] hands in innocent blood." Jesup first attempted to justify his conduct but later tried to make amends by pressing the government to honor the promises made to Indians who had supported the removal effort, particularly the Creeks who had served with the army in 1836 and 1837, and to the Seminoles whom he had sent west, writing in 1844 that "as the Commander of the Army in Florida I assured them in good faith that the country [in the Oklahoma region] set apart by the treaty was ready for their reception. I consider it due to my honour, as well as that of the Country . . . to urge upon the government the prompt fulfillment of the treaty." Acting as government officer, military commander, and gentleman, Jesup conflated personal and national honor in the execution of his duties, simultaneously embodying the closely allied processes of state, class, and occupational formation in his own language and behaviour.[35]

The officer corps drove forward despite every irritant; indeed, resignations declined precipitously during just the years (1838 and 1839) when demoralization and discontent became pervasive. Army officers continued to serve for three basic reasons: the security of their careers, the comparatively neutral attitude most of them had toward partisan politics, and their occupational and professional cohesion, which was actually strengthened by their collective misery. These factors came together in the same sense of nonpartisan accountability to the federal government simultaneously in evidence among officers along the Canadian border (where the army was charged with suppressing filibustering), and on that with Mexico a half-decade later, an ethos commonly expressed in a language of duty, honor, and service to the "national" interest embodied in the central government. Lieutenant William Warren Chapman resented the government's "cold ingratitude" but assured his fiancee that "I remain in Florida because it is my duty to do so," while another officer wrote to the *Army and Navy Chronicle* that only "the consciousness [that] 'I have done my duty'" allayed "the stigma of [civilian] ingratitude." Pondering policies he considered atrocious, even Nathaniel Hunter referred to the "duty of a soldier to obey." The majority of the officer corps wanted to carry matters to a clear conclusion, whether that meant removal or peace, to demonstrate its faithful performance of

---

[35]"Omicron," "General Jesup, the Secretary of War, and the Military Academy," ANC 6 (March 1, 1838): 138; Hunter, Diary, I, pp. 27-28, in "Captain Nathaniel Wyche Hunter and the Florida Indian Campaigns," 73-74; Jesup to Secretary of War William Wilkins, May 22, 1844, quoted in Kieffer, *Maligned General*, p. 233. The origins and scope of this order are unclear from Hunter's entry; the editor writes that it came from theater commander Zachary Taylor, but provides no citation, and none of the standard secondary works refer to such an order. Hunter's regimental commander was William S. Harney, who may have given such an order verbally.

the duties it had been assigned, however onerous or distasteful its members found them.[36]

Another factor that encouraged yet simultaneously moderated dissent was the availability of a public, yet usually anonymous, forum for the officer's pride and frustration in the *Army and Navy Chronicle*. The *Chronicle*'s most significant effect was to buttress the officer corps' collective identity as a professional body and to provide a safe channel for expressing the frustrations engendered by war and civilian antipathy. The weekly paper was partially dependent on federal subsidies in the form of payments for relaying official news and orders, but it had no set editorial policy regarding the war: it was the army's forum, open to any officer's opinions. By 1835 the career officer corps had developed an image of itself as an expert, personally disinterested body of national servants, an identity that encouraged officers to speak out on policies related to their duties. The *Chronicle* served as their primary sounding board at a crucial moment in the development of the army's professional culture, a vehicle for maintaining much of

---

[36]Chapman to Helen Blair, February 27, 1838, in "A West Point Graduate in the Second Seminole War," 468; "Battle of the Kissimmee—The Army" (subtitled "honor to whom honor is due"), ANC 6 (March 1, 1838): 141; Hunter, Diary, I, p. 28, in "Captain Nathaniel Wyche Hunter and the Florida Indian Campaigns," 74. My essay "U.S. Army Officers Fight the 'Patriot War': Responses to Filibustering on the Canadian Border, 1837-1839," *Journal of the Early Republic* 18 (Fall 1998): 485-519, explores the army's efforts, and its frustration with civil officers and militiamen, along the Canadian frontier during the so-called "Patriot War" of 1838-1839. Note that here, as elsewhere in my work, I am measuring military accountability to contemporary civilian control, which meant that of white males with strong ethnoracial biases, not to modern moral standards. It was entirely possible, indeed from today's perspective it was the norm, for officers to perform accountably to the government to which they had sworn an oath while executing racist policies of ethnic cleansing. This paper points out some of their qualms in doing so, but it must not be forgotten that the army served as a leading agent of Anglo imperialism throughout the nineteenth century. Given that well-known reality, I have concentrated on the ways in which officers negotiated accountability to the constitutionally established national government, a process that illustrates manifold tensions in American federalism, class, state, and occupational formation, and the course of U.S. expansion.

the cohesion that would otherwise have been lost in the resignation crisis of 1835-1837.[37]

From an institutional perspective, dissent among army officers was possible because the seniority system of promotion meant that partisan politicians could not punish them (or hold them directly accountable) for their statements without using the cumbersome formalities of court martials, employing vague charges such as "unofficerlike conduct." This would obviously have been a political move, which senior officers attempting to keep the army apolitical would have resisted, with assistance from congressional inquiries by friends of the accused, particularly those northerners with ties to opponents of the removal policy. Given the close social and personal connections between many officers (even junior ones) and officehold-ers, even charges of direct disobedience or disrespect to superiors were commonly defused through technicalities. The ultimate basis of the army's personnel policies toward officers was still the model of the independent gentleman claiming his rights and prerogatives in an eighteenth-century language of personal honor and integrity, not the idiom of spoilsmen or bureaucrats.

This "independence" and the ability to dissent actually did a great deal to alleviate civil-military tensions, for officers were able to let off steam while continuing to perform their assigned tasks, an opportu-nity that provided the psychological breathing space necessary for them to move forward with policies they found distasteful. The resignations of the mid-1830s notwithstanding, the officer corps' fledgling professional ethos enabled the federal government to maintain a force that owed its allegiance to the national center, rather than commissioning large numbers of southern men (those most willing to volunteer for service in Florida, and most likely to accept commissions given its prospect), whose first loyalties lay with their section and its institutions, directly from civilian life (without passing

---

[37]The officer corps no longer sustained the paper once it reverted to everyday army news and occasional reform proposals: after several years of near-insolvency, the *Chronicle* folded for lack of subscribers in 1844.

through the Military Academy). The career officer corps was one of the few forces in Jacksonian America that consistently acted to maintain and extend the authority of the national government, one of the few surviving manifestations of a supposedly disinterested national elite providing direction from the center of the federal system. Knowing this, the central government did not attempt to stifle the expression of dissent among its officers, who returned the favor by limiting their dissent to private letters, requests for leave, and the anonymity of the *Army and Navy Chronicle*. This mutual self-restraint helped to preserve both individual careers and the regular army's monopoly over the direction of American military force, one of the few buttresses of national sovereignty in frontier and borderlands regions.[38]

Officers also reacted by showering each other with praise and developing internal rituals to cope with the losses they suffered. (Foremost among these was the custom of group memorials paying tribute to dead comrades in the *Army and Navy Chronicle*.) Other

---

[38]See Skelton, *An American Profession of Arms*, 144, regarding appointments directly from civil life (i.e., those bypassing West Point training). This practice was almost unheard of between 1820 and 1832, but the need to officer the dragoon regiments raised in 1833 and 1836, replace the men who resigned between 1835 and 1837, and fill the new slots created in 1838 led to a wave of these appointments: 102 between 1837 and 1839, forty-three percent of the commissions issued in that time. (By 1840 about one out of six regular officers had been so commissioned.) Officers' reluctance to serve in Florida undoubtedly contributed to these appointments, if only because West Point could not graduate enough cadets to supply the vacancies, but they were forced on the Van Buren administration by circumstances rather than preference. Accepting at least part of the officer corps' self-definition, the administration refused to use the appointments for overtly partisan purposes, and they did not alter the fundamental character or ethos of the corps as a whole.

The officer corps' success in extending and maintaining federal sovereignty over the borderlands suggests that not all of the organizing programs put forward by nationally minded elites during the generation after the War of 1812 were failures, a caveat worth bearing in mind by historians exploring the tensions between decentralized society and federal nation in the early republic. I am deeply indebted to Lacy Ford for this insight. See Robert H. Wiebe, *The Opening of American Society from the Constitution to the Eve of Disunion* (New York, 1986), for an extended meditation on the balance between centralization and decentralization throughout the Middle Period, and Richard R. John, *Spreading the News: The American Postal System from Franklin to Morse* (Cambridge, Mass., 1995), for a monograph with arguments and implications broadly parallel to my own.

veterans sought vindication through victory, demanding further campaigns to that end: even "Sam Jones" argued that "it is due the army, to Florida, and the United States generally, that this protracted war should be closed! It is due the army because it has already spent too much of its time here for its own comfort and advantage." The officer corps was satisfied with its performance, and that had to suffice: "The army has done well what was given it to do, and is unwilling to take any of the responsibility of failure," proclaimed "An Officer of the Line." These words demonstrate both dedication to performing the tasks assigned by the nation-state and unwillingness to be held responsible for their consequences; through this fusion, a sense of martyrdom and alienation served to shore up rather than undermine officers' willingness to fight. The potential for strains in American civil-military relations was eased by officers' ability to express their dissent in public forums without fear of reprisal: subordinates refusing the full burden of accountability for their beliefs, they received a hearing without being forced to choose between Florida and resignation.[39]

The frustration and antagonism that characterized civil-military relations during the Second Seminole War was both deceptive and exceptional. Army officers had secure incomes, social respectability as gentlemen (in the eyes of national elites and the local middle classes outside frontier regions), and the power to command.[40] The social sanction and legitimacy embodied in recognition by public opinion was the only thing they lacked. Officers felt unappreciated and put

---

[39]"Sam Jones," "Florida War," ANC 9 (October 31, 1839): 285; "An Officer of the Line," "Florida War," ANC 9 (August 29, 1839): 132.

[40]This is not to suggest that officers were drawn uniformly from elite or "upper middle class" backgrounds, but their social origins were disproportionately urban, professional, and office holding—very few of the men who were admitted to and graduated from West Point after 1820 were from farming or planting families on the frontier. See Skelton, An American Profession of Arms, Tables 9.4 and 9.5 (pp. 159-60) for comparisons with the civilian population. See Richard L. Bushman, The Refinement of America, 1750-1850: Persons, Houses, Cities (New York, 1993) for an analysis of what might be called "the gentrification of the middle class" that presses historians to recognize the survival of aristocratic values in the early republic, a survival clearly present in the ethos of the regular officer corps.

upon, but they were becoming accustomed to enduring frustration and criticism, and they had been deliberately socialized in an ethos of service, sacrifice, and duty to the national union. Though largely foreign to the everyday lives of civilians, these beliefs served a valuable function during the attacks on the army during the 1830s and '40s, for they enabled officers to turn criticism on its head by proclaiming themselves disinterested, self-sacrificing servants of the union—in a sense, and at some distance, nonpartisan representatives of the general public will, "the people" which they identified with the central government that gave them employment. They upheld distance from the influence of public opinion as the very measure of their disinterestedness, and hence their ability to act "independently" of narrow local interests in order to serve those of the nation as a whole.

By the 1840s many officers had come to see themselves as the nation's policemen, whose duties to the union required preserving law and order among unruly frontiersmen. Yet their distaste for the individualism of frontier settlers was also moderated by their socialization in genteel moderation and partisan neutrality. Army officers were not isolated from their society: the officer corps reflected a divided society, and its members held Whiggish attitudes and values without seeking to declare or act directly on Whig allegiances. As a group officers were neither reformers nor humanitarians, neither advocates of the American System nor those of the evangelical empire; the minority with identifiable partisan loyalties appear to have been about equally divided, and the Democrats among them were neither decentralizers nor anti-institutionalists. Their growing accountability to civilian political processes was stimulated not by ideological devotion to the glories of republicanism and democracy but by their interests as members of an institution dependent on those processes for its survival—by the desire for security and the implicit threat of sanction rather than overt ideological allegiance or partisanship.[41]

Many of the same attitudes found among officers during the Seminole conflict were shared by their compatriots on the Mexican border in 1845 and 1846, but the promise of a shorter, faster-paced war with decisive victories, promotions, and public acclaim was sufficient to allay most doubts, and dissent never became prominent among officers during the occupation of Texas or the war with Mexico. That war was fought against enemy regulars by unitary field armies in set-piece battles, while the volunteers were held firmly under the command of career professionals: it was the closest American approximation to the romantic ideal of Napoleonic warfare before 1861, and it had a momentum that encouraged officers to look forward to civilian recognition and fame. Career officers were not the ardent proponents of Manifest Destiny that many historians have portrayed, but the war was fought against a nation initially seen as European in culture, and hence a worthy opponent whose defeat would bring civilian acclaim, yet one for whom the officer corps had few sympathies, either romantically or in contrast with Anglo settlers,

---

[41]To argue that army officers were isolated or alienated from the culture they lived in exaggerates the uniformity of that culture. Officers did not lack ties to political elites, but their demands on civilian society were usually limited to increases in military spending and compensation, the hope for faster promotions, professional command over the militia and volunteers in time of war, attempts to control entry into and the values of the officer corps by requiring specialized training and socialization at West Point, and a longing for public recognition and acclaim. Career officers rarely expressed republican or other ideological sentiments in any detail or in any form save that of antipartisanship, which suited their ethos of disinterested patriotism and nationalism and complemented their desire for career security regardless of electoral change. Regular army officers wrote very little about republicanism or democracy: this is not to say that they didn't believe in "free institutions" in a generic way, but to call officers ideological would stretch the meaning of the word to encompass virtually any social group or set of attitudes. Given their education and political connections, which precluded ignorance of the issues, we must attribute much of the officer corps' inarticulateness on politics and ideology to its nascent professional ethic, which stressed national service in the ostensibly neutral form of "duty." See William B. Skelton, "Officers and Politicians: The Origins of Army Politics in the United States Before the Civil War," *Armed Forces and Society* 6 (Fall 1979): 22-48, and idem., *An American Profession of Arms*, ch. 15, for more detailed analyzes of "army politics."

who were left behind when the army crossed the Nueces. The army's stay in Texas was short, its civilian contacts limited; officers feared exposure to the climate and disease and lamented their separation from wives and family. There was a small wave of resignations as war approached, but the army never became bogged down and exposed to these problems as it had in Florida. Many officers voiced reservations at some point between the annexation of Texas and the invasion of Mexico, but they no longer had the *Army and Navy Chronicle* (which had gone out of business in 1844) to express them in, and the level of dissent was far lower than five years before.[42]

The differences between these wars and the officer corps' reactions to them lay in the forms of warfare and the groups—particularly the clamorous settlers in Florida, and their absence from Mexico—that military commanders had to deal with, not in their individual responses to personal inconvenience. The circumstances of the Second Seminole War aggravated civil-military friction, but the war was not its underlying source, for these disputes embodied deeper social tensions and questions of allegiance to locality, section, and nation. Yet the Seminole conflict proved a testing ground, a crucible where professional soldiers gained valuable experience dealing with the complexities and frustrations of balancing among a diverse array of ethnicities, constituencies, and antagonists. Veterans bewailed "Unhappy Florida! [Whose] soil has drunk the heart's blood of the army!" but these trials provided the officer corps with hard-won lessons in patience and accountability to civilian control.[43] The

---

[42]The army was stationed in Texas for nearly a year before the fighting began, and some of the officers waiting for active operations came to wish that they were in Florida, safe and sound on established posts with their families, but the economy was no longer booming as it had been before the Panic of 1837, leaving fewer alternatives for officers who might otherwise have resigned. See Skelton, *An American Profession of Arms*, ch. 17, and my essays "The Uncertain Road to Manifest Destiny," and "Manifest Destiny and Military Professionalism: A New Perspective on Junior U.S. Army Officers' Attitudes Toward War With Mexico, 1844-1846," *Southwestern Historical Quarterly* 99 (April 1996): 466-98, for discussions of officers' attitudes concerning Texas and Mexico.

[43]"Notes and Reminiscences of an Officer of the Army, No. 9," ANC 11 (September 24, 1840): 202.

resignations of the mid-1830s, the difficult experiences of the Seminole war, and the economic depression of the late 1830s and early 1840s left an officer corps whose loyalties had been tempered in the forge of adversity, a cohesive group willing to lead the nation's armies wherever the government sent them, regardless of the nature of their assignments, in return for secure careers. Army officers served the cause of sectional and national aggrandizement in Florida, but they thought and acted as members of a bureaucratically structured and constitutionally accountable organization under national control, not as individuals or representatives of a single sectional and economic interest like Andrew Jackson and their predecessors two decades before (i.e., as southern whites advancing the frontier of commercial plantation agriculture and chattel slavery), and they did so without espousing the fervent racism that characterized officers during the 1810s and civilian frontiersmen and expansionist politicians throughout the century. In the final analysis, the personal security guaranteed by stable careers in a large-scale organization led career officers to accountability and restraint rather than recklessness and belligerence in their attitudes toward Indian removal and territorial expansion.[44]

---

[44]My essay "The Uncertain Road to Manifest Destiny: Army Officers and the Course of American Territorial Expansionism, 1815-1846," in Christopher Morris and Sam W. Haynes, eds., *Manifest Destiny and Empire: Essays on Antebellum American Expansionism* (College Station, 1997) provides social and institutional explanations for the changes in officers' perspectives on expansion between 1820 and 1846. Perhaps the best evidence for decreasing sectional motives among the officer corps lies in the struggle between soldiers and civilians over the disposition of free blacks, escaped slaves, and maroons captured with or from the Seminoles. See Kenneth Wiggins Porter, "Negroes and the Second Seminole War, 1835-1842," *Journal of Southern History* 30 (November 1964): 427-50, and *The Black Seminoles: History of a Freedom-Seeking People*, rev. and ed. by Alcione M. Amos and Thomas P. Senter (Gainesville, 1996); Daniel F. Littlefield, *Africans and Seminoles: From Removal to Emancipation* (Westport, Conn., 1977) and *Africans and Creeks: From the Colonial Period to the Civil War* (Westport, Conn., 1979); and Kevin Mulroy, *Freedom on the Border: The Seminole Maroons in Florida, the Indian Territory, Coahuila, and Texas* (Lubbock, 1993). My essay "Thomas Sidney Jesup: Soldier, Bureaucrat, Gentleman Democrat," in Michael A. Morrison, ed., *The Early American Republic* (Scholarly Resources, forthcoming, 2000) assesses Jesup's career, and I am presently at work on a manuscript exploring the relationships between officers and maroons in greater depth.

2

ESTABLISHING A SEPARATE IDENTITY: TEXAS'S OFFENSIVE STRUGGLE WITH THE INDIAN NATIONS, 1861-1862

Clayton E. Jewett

In early 1861, Atascosa County resident José A. Navarro wrote a letter to his son revealing the complex situation between Texas and the Indians. "The Indians are aware of our political differences," he said, and view Texas "as much revolutionized and weakened as Mexico." "And with that belief," Navarro warned, "they will rush, without doubt to redden their spears in human blood, with that ferocity and savageness which they breathe in their blood-shot eyes." Navarro feared that if Texans did not resist the Indians in armed fashion and pursue them into their territory a "destructive Indian war" would lead to the ruin of Texas. Most Texans viewed the Indians as a ruthless race bent on destruction and death, and believed only the adoption of offensive action could successfully counter the Indian threat.[1]

---

[1]*Southern Intelligencer*, 27 March 1861. This article is part of a larger work seeking to understand the beliefs and attitudes of Texans during the Civil War. Throughout the paper I employ the term "Indian" instead of "Native American." Though some scholars may oppose this term, my work is written from the perspective of nineteenth-century Texans, and this is the term used in the press, personal correspondence and official correspondence of that era. The limited primary Native American sources make it difficult to ascertain fully their point of view in this conflict.

Scholarship addressing the relationship between Anglo Americans and Indians during the Civil War has generally focused on the conflict between Indian nations and the Confederacy. Historians have emphasized divisions between slaveholders and non-slaveholders and the Indian's military contribution to the Confederate cause. The examination of Texas's relationship with the Indians, though, reveals tensions within the Confederacy that are more complex than previously thought.[2]

Texas's trouble with the Indians existed before the days of the Republic. While Indians played a significant role in the development of Texas by participating in commercial and political relations with Anglos and Hispanics, they also fought to stave off encroachment upon their lands. When Texas became a Republic in 1836, relations between Anglos and Indians appeared to improve. Sam Houston, the first President of the Republic, attempted to improve prospects for peace by enforcing trade laws, removing white trespassers from Indian land, upholding Indian hunting rights, and negotiating fair treaties. Favorable relations, however, did not last. Under the presidential leadership of Mirabeau B. Lamar, Texas adopted a policy of forced removal. As a result, brutal attacks upon the Indians ensued, and Texas alienated most of the Indian tribes in the region. Indians did not sit patiently, but sought revenge upon their perpetrators and sacked many towns as far south as Galveston. Sam Houston attempted to remedy the situation when reelected in 1841. On an official level, Houston perhaps succeeded, but skirmishes continued to exist. When the United States annexed Texas in 1845, it assumed the role of frontier protector. Texas-Indian relations fared no better though as the United States became preoccupied with the Mexican

---

[2]Emory Thomas, *The Confederate Nation, 1861-1865* (New York: Harper & Row, 1979); Annie Heloise Abel, *The American Indian as Slaveholder and Secessionist* (1915; reprint Lincoln: University of Nebraska Press, 1992); R. Halliburton Jr., *Red Over Black: Black Slavery Among the Cherokee Indians* (Westport: Greenwood Press, 1977); Wilfred Knight, *Red Fox: Stand Watie and the Confederate Indian Nations During the Civil War Years in Indian Territory* (Glendale: Arthur H. Clark Company, 1988); Nancy Hobson, "Samuel Bell Maxey as Confederate Commander of Indian Territory," *Journal of the West* 8 (July 1973).

War. In the 1850s, pressure mounted as white expansion increased, and relations between the Indians, Texas, and the Federal government began to deteriorate. Though slavery seized much of the nation's attention, Anglo and Indian atrocities continued to preoccupy the frontier. Prior to the Civil War, a clear pattern to Texas-Indian relations did not exist.[3]

The relationship between Texans and Indians, however, became more fractious with the onset of the sectional crisis. When United States troops evacuated western forts in May 1861, the Indians became alarmed over the confusion. Well aware of the political differences existing between the North and South, Indians expressed deep concern for their safety and how the outbreak of the Civil War affected them. Their concern for safety intensified when evacuating federal troops told them of armed Texans "coming to destroy them."[4] As a result of the crisis, the Indians "evinced a boldness and daring never before shown," and Texas citizens blamed the evacuation of federal troops for affording Indians "a general license to rob and murder at their pleasure." Texas Governor Francis Lubbock believed that "the greatest immediate danger we apprehended was from Indian hostilities." The rise in Indian hostility most likely resulted from renewed fears of white expansion that led them to feel threatened. Thus, guerilla war offered one of the few options available to the Indians. In turn, Texas citizens believed that secession and the subsequent removal of federal forces placed their region in jeopardy, and that only an offensive war could secure their well being.[5]

---

[3]William Banta, *Twenty Seven Years on the Texas Frontier* (1893; reprint, Council Hill, Oklahoma: L. G. Park, 1933); W. W. Newcomb Jr., *The Indians of Texas: From Prehistoric to Modern Times* (Austin: University of Texas Press, 1961); J. W. Wilbarger, *Indian Depredations in Texas* (Austin: Hutchings Printing House, 1889); and James M. Day, ed., *The Indian Papers of Texas and the Southwest* (Austin: Texas State Library, 1995), (hereafter Indian Papers).

[4]*Clarksville Standard*, 22 June 1861.

[5]*San Antonio Weekly Ledger and Texan*, 6 April 1861; C. W. Raines, ed., *Six Decades in Texas or Memoirs of Francis Richard Lubbock Governor of Texas in War-Time, 1861-1863* (Austin: Ben C. Jones & Co., 1900), 337. For a detailed account of federal evacuation from Indian territory see Dean Trickett, "The Civil War in Indian Territory," *Chronicles of Oklahoma* 17 (1939).

Historically war and destruction are integral parts of nation building, and those individuals who understand the need for an offensive posture with their enemies truly comprehend the task of defining and building a nation. An offensive approach involves more than armed resistance; it encompasses pursuit both as a reaction to attacks and as a distinctive approach to war. The acceptance of the necessity of offensive posturing, however, as José Navarro's letter reveals, reached beyond top military strategists to the ordinary citizen. Unable to rely previously on United States or current Confederate assistance with the Indians, Texas citizens forged their own relationship with the Indian tribes.[6] A fight for economic survival and growth defined the relationship between Texans and Indians. Fired by the passion of protecting their life and property, the relationship between the two races is best characterized by mutual hatred and destruction. Both groups stole the other's property, murdered each other's families, and sought the extinction of the other. For Texas, from 1861 through 1862, a war more serious and defining than the sectional conflict took place on its borders, contributing to the formation of a separate identity from that of other southern states. This process did not occur evenly throughout the state, nor was a separate identity imposed on the common citizen by the political elite. Instead, at various times throughout 1861 and 1862, different regions and different classes exhibited this separateness, and by 1863 a distinct Texas identity emerged in the midst of the Civil War.[7]

---

[6]Samuel J. Watson, in " 'This thankless . . . unholy war': Army Officers and Civil-Military Relations in the Second Seminole War," suggests that a primary reason for the failure of the U.S. government to protect citizens from Indian depredations in earlier years was due to the attitude of army officers. Whether this sentiment continued, affecting the Texas frontier is unknown, but worthy of investigation.

[7]Charles Royster, *The Destructive War: William Tecumseh Sherman, Stonewall Jackson, and the Americans* (New York: Random House, 1993). Other factors contributed to a separate identity as well, including Texas's conflict with the Trans-Mississippi Department, the battle over cotton, and Texas's political effort to sustain state institutions and support the citizenry at the expense of the Confederacy. I deal thoroughly with these issues in my dissertation, "On Its Own: Texas in the Confederacy," (Catholic University of America) written under the direction of Jon L. Wakelyn.

The sectional crisis brought fear and insecurity to everyone involved, including Indians. As wards of the federal government, and as slaveholders, the five organized tribes and smaller bands of Indians west of Arkansas and north of Texas were forced to choose sides in the sectional crisis. Aware of the political crisis and potential threat to their lives and property, the legislatures and general councils of the Cherokee, Chocktaw, Chickasaw, Creek, and Seminole nations, along with various Comanche tribes, each gathered to deliberate their stance on the crisis. Though internal division existed within each tribe over the issue of neutrality, eventually each of the organized Indian nations sided with the Confederacy to secure their own rights and to place themselves in an economically advantageous position.[8]

In reaction to the Indian's allegiance, and in an attempt to maintain the fidelity of the organized tribes for its own benefit, the Confederate government sought to negotiate treaties with the Indian tribes. President Jefferson Davis commissioned Albert Pike, a man experienced in dealing with the Indians, especially in legal matters, and fluent in several Indian languages, for this purpose. Often dressing in traditional Indian wear, his popularity among the tribes helped the Confederacy secure the desired treaties. Between July and August 1861, the Confederacy negotiated treaties with the Creek, Choctaw, Chickasaw, and Cherokee Nations and several Comanche tribes that had a direct impact on Texas-Indian relations. These

---

[8]*San Antonio Daily Ledger and Texan*, 13 March 1861; *Galveston Tri-Weekly News*, 18 July 1861; "Resolutions of the Senate and House of Representatives of the Chickasaw Legislature Assembled," *War of the Rebellion: Official Records of the Union and Confederate Armies* (Washington: Government Printing Office, 1883), series I, volume III, 585-587, (hereafter OR); Arrell M. Gibson, *The Chickasaws* (Norman: University of Oklahoma Press, 1971); "Resolutions expressing the feelings and sentiments of the General Council of the Choctaw Nation in reference to the political disagreement existing between the Northern and Southern States of the American Union," OR, series I, volume I, 682; W. David Baird, *The Choctaw People* (Phoenix: Indian Tribal Series, 1973), 126-128; "Proclamation by the Principal Chief of the Choctaw Nation," OR, series I, volume III, 593.

treaties attempted to set boundaries on political and legal rights, and foreign and tribal relations.[9]

Under the guise of "perpetual peace and friendship," the Confederate government established itself as "the protectorate of the several nations and tribes." The Confederacy promised to protect the Indians from domestic strife, hostile invasion from Union forces, and from aggression by other Indians. The tension within Indian tribes kept the Confederacy alert to securing favorable relations. The Confederate government also believed that to ensure such favor and loyalty that it must squelch divisions between the Indian tribes. Most of all, the Confederacy had to guarantee that no harm would come to them from the North. Without the assurance of full protection of their lives and property, the Confederate government stood little chance of persuading the organized tribes to fully support the southern cause.[10]

An intriguing aspect of the Confederate-Indian treaties pertains to articles regarding the political and legal rights of the Indians. The Confederate government gave general amnesty to all Indians who violated United States or Confederate laws prior to the signing of the treaties. Thus, those Indians charged with an offense received full pardon from the President, and those who were imprisoned or held on bail received full discharge. The Confederate government, though, had no power to force individual states to abide by this agreement, and the most Richmond could promise each Indian tribe was their intention and effort to request the state of Texas to grant the same amnesty and pardons from the governor. Thus, from the onset a

---

[9]OR, series IV, volume I, 785; Alvin M. Josephy Jr., *The Civil War in the American West* (New York: Random House, 1991), 323-324; Trickett, "Civil War in Indian Territory," 404-407.

[10]OR, series IV, volume I. For the Creek Treaty, 426-443; Choctaw and Chickasaw Treaty, 445-466; Seminole Treaty, 513-527; Comanche Treaties, 542-554; and Cherokee Treaty, 669-687. (Hereafter, *Creek Treaty, Choctaw and Chickasaw Treaty, Seminole Treaty, Comanche Treaty, Cherokee Treaty*). For Indian relations with the Union see Gary E. Moulton, "John Ross and W. P. Dole: A Case Study of Lincoln's Indian Policy," *Journal of the West* 8 (July 1973).

division appeared between formal Confederate-Indian-Texas relations.[11]

Confederate treaties with the Comanche Indians dealt thoroughly with Texas-Indian relations, and further exposed the feeble relationship. The Comanche treaties declared that "it is distinctly understood by the said several tribes and bands, that the State of Texas is one of the Confederate States, and joins this Convention, and signs it when the Commissioner signs it, and is bound by it; and that all hostilities and enmities between it and them are now ended and are to be forgotten and forgiven on both sides."[12] Given the presence of Texas forces in Comanche territory, and the tradition of hostility between the two groups, the Confederate government believed it necessary to specifically mention Texas in its treaty with the Comanches. Through such treaty articles, Richmond sought to reassure the Comanches that the entire Confederacy including Texas would support and protect them. This aspect of the treaty greatly pleased Pike for he knew that any ceasing of hostility between Texas and the Indians benefitted the South.[13]

The Confederate government also promised the Comanche tribes that "all the Texan troops now within the limits of the said leased country shall be withdrawn across the Red River, and that no Texan troops shall hereafter be stationed in forts or garrisons in the said country or be sent into the same, except in the service of the Confederate States, and when on the war-path against hostile Indians."[14] While the Confederate government could force Texas troops out of the territory, it could do little to actually ease the existing hostility. Keenly aware of this, Pike strove to bring peace between the Indian tribes and Texans. Pike believed that peace between the two groups could be achieved if Texans retreated from their offensive posture. Pike implored the citizens of Texas "not to cross the Red River, into the country leased from the Choctaws and

---

[11]*Creek Treaty; Choctaw and Chickasaw Treaty*, article LXIV.
[12]*Comanche Treaties*, articles X and XI.
[13]Josephy, *Civil War in the American West*, 328.
[14]*Comanche Treaties*, articles XXIV and XXVII.

Chickasaws, in armed bodies." He told Texans they had no reason or right to be in Comanche territory and that all parties would benefit from their withdrawal and ceasing of hostilities. In his view, the Indians wanted peace and the burden for it fell upon Texas citizens. It became their responsibility to keep mounted men and volunteers from interfering in negotiations, regardless of what they believed best.[15]

The Confederate government's attempt to regulate Texas's activity to pacify the organized Indian nations bespeaks the tumultuous relationship between Texans, the Indians, and the Confederacy. Furthermore, it reveals the Confederate government's opposition to Texas's designs for expansion and reveals a paradox regarding the protection of life and property.[16] Unable to protect frontier citizens, the Confederate government simultaneously attempted to restrict Texans from protecting themselves in an offensive manner. Tension existed between Texas and the Confederate government with both sides blaming the other for continuing hostilities. Richmond's attempt to negotiate peace through treaties, however, mattered little to Texans. They placed no faith in Confederate negotiations with the Indians. Many Texans believed that "you cannot get a fair and favorable contract with a white man while he thinks he holds you in his power and to suppose that these savages will make and respect treaties favorable to us, while they believe themselves our masters, is absurd." Texans believed that hostilities would continue to exist despite treaty negotiations.[17]

For the Indians, making war upon Texans did not violate the treaties they signed with Pike. Indians viewed whites in the same manner as themselves—one race divided into separate tribes. Indians

---

[15]*San Antonio Weekly Herald*, 21 September 1861; also see *McKinney Messenger, and Texas State Gazette.*

[16]For Texas expansionism see Josephy, *Civil War in the American West*; William C. Binkley, *The Expansionist Movement in Texas, 1836-1850* (New York: DeCapo Press, 1970); Donald S. Frazier, *Blood and Treasure: Confederate Empire in the Southwest* (College Station: Texas A&M University Press, 1995).

[17]*Texas State Gazette*, 31 August 1861.

looked upon Texans as another 'white tribe' in the Confederacy. Therefore, agreements signed with easterners did not necessarily bind Indians to the same relationship with western whites. As a result, the Indians took advantage of the tumultuous situation and became "more hostile and much bolder than for many years." Texans placed the blame for this on faulty U.S. government relations that the Confederacy continued to uphold. For years the government had "neither sought to conciliate them by kindness nor chastise them into wholesome fear." Texans believed that the bounty approach of the federal government fostered a belief in the Indians that the white man feared their prowess. This led the Indians to view themselves as "masters of the whole interior region." In turn, Indians struck out against Texans, marauding throughout the state to secure their material well being. The *San Antonio Tri-Weekly Alamo Express* reported that "large parties of bold, bloodthirsty Indians scour the country, committing murder and rapine, being embolden by the withdrawal of the Federal troops."[18] The Indians' worldview, combined with a deep-seated belief in self-preservation, therefore helps explain their sentiment toward Texas. Furthermore, it sheds light on Richmond's ignorance of the hostilities that increased due to the sectional conflict.[19]

During this period, Indian attacks knew no age or gender barrier, and Texas suffered atrocities from the organized Indian nations and 'hostile' tribes. Indians were not passive victims but rather aggressive perpetrators, and Texans held them suspect.[20] For example, the *Marshall Texas Republican* reported the story of an attack on two children that occurred in Uvalde County in October 1861. Joseph B.

---

[18] *San Antonio Tri-Weekly Alamo Express*, 13 March 1861.

[19] Lucy A. Erath, *The Memoirs of Major George B. Erath, 1813-1891* (Austin: Texas State Historical Association, 1923), 22; Trickett, "Civil War in Indian Territory," 316. After the Civil War ended, Indians continued to view whites in this manner. See Erath, 98. For an alternative view arguing that Native Americans were loyal to the Confederacy and upheld the treaties see Kenny A. Franks, "The Implementation of the Confederate Treaties with the Five Civilized Tribes," *Chronicles of Oklahoma*, 51 (1973).

[20] Texans referred to the organized Indian nations as the "civilized" tribes and referred to all other tribes as "hostile" Indians.

Long, only six years old, was out herding the family's cattle, only a half mile from the house, with his brother Andrew. Out of nowhere, five Indians on horseback attacked the two children. They demanded, in plain English, that Joseph give them his clothes, and the little boy complied. Standing there stark naked, the Indians shot an arrow into his side. When Joseph started to run, the Indians launched another arrow into his back. The little boy, wise for his age, fell and feigned death. Thinking the boy dead, the Indians departed and started after his brother Andrew. While chasing him, the Indians came upon Julia Ann, a little girl of eleven years, driving up the family horses. The Indians immediately attacked her, pulling her off her horse by her hair and beating her. Her father's quick reaction, however, saved her life. Upon seeing his daughter in the grasp of the Indians he gave chase, and the Indians let Julia Ann free. The Indians, though, departed with all the family's horses, and Joseph died the next day.[21]

Throughout 1861 and 1862 such incidents occurred across the state. Over forty Texas counties suffered from Indian attacks. These incursions transcended regional boundaries. (See map of *Indian Attacks in Texas 1861-1862*, p. 77.) "Civilized" Indians crossed the Red River and assaulted northern counties, raids existed all along the western frontier, and "hostile" Indians crossed from Mexico to invade many south Texas counties. The highest concentration of Indian raids existed along the western frontier, especially in Llano, Blanco, Gillespie, Uvalde and Atascosa counties, within close proximity of the capital. The location of these encounters kept Texas politicians aware of the constant danger that Texas citizens faced. Indian raids, however, also extended deep into Texas, beyond the border-frontier regions, and into slaveholding territory. Counties such as Cass, Titus, Cherokee and Lavacca were among those slaveholding areas that suffered the loss of lives and property. Thus, Indian raids were not a

---

[21]*Marshall* [Texas] *Republican*, 23 November 1861; *San Antonio Weekly Herald*, 19 October 1861.

concern solely for frontiersmen, but a serious economic threat that slaveholders and a majority of Texans faced.[22]

Texas's problems with the Indians took on a dual nature. Not only were Indians driven by their desire for the spoils of war to secure their economic well-being, but they were also fueled by the promptings of northern abolitionists. Abolitionists worked fervently among the Indian tribes to rally support around the Union cause.[23] Several influential Creeks, in fact, changed their loyalty from the Confederacy to the Union. Citizens in Wood County complained in November 1861 that abolitionists were especially strong among the Choctaw Indians. They established friendly relations with many of the Indians and "were doing everything in their power to train the mind of the Choctaw to hate slavery and everything, and every person connected with it, or upholding it." Though frontiersmen had more of a vested interest in livestock and agriculture, their citizenship as Texans joined them, in the mind of the Indian, with those linked to slavery. As such, they suffered the effects of Indian attacks influenced by northern abolitionists. Furthermore, the effect of abolitionists no doubt influenced the Indians to raid into slaveholding territory where oftentimes even slaves suffered death. The Indian nations did not necessarily heed the abolitionist platform, but rather understood the intensity of the American crisis and took advantage of opportunities to gain financially. Their acceptance of northern abolitionists was mixed, and oftentimes they attacked and plundered abolitionist missionaries entering their territory.[24]

Many Texans feared that the Creeks, Choctaws, and other Indian tribes intended to take over Texas, and the *Galveston Weekly News* reported that this was "no idle boast." Newspapers across Texas gave detailed accounts of the Indian attacks and kept those individuals

---

[22]Map of *Indian Attacks in Texas 1861-1862*. Texas newspapers provided that data for Indian attacks.

[23]Morris L. Wardell, *A Political History of the Cherokee Nation, 1838-1907* (Norman: University of Oklahoma Press, 1938), 120-121.

[24]*Marshall [Texas] Republican*, 2 November 1861; *San Antonio Weekly Ledger and Texan*, 1 June 1861; Abel, *American Indian as Slaveholder*, 132; Halliburton, *Red Over Black*, 93-104.

who did not suffer such hazards keenly aware of the dangers that fellow citizens faced. In their raids upon Texans' property, Indians primarily sought to steal horses. In virtually every raid made into Texas counties, Indians were successful in their quest. Oftentimes, Indian tribes banded together to maximize their results. To further make their raids successful, Indians occasionally dressed in Union clothing. Indians were ingenious in their disguise, and dressing as a white man allowed them to move closer without detection. This mode of dress further reveals that Union forces often supported Indian raids into Texas.[25]

Such unified efforts allowed Indians to capture a significant number of horses. In some cases, Indians rounded up several hundred horses at a time, virtually depleting counties of their entire horse population. In one instance, "hostile" Indians stole five-hundred horses from Starr County residents, over ninety-percent of the county's entire horse population. Palo Pinto, San Saba and Burnet counties also suffered a high loss of livestock. The majority of horse raids occurred along the western frontier and the southern border region. (See map of *Horses Stolen 1861-1862*, p. 78.)[26] Approximately twenty-three counties suffered the loss of livestock which greatly effected the economic well being of Texas citizens. Horses were essential to a family's daily livelihood. They not only provided the primary means of transportation, but were necessary for managing cattle. Indians stole horses not only for personal use, but for sale at market. Western markets, Mexico, and northern forces all benefitted from the plunder. Stealing horses not only was a distinct part of their offensive strategy, but also a means to further orient the Indians to the market economy. In their attempt to survive, they partially

---

[25]*Galveston Weekly News*, 26 March 1861; *Galveston Weekly Civilian and Gazette*, 15 January 1861; *Marshall Texas Republican*, 21 May 1862.

[26]Map of *Horses Stolen 1861-1862*; Agriculture of the United States in 1860, The Eighth Census (Washington: Government Printing Office, 1864). Hereafter cited as Agriculture Census.

accommodated themselves to the world against which they struggled.[27]

More devastating than the loss of livestock, however, was the loss of life. No measure can be placed on the cost of lives and the effect of such loss at a time when many counties sent men to war. The calamity of Indian aggressions only compounded the difficulties in each county. Approximately thirty counties lost men, women, and children due to Indian attacks. The loss of life due to Indian attacks was widespread throughout the state. (See map of *Lives Lost 1861-1862*, p. 79.) Both frontier and slaveholding counties had citizens killed and injured.[28] Assaults on Texas citizens were often of the most brutal nature. In one instance, Indians attacked and killed a man in Weatherford. "As soon as he fell," reports stated, "he was surrounded by Indians, who commenced torturing him with arrows. . . . When his body was found, his tongue and eyes had been cut out, most probably while still alive. . . . Behind every pine tree in the vicinity was blood." The brutality of the conflict cannot be overemphasized. The Indian tribes undertook an offensive strategy to murder Texas citizens and steal their property. They devastated families and counties for their own personal gain.[29] The brutality of attacks and the loss of life stirred mingled feelings for Texans. Blanco county residents were torn at the loss of a child killed by Indians. The citizens felt "deep pity for the lad, boiling indignation against his brutal murderers, and deep-rooted disgust at the majority of our rulers who have never bestowed a second thought upon frontier protection."[30]

Citizen outrage toward the government in such situations is understandable. Nevertheless, the Texas state government did make

---

[27]T. R. Havins, *Something About Brown: A History of Brown County, Texas* (Brownwood, Texas: Banner Printing Company, 1958), 22-23; Sandra Myres, "The Ranching Frontier: Spanish Institutional Backgrounds of the Plains Cattle Industry," *Essays on the American West* (Austin: University of Texas Press, 1969), 24; Sara Kay Curtis, "A History of Gillespie County, Texas, 1846-1900" (M.A. thesis, University of Texas at Austin, 1943), 63.

[28]Map of *Lives Lost 1861-1862.*

[29]*Texas State Gazette*, 26 October 1861.

[30]*Marshall Texas Republican*, 22 February 1862.

an effort to deal with the Indian problem. The Confederate govern-ment's delay in ratifying the treaties undermined relations between Texas and the Indians, forcing state politicians to act regarding the safety of Texas citizens. By the end of 1861, the Indian problem emerged foremost in the minds of Texas politicians, and the legisla-ture resolved to have a committee from both Houses to "act jointly on measures of frontier defense."[31]

During the political debate that followed over the frontier and the Indian problem, Governor Francis Lubbock addressed a joint session of the legislature. Lubbock told Texas politicians on November 15, 1861, that "our Indian troubles should occupy your attention," for it is "no unfrequent occurrence to hear of murders being committed and property stolen by our Indian enemies." Lubbock also criticized the Confederate government and further remarked, "a civilized Govern-ment could not be expected to make treaties with a power with which it is at war, so long as success attended its arms—much less can it be hoped of a savage foe, who believe that they are superior in the mode of warfare pursued." Lubbock and most Texans alike fully understood the offensive posture of the Indian tribes and the failure of the Confederate government adequately to handle the situation. Because the organized tribes, under the protection of the Confederate government, continued to receive subsidies while simultaneously robbing and murdering Texas citizens, Lubbock placed no faith in the Confederacy's Indian policy. The governor railed against the presence of Indians in Texas territory and told the state legislature "to declare by positive enactment," that the Indians "whenever and wherever found on our soil they will be deemed and treated as enemies." Lubbock believed that too many Texas citizens had been affected in disastrous ways as a result of Indian raids and that "it will require years for the people to forget their numerous atrocities."[32]

---

[31]James M. Day, ed., *Senate Journal of the Ninth Legislature of the State of Texas* (Austin: Texas State Library, 1963), 43, (hereafter *Senate Journal—Ninth Regular Session*).

[32]James M. Day, ed., *Journal of the House of Representatives of the Ninth Legislature of the State of Texas* (Austin: Texas State Library, 1963), 49-51, (hereafter *House Journal—Ninth Regular Session*); *Senate Journal—Ninth Regular Session*, 51-52.

Due to Richmond's ignorance and neglect of Texas's situation, Lubbock beseeched the legislature to adopt a meaningful and effective strategy for the protection of Texas. Lubbock had in mind the adoption of an offensive strategy and opposed the continued approach of treaty making. "It is my deliberate opinion," he told the legislature, "that we will never have treaties with the Indians on our border, on which we can rely, until they are made to feel the blighting effects of war, visited upon them at their own homes, and around their own firesides." For Lubbock, as for most Texans, adopting an offensive strategy proved the only means to secure life and property within Texas's borders.[33]

The Texas legislature heeded Lubbock's words only to a certain extent. On November 19, 1861, George B. Erath, chairman of the Senate Committee on Indian Affairs, presented a committee report. The committee found that the Confederate troops on the frontier had done less than an adequate job. The committee criticized the Confederate troops for their lack of a full offensive against the Indians. They did, however, acknowledge that the Indians hampered their duties. Nevertheless, this did not provide a satisfactory excuse for the lack of protection. Due to the Confederate troops' failure, the committee suggested that the system of frontier protection be bolstered by men under state authority who would be placed in smaller groups "on the outskirts of the settlements at points so near each other that the distance between any two stations could be traversed every day."[34] The Senate Committee on Indian Affairs comprised eight individuals from various districts representing fifty counties from across the state, and geographical analysis of the committee reveals that politicians represented counties from every economic region of the state. Both frontier and slaveholding counties had representatives on the Committee on Indian Affairs. Thus, the committee's criticism of the Confederate government and the political effort to protect Texas citizens came not only from frontier politicians

---

[33]Ibid.
[34]*Senate Journal—Ninth Regular Session*, 88-89.

but also from those politicians representing slaveholding interests, revealing a unified effort to protect the welfare of the state and the citizenry.[35]

On December 10, 1861, the Texas Senate announced in chamber that the House of Representatives passed a bill to provide for frontier protection, and began debate on the issue the next day. Debate over frontier protection involved several intermingled issues including questions on the authority over troops, the financing for frontier protection, and the location of troops. In dealing with the mustering of troops, E. B. Scarborough from Cameron County[36] proposed to strike a section of the House bill specifically referring to mustering troops from Nueces, Webb, Cameron, Starr, Zapata, San Patricio, and Goliad counties and instead proposed that the governor muster companies from any part of the state as he so directed. Mr. Scarborough's resolution passed, placing significant power for the control of state troops in the hands of the governor.[37]

The eighth section of the frontier bill dealt with financial responsibility of these proposed troops. The critical aspect of the debate revolved around whether the state or the Confederate government had financial responsibility for the troops. Texas politicians hoped to raise troops for frontier protection while placing the burden of financial support on the Confederate government. In addition they desired that these troops remain on Texas soil, free from Confederate control. Texas politicians did not view this as a contradiction. They believed that the Confederate government had the responsibility for protecting the frontier and could accomplish this goal by financing state troops mustered specifically for this task. The

---

[35]Map of *Texas Committee on Indian Affairs*. Committee on Indian Affairs: George B. Erath, N. G. Shelley, Erastus Reed, H. C. Cook, Robert H. Guinn, Pryor Lea, A. F. Crawford, and John T. Harcourt.

[36]E. B. Scarborough, a Georgia native who worked as a planter and printer, represented District 32 that comprised Cameron, Hidalgo, Starr, Zapata, Webb, Encinal, and Duval counties located on the South Texas-Mexico border.

[37]*Senate Journal—Ninth Regular Session*, 117.

Senate debated these critical issues much of the day, but adjourned without a decision.[38]

The next day, December 12, the Senate entertained again the question of frontier protection. Attempting to bring compromise to the issue over financial responsibility and state control over troops, Robert H. Guinn, who served on the Committee on Indian Affairs,[39] offered an amendment "that said regiment shall not become a charge against the State until the Confederate government musters out of service the regiment now stationed upon the frontier or refuses to accept this regiment in lieu thereof." By a vote of eighteen to ten, however, the Senate laid Mr. Guinn's proposal on the table. The majority of Senate members therefore believed that providing for the protection of the frontier took precedence over financial concerns at that moment, and agreed to provide frontier protection regardless of financial costs. The Senate did agree, though, that state troops should not become a charge against the state "until they are mustered into service or placed under orders."[40]

The Senate then sent the amended version of the bill back to the House of Representatives, and politicians there informed the Senate that they agreed to all the changes in the frontier bill except those pertaining to section eight. Politicians believed that the Confederate government should take full responsibility for the proposed troops. As a result, the House appointed a three-man committee to resolve the differences between the two legislative branches. On motion from George B. Erath, however, the Senate insisted on its version of the bill and also appointed a three-member committee to deal with the differences.[41] On December 17, the Senate passed a resolution dealing

---

[38]Senate Journal—Ninth Regular Session, 124; David Paul Smith, "Frontier Defense in Texas, 1861-1865" (Ph.D. diss., North Texas State University, 1987), 96-98.

[39]Robert H. Guinn, a lawyer from Tennessee, served as President pro tempore of the Senate and represented District 10 that comprised Cherokee County in East Texas, approximately forty miles from current day Nacogdoches, Texas.

[40]Senate Journal—Ninth Regular Session, 132-133.

[41]Senate Journal—Ninth Regular Session, 132-133. George Erath, a native of South Carolina who worked as a farmer and surveyor, represented District 28 that comprised Fall, Coryell, Bosque, McLennan, Comanche, Brown, Hamilton, Ellis, Eastland, Callahan,

with the eighth section: "that no portion of said troop shall become a charge against the State until organized as required by the fifth section of this Act and placed under orders." The next day, the House adopted the committee report and this version of the eighth section. The final version of the bill for frontier protection called for a twelve-month enlistment of ten companies. On Governor Lubbock's insistence, the recruited men were to be stationed near their home counties to remain close to their families. In addition, these troops were to remain on Texas soil. Furthermore, Texas politicians still hoped to place the financial responsibility for the troops on the Confederate government.[42]

The Confederate government, however, refused to accept Texas troops into Confederate service under this agreement. Though the bill came up for debate and passed in the Confederate Congress, President Davis vetoed the bill because it limited executive control and complicated the military administration of the Confederacy. Davis's veto and neglect of Texas's concerns was a foreshadowing of events to come. Due to Davis's veto, the financial burden for frontier protection fell to the state. Not all Texans were happy with this decision, and many citizens believed the legislature's decision to maintain troops at state expense "foolish and unconstitutional." Despite minor criticism, Texas politicians did take action toward addressing the Indian issue. Furthermore, the effort of the House and Senate to cast aside differences and settle the critical issue of frontier protection reveals the unity of Texas politicians to secure the welfare of the citizenry and the protection of their lives and property.[43]

In December 1861, the Confederate government deliberated Indian relations when President Davis submitted the Pike treaties to Congress. The ratification process included debate among the

---

Coleman, Taylor, Hill, and Runnels Counties located on the central Texas frontier.

[42]*Senate Journal—Ninth Regular Session*, 142, 148; Smith, "Frontier Defense in Texas, 1861-1865," 95-97.

[43]Smith, "Frontier Defense in Texas, 1861-1865," 98-99. These events, including control over state institutions and the cotton trade are detailed in my dissertation. For specific criticism of the Texas legislature see *Texas State Gazette*, 3 September 1862.

Confederate representatives that resulted in several amendments to the treaties. On December 31, 1861, Congress considered the treaty with the Comanche Indians and moved to have article twenty-seven completely stricken from the treaty. Striking out article twenty-seven, "that all Texan troops now within the limits of said leased country shall be withdrawn across the Red River," was significant for it allowed Texans to fully employ an offensive posture against the Indian tribes. All of the Texas representatives in Congress, except William Ochiltree, supported the presence of Texas state troops within Indian territory, regardless of their mission. The sanction from Richmond allowing Texas to wage war against the Indians using state troops contributed to the solidifying of state identity and reinforced Texas's designs to pacify or eradicate the Indians for their own economic security. Previous to the ratification of the treaty, though, Texas had already adopted the extra-legal position of pursuing Indians across the Red River. Therefore, the political endorsement from Richmond was essentially of little consequence except to solidify a process already transpiring. It did, however, reveal that Texas representatives in Congress, at this stage in the crisis, still had contact with and supported the desires of their constituents.[44]

During the evening session that same day, Congress debated several articles in the Choctaw and Chickasaw Treaty. Two of these articles under debate, articles forty-three and forty-four, established the power of state courts and laws to deal with Indian problems. Though the original version of the treaties stipulated that Indians would receive full rights and representation in court, the amended version left the final decision to individual states. Thus, each state in practice could refuse the Confederate request to abide by the original agreement of Indian representation in the treaties. For Texas this was a significant piece of legislation enabling it to exercise full political power over foreign individuals. In the face of hostilities, this enabled Texas to take legal measures against Indians. Still, this was of little

---

[44]*Journal of the Congress of the Confederate States of America, 1861-1865*, volume 1 (Washington: Government Printing Office, 1904), 632-633, (hereafter JCCSA).

consequence since Texas had routinely engaged in extra-legal measures to deal with the Indian problem. Richmond's political support of state interests came too late for Texas's Indian crisis. Moreover, Indian hostilities all but nullified Texas's desire to follow Confederate treaties.[45] Each of these approved amendments were significant pieces of legislation affecting relations between Texas and the Indian nations. The Indian tribes, however, were not pleased with the amendments, and Pike labored for three days to convince them to accept the treaties. Despite his efforts, Congress did not uphold the treaty agreements. Their failure to do so resulted from multiple factors including a lack of finances, disruptive military campaigns, and a concern for its own continued existence.[46]

Despite Richmond's efforts to secure relations with the Indians, their failure adequately to solve the crisis led Texas citizens to rail against the Confederate government for its neglect, expressing the same sentiments as their political leaders. Citizens from Coryell County expressed outrage at the Confederate government. Not only did they battle abolitionists and "Reserve Indians," but they believed they were in a struggle with the Confederate government who they blamed for purchasing stolen horses from the Indians and paying them in arms and ammunition far superior to any of those owned by Texas citizens.[47] In May 1862, the *Houston Telegraph* ran an editorial further criticizing Richmond. While Texans knew that the Confederate government had to give attention to strategic points in the Confederacy, they complained that the government ignored vital points and interests in Texas. "That we can look for little or no help from the Government is obvious," the paper complained, "from the fact that

---

[45]*JCCSA*, volume 1, 633-634. The Congress also debated the same issues regarding the Creek treaty, articles 28, 30, and 40, with the same conclusions, *JCCSA*, volume 1, 634; and debated the Cherokee treaty on December 23, 1861 (articles 35, 44, 33) with the same results, *JCCSA*, volume 1, 610-611.

[46]Josephy, *Civil War in the American West*, 3 37; Franks, "The Implementation of the Confederate Treaties with the Five Civilized Tribes," 33; Kenny A. Franks, "The Confederate States and the Five Civilized Tribes," *Journal of the West* 8 (July 1973).

[47]Zelma Scott, *A History of Coryell County, Texas* (Austin: Texas State Historical Association, 1965), 60.

the general defense of the whole country demands their exclusive attention to the military strategic points, none of which lie in this State." Texans believed that the economic interests of their state were as vital as the military interests of the South. Citizens worried that "the strategic cattle pasture extending from here to the Rio Grande, the strategic commercial channel passing through Brownsville, the strategic strip of empty territory west of San Antonio, and extending to El Paso; and, above all, the strategic wheat fields of Northern Texas, stand a good chance to be left to the care of old men and boys." Texans believed these economic interests were vital to their "destiny" and deserved full protection. Due to Richmond's neglect, Texans placed their trust in the state and local agencies. "We have the utmost confidence in our own authorities," the *Telegraph* declared, "both military and civil."[48]

Due to the continuing hostilities, requests poured into Lubbock's office asking for action against the Indians.[49] Indian attacks became so severe in some areas that open hostility existed between outraged citizens and government troops. Citizens still looked to the state government for protection of life and property, but they increasingly realized that the responsibility for protection lay in their own hands. This realization came in part due to the failure of the Texas Rangers. Citizens railed against the poor job of the Rangers and the *State Gazette* asked, "Where are our Rangers? Wonder if there were not some eight or ten at this place drinking and cutting up worse than Indians during this time: while our citizens are fighting for the recovery of their stolen property."[50]

Despite the criticism and strife, the state legislature did attempt to remedy the Indian problem, but it did not fully succeed in this task. This, according to George B. Erath, resulted in part from their little experience in legislating and fully comprehending the task of adopting specific measures necessary to safeguard Texas citizens.[51] The minute

---

[48]*Houston Tri-Weekly Telegraph*, 9 May 1862.
[49]*Indian Papers*, volume 4, 67-68; *Marshall Texas Republican*, 22 February 1862.
[50]*Texas State Gazette*, 22 February 1862; *San Antonio Weekly Herald*, 1 March 1862.
[51]Erath, *Memoirs of Major George B. Erath*, 95.

man system that it adopted, however, proved more favorable than that of Confederate protection, which accomplished little. Nevertheless, in the aftermath of attacks some citizens complained that the state government failed in its programs and its commitment to protect the lives and property of its citizens. Many Texans believed that the Texas Rangers and the Minute Company system adopted by the legislature failed to protect the Texas frontier.[52]

The Indian problem became so grave that many Texans feared to venture from their homes. "The man thus situated," one citizen complained, "dare not go out of the smoke of his own chimney without constant uneasiness and misgiving lest his wife and little ones may be massacred in his absence." Texas citizens believed that "the Indians must be worried and hunted down, killed to the last man, or driven so far beyond our borders that we shall hear no more of them. They should be sought in their hunting grounds, when killing their stock of buffalo meat—should be allowed no rest nor respite—should be granted no truce nor treaty. The cruel war they are waging against us—and cowardly as well as cruel, for they attack none but the weak and defenseless—will last so long as an Indian is left." Texans expressed severe doubts about the ability of the troops to protect a vast frontier, and realized the necessity of more localized efforts.[53]

The brutality of the conflict is beyond contemporary imagination and the fact that Indians held no respect for age or gender only compounded the harsh realities that families faced. Throughout 1861 and 1862, Texans sought to counter the Indians with offensive measures. "Let them be taught that their existence depends on their good conduct," the *Austin Texas State Gazette* reported, "and that their arid plains and mountain vastness will not protect them from the just vengeance of the Government; and then, and not till then, may we expect such treaties, and such faith in the observance of treaties as will result in continued friendly relations between the two races." Texans did not have faith in Pike's negotiations with the

---

[52]*Marshall Texas Republican*, 11 February 1862, 22 February 1862, 1 March 1862.
[53]*San Antonio Weekly Herald*, 1 February 1862.

Indian nations, nor did they agree that they should retreat from their offensive posture. The only effective way to deal with the Indians, they believed, involved incorporating the same tactics used by the Indians.[54] Citizens felt they had no choice but to launch their own offensive measures, and Texans committed themselves to tracking down Indians and taking the war to their enemy. Their offensive posture was not merely a reaction to specific attacks, but a general practice whenever Texans believed Indians lurked in the vicinity. For example, after hearing rumors of Indians present in the area in March 1861, citizens from Webb and Zapata Counties immediately searched the known Indian trails and killed several Indians. A similar situation occurred in February 1862, when Parker County residents tracked down and killed several Indians who stole sixty-three horses from local citizens. In addition, Texas citizens often pursued the Indians into Choctaw, Chickasaw, and Cherokee territory where they succeeded in killing a significant number of Indians. In one case, the *Austin Texas State Gazette* reported in February 1862 that three hundred Indians were killed in a single battle.[55] In their pursuit of the enemy, Texans tortured and killed any Indian they happened upon, whether or not they were responsible for raids. Texans exhibited complete wantonness in their objective and often returned with Indian scalps as a show of force and victory.[56]

More than fifty percent of the counties that suffered from Indian attacks adopted offensive measures. (See map of *Offensive Measures 1861-1862*, p. 80.) In counties across the state, concerned citizens searched for Indian trails hoping to catch, torture and kill the enemy. Often they left loved ones unprotected for days, a jeopardizing dilemma, but a necessary one. In their pursuit, Texans injured and

---

[54]*Austin Texas State Gazette*, 31 August 1861; Theda Perdue, *Nations Remembered: An Oral History of the Five Civilized Tribes, 1865-1902* (Westport: Greenwood Press, 1980), 5.

[55]*Austin Texas State Gazette*, 1 February 1862. For additional pursuits into Indian territory see *Austin Texas State Gazette*, 26 November 1861; *Galveston Weekly News*, 23 July 1861; *Galveston Tri-Weekly News*, 14 December 1861; *Marshall Texas Republican*, 11 January 1862; *Dallas Weekly News*, 5 July 1862.

[56]*San Antonio Tri-Weekly Alamo Express*, 18 March 1861; *Austin Texas State Gazette*, 22 February 1862; *Marshall Texas Republican*, 1 March 1862.

killed a significant number of Indians. Geographical analysis of the offensive measures and Indians killed reveals that over eighty percent of the counties succeeded in mounting effectual campaigns of locating, fighting and killing Indians. Texans were just as brutal and savage as the Indian in their pursuit, and the offensive posture that united Texans served as the basis for a separate identity from that of other Confederate states.[57]

Efforts to combat the Indians, however, extended beyond those counties directly affected by atrocities. Throughout this period citizens turned to other counties for aid to combat the hostility. All Texans were aware of Indian encounters; if their county had not experienced skirmishes within the last decade, they were at least informed through the press of the hardship that fellow citizens faced. Reports of Indian atrocities were so horrendous and so well known throughout the state, that citizens from counties not directly affected gathered to offer support for the afflicted counties. Houston and Galveston stood out as being especially generous in their efforts to aid fellow Texans; citizens there often contributed arms and supplies for the frontier. In Seguin, the *Southern Confederacy* reported that "the Indian excitement on the bleeding frontier, has roused the patriotism of some of our gallant citizens," and urged residents to aid frontier citizens. Similar situations occurred across the state, and the frontier countrymen knew that those citizens gave well beyond their means.[58]

More often than not, though, counties raised their own financial and material support for defense. Unable to rely on the Confederate or state government for adequate assistance, individual counties collected money, arms, blankets, food and other basic necessities to aid men willing to brave confrontation with the Indians. The willingness of counties to sacrifice money and material for the

---

[57]Map of *Offensive Measures 1861-1862*; Map of *Indians Killed 1861-1862*; *Marshall Texas Republican*, 1 June 1861. Texans also pursued and killed the Indians in their territory. See *Austin Texas State Gazette*, 17 August 1861, 24 August 1861; *Dallas Weekly Herald*, 5 July 1862.

[58]*Dallas Weekly Herald*, 9 January 1861; *San Antonio Tri-Weekly Alamo Express*, 13 March 1861; *Seguin Southern Confederacy*, 22 March 1861.

protection of their lives and property speaks to the significance of the Indian crisis in their daily life, and reveals a desire on the part of individual citizens to take offensive measures for their security. Furthermore, the decision of other counties to assist their brothers and sisters in the struggle against the Indian reveals a unified state bound in a common struggle. Instead of placing their faith and trust in the general government, the Indian problems led most Texans to distrust the Confederate government, to look to their own defense, and to identify with local as opposed to larger Confederate issues.[59] Likewise, the Indians could not rely on the Confederate or Texas government. White expansion led to a relationship of hostility and broken promises. Ironically, the Indian's struggle paralleled that of Texas and the Confederacy. The Indians believed they were assaulted on all sides. They sought to halt encroachment from outsiders and fought to retain their way of life. Struggling against long odds, guerilla war provided an opportunity to attain this goal. In this process, the Indians came to distrust outside forces completely. This further served to unify Indian tribes and proved a foreshadowing of the embittered conflicts that later surfaced in their quest for survival against invasion and assimilation.[60]

By 1863, Union forces invaded much of the territory belonging to the Cherokee and Creek nations, forcing those Indians into Choctaw and Chickasaw territory. The additional presence of Indians along the Red River served to continue the tumultuous relationship as Indians pressed increasingly upon Texas soil for their own economic gain. In addition, Indian raids continued in south Texas and on the western frontier. Though hostilities between Texans and Indians existed throughout the Civil War, by 1863 Texans became more concerned

---

[59]*Galveston Weekly News*, 5 February 1861; *San Antonio Weekly Alamo Express*, 9 March 1861; *San Antonio Tri-Weekly Alamo Express*, 8 March 1861.

[60]On the Indians after the Civil War, see Frederick E. Hoxie, *A Final Promise: The Campaign to Assimilate the Indians* (Lincoln: University of Nebraska Press, 1984), Janet A. McDonnell, *The Dispossession of the American Indian, 1887-1934* (Bloomington: Indiana University Press, 1991), Robert Wooster, *The Military and United States Indian Policy, 1865-1903* (New Haven: Yale University Press, 1988).

with the state's relationship to the Confederacy. Due to Union control of the Mississippi River, the Confederate government organized the Trans-Mississippi Department, the official military and political voice of Richmond in the West, under the direction of Edmund Kirby Smith. The Indian problems that Texas faced from 1861 through 1862, though, fostered the establishment of a separate identity for Texans. This in turn directly affected Texas's relationship with the Trans-Mississippi Department and the Confederate government as Texas faced new issues of control and authority that continued to threaten their economic well-being.[61]

---

[61]Josephy, *Civil War in the American West*, 375.

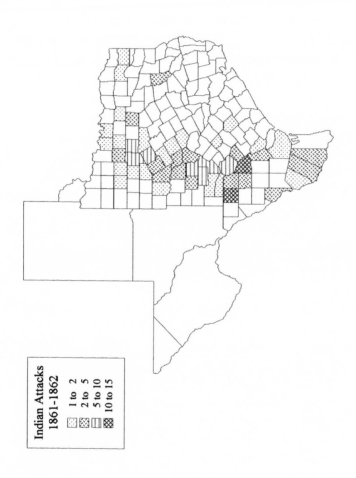

Indian Attacks
1861-1862

⬚ 1 to 2
⬚ 2 to 5
⬚ 5 to 10
⬚ 10 to 15

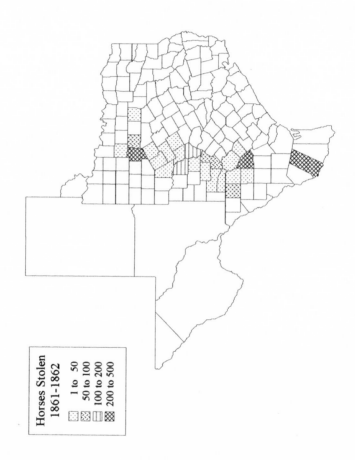

Horses Stolen
1861-1862

1 to 50
50 to 100
100 to 200
200 to 500

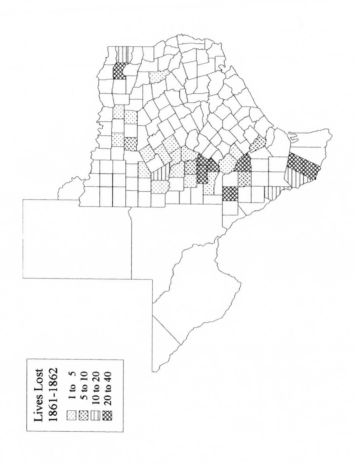

Lives Lost
1861–1862

1 to 5
5 to 10
10 to 20
20 to 40

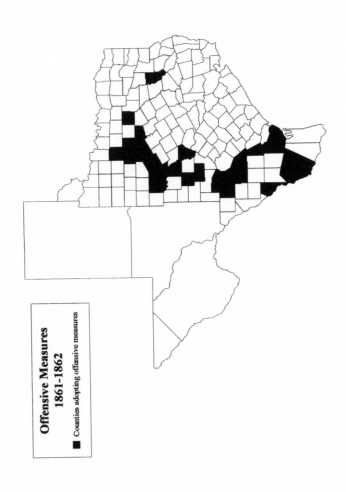

Offensive Measures
1861-1862

■ Counties adopting offensive measures

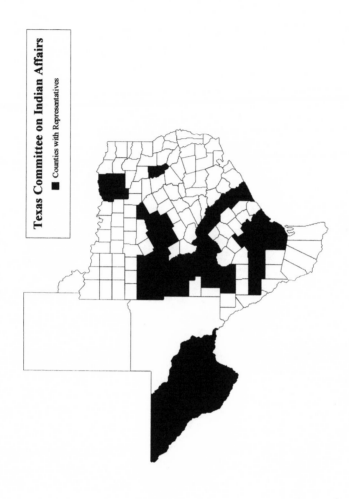

Texas Committee on Indian Affairs
■ Counties with Representatives

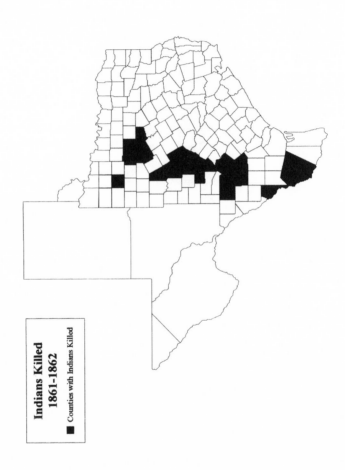

Indians Killed
1861-1862

■ Counties with Indians Killed

II.

Development of African-American Identity in the Reconstruction South

3

"I HAVE NEVER BEEN FREE AND I AM GOIN' TO TRY IT": THE DEVELOPMENT OF BLACK FAMILIES IN WAKE COUNTY, NORTH CAROLINA, 1865-1870

David H. McGee

At the end of the Civil War, Bertcha Lane faced her "old marster" and informed him that she was leaving his Wake County plantation. Her former owner, Charles Manly, a skilled politician who served two terms as governor of North Carolina during the antebellum period, tried to talk her into staying. He warned Bertcha that she did not possess the means to "feed all her children, pay house rent, and buy wood." Charles tempted Bertcha and her family with the offer of a free house and free wood if they would remain with him. She declined, stating "I am going to leave, I have never been free and I am goin' to try it. I am goin' away and by my work and the help of the lord I will live somehow." Bertcha Lane felt the exhilaration of her new freedom and was determined to find out what it meant, regardless of possible dangers.[1]

Across Wake County and the rest of the South, blacks echoed Bertcha Lane's feelings about exploring their newfound liberty. But what did "freedom" mean to these newly emancipated people? One historian, Eric Foner, defined it as a "desire for independence from

---

[1]George P. Rawick, gen. ed., *The American Slave: A Composite Autobiography*, vol. 15, *North Carolina Narratives*, pt. 2 (Westport, Conn.: Greenwood Publishing Company, 1972), 181.

white control, for autonomy both as individuals and as members of a community itself being transformed by emancipation." Many other historians have described the African-American struggle for freedom mainly in political, legal, or economic terms. Although these writers did not ignore social issues, they frequently judged Reconstruction a success or failure (or a mixture of both) based on their view of how well blacks achieved some measure of political and economic autonomy or independence.[2]

But for many southern blacks in the years immediately following the Civil War, their search for freedom centered around more tangible gains. A key element of this quest was the desire of African-Americans to create a stable family life that had so often been denied them during slavery. Historians such as Jacqueline Jones, Herbert Gutman, and Leon Litwack have described the lengths freedpersons went in their efforts to build lasting familial relations following emancipation. For the former slaves, the ability to have loved ones close by without the constant threat of separation played an important role in defining freedom.[3]

This study examines how African Americans in Wake County, North Carolina, went about creating (or recreating) their families and what factors influenced their decisions to live in a rural or urban

---

[2]Eric Foner, *Reconstruction: America's Unfinished Reconstruction, 1863-1877* (New York: Harper and Row, 1988), 78. Other significant works which have focused almost solely on the political, legal, or economic aspects of slavery include: John Hope Franklin, *Reconstruction after the Civil War* (Chicago: University of Chicago Press, 1961); Kenneth Stampp, *The Era of Reconstruction after the Civil War* (New York: Alfred Knopf, 1965); Roger L. Ransom and Richard Sutch, *One Kind of Freedom: The Economic Consequences of Emancipation* (New York, 1977); and Anderson and Moss, eds., *The Facts of Reconstruction: Essays in Honor of John Hope Franklin* (Baton Rouge: Louisiana State University Press, 1991).

[3]Jacqueline Jones, *Labor of Love, Labor of Sorrow: Black Women, Work and the Family, from Slavery to the Present* (New York: Vintage Books, 1985), 58; Herbert G. Gutman, *The Black Family in Slavery and Freedom, 1750-1925* (New York: Vintage Books, 1976), ch. 9; Leon Litwack, *Been in the Storm So Long: The Aftermath of Slavery* (New York: Alfred A. Knopf, 1979), 229-247. Brenda E. Stevenson's study of antebellum family and community life in Loudon County, Virginia provides an excellent description of the struggles that African-American families (both slave and free) to maintain stable families. *Life in Black and White: Family and Community in the Slave South* (New York: Oxford University Press: 1996), chapters 7, 8, and 10.

setting. Focusing on family life provides an opportunity to examine one of the ways the newly liberated blacks developed their vision of freedom in an environment where a significant number of whites continued to treat freedpersons as if they were still slaves. Francis Butler Simkins noted that in the years following the Civil War, the "family was the core of Southern society; within its bounds everything worth while took place." Although Simkins was discussing southern whites, his observation remains valid for the freedpersons as well. The family became the keystone of an independent black community.[4]

Two factors make Wake County a good locale for such an investigation. First, the county contains both the state capital of Raleigh and a large farming area. This allows a comparison of family and household development in both urban and rural areas. Second, the North Carolina legislature passed a law in 1866 which required all blacks who had been cohabiting during slavery to have their marriages legalized before a justice of the peace or clerk of court. The records left by this law furnish information on the number of slave couples who legitimized their relationship and the length of their marriage. The records of cohabitation, combined with census data and the fifty-six interviews of former Wake County slaves taken by Works Progress Administration workers during the 1930s, provides a good overview of the development of African-American families following the Civil War.[5]

After emancipation, many freedpersons rapidly set forth to develop or reconstruct their families. The speed with which this process took place often depended on the location of the various

---

[4]Francis Butler Simkins, *A History of the South* (New York: Alfred A. Knopf, 1965), 388.

[5]Roberta Sue Alexander, *North Carolina Faces the Freedmen: Race Relations During Presidential Reconstruction, 1865-1867* (Durham, NC: Duke University Press, 1985), 59, 62; Wake County, North Carolina, Record of Cohabitation, 1866, North Carolina Division of Archives and History (hereafter referenced as NCDAH). The statute requiring the registration of slave marriages passed the North Carolina legislature only after another bill which would have automatically legalized slave marriages failed. The sponsor of the original proposal argued that his marriage ordinance would prevent black men from marrying more than one woman, which he claimed the males liked to do. John Richard Dennett, *The South As It Is: 1865-1866* (New York: Viking Press, 1965), 164.

family members. If a couple had "married abroad" (while living on different plantations) the first task was to find a way to reunite their family. According to Charlie Dickens, it took nearly a year before his father came to Wake County and carried the family back with him on a "steer cart" to a neighboring county. Other families, like that of Clara Jones, reunited swiftly. Jones's husband moved right after the end of the war to the plantation where she lived and started "ter farmin' wid a purpose."[6]

The number of couples like the Dickenses or the Joneses who married abroad cannot be determined precisely. A perusal of the Wake County Record of Cohabitation shows that only thirty-six out of 659 couples had different last names at the time their marriage was legalized. This suggests that most couples lived on the same plantations before emancipation. Yet accounts from the Works Progress Administration (WPA) interviews with former slaves present a completely different picture. Of the forty-seven Wake County narratives that described where a couple lived before emancipation, twenty-one stated that husband and wife lived at separate locations. Roberta Sue Alexander compared the Records of Cohabitation and the WPA narratives for twenty-eight North Carolina counties. She also concluded that the slave narratives present a more accurate picture of how many slaves married abroad.[7]

Not all former slaves acknowledged marriages formed while they had been in bondage. After emancipation occurred in North Carolina, some freedpersons took advantage of their new freedom to escape unwanted spouses or families. A number of reports reached the local Freedmen's Bureau of husbands or wives deserting their spouses. The agency also reported that it had received numerous complaints from black women that their husbands would not support them or their children. One Wake County slave, Edmund Rand, left the

---

[6]White, Ar'n't I a Woman, 154; Rawick, The American Slave, vol. 14, 255-57; vol. 15, 33.

[7]Alexander, North Carolina Faces the Freedmen, 58; Wake County Record of Cohabitation, NCDAH; Rawick, The American Slave, 14 and 15.

plantation and his family as soon as the war ended. Not to be outdone, his daughter Emma Blalock left shortly afterwards.[8]

Those freedpersons looking to reunite their families often faced the additional challenge of locating and recovering their children. Besides finding children who had been sold away from their kin under slavery, blacks were pressured by former masters who tried to keep the youngsters as "apprentices." Burton Freeman yielded to the insistence of his former mistress and let his son stay with her after the war. Not until 1868 did Freeman come and take his son home with him. The United States Army found itself forced to intervene at times. General Newton Palmer, commander of the federal troops in the Raleigh area immediately after the war, ordered a black boy returned to Mrs. B. C. Beckwith because the child was "incapable of self-support."[9]

In certain cases, the Freedmen's Bureau had to step in to protect children against abusive indentures. In Raleigh, Lt. F. D. McAlpine informed Alonzo Mial that a complaint had reached his office about Mial attempting to get possession of two freed children. McAlpine cautioned him to leave the children alone unless he had a legal claim to them. "If these children do not want to live [with] you, or if their relatives do not want you to have them, they must not be induced by you to leave their relatives or friends." McAlpine went on to warn Mial against threatening the family, declaring that "threats in regard to killing only hurt those who make them." The problems black parents in Raleigh had in keeping their children echoed the troubles faced by many African-American parents throughout the South. Historian Leon Litwack has described the apprenticeship laws used by

---

[8]Alexander, *North Carolina Faces the Freedmen*, 65; Rawick, *The American Slave*, vol. 14, 107. Peter Kolchin argues that the end of slavery in Alabama initially weakened the "precarious bonds" that held members of African American families together. Peter Kolchin, *First Freedom: The Responses of Alabama's Blacks to Emancipation and Reconstruction* (Westport, Conn.: Greenwood Press, 1972), 59-63. In contrast to Kolchin's assertion and the reports from the Raleigh office of the Freedmen's Bureau, only one of the fifty-six slave narratives from Wake County mention the breakup of a family after emancipation.

[9]Alexander, 65; Order from Gen. Newton Palmer, June 1, 1865, B. C. Beckwith Papers, NCDAH; Rawick, *The American Slave*, vol. 14, 320.

some whites to keep control of their labor source as "close to legalized kidnapping."[10]

Other threats to the creation of a stable family life came as a significant proportion of whites throughout the South systematically abused blacks and used the law to deprive them of their autonomy. Black-oriented newspapers published numerous reports concerning mistreatment of freedpersons. These accounts included stories ranging from persecution by plantation owners—beatings, refusal to pay justly earned wages, and even denying emancipation to the slaves well after the war ended—to whipping and torture "in the most fiendish manner for even expressing a desire to be free," and later the terror of the Ku Klux Klan. But the most serious consequences arose from a double standard of law enforcement which brought swift punishment for freedpersons charged with minor crimes—such as disturbing a religious service or a public "affray"—for which whites were seldom prosecuted. But the unequal enforcement of the laws was only half the problem. If a convicted black did not have the money to pay the fines or court costs, another person could pay the penalties in their stead. In such instances the county court allowed blacks to be indentured to pay the debt. These indentures, which usually lasted one to three years, effectively returned the black person to slavery for a limited time.[11]

Not all whites proved unsympathetic to black efforts to create a stable family life. In addition to occasional assistance from the

---

[10]Lt. F. D. McAlpine to Alonzo T. Mial, October 31, 1866, Alonzo T. Mial Papers, NCDAH; Gutman, The Black Family, 402; Kolchin, First Freedom, 63-67; Litwack, Been in the Storm, 237-38.

[11]Orville Vernon Burton, In My Father's Household Are Many Mansions: Family and Community in Edgefield, South Carolina (Chapel Hill: University of North Carolina Press, 1985), 227; H. C. Vogell (Freedman's Bureau) to Alonzo Mial, August 1 and August 20, 1867, Alonzo T. Mial Papers, NCDAH; National Freedman (New York), September 15, 1865, 266; Journal of Freedom, October 7, 1865; Rawick, The American Slave, vol. 14, 200; Freedmen's Record (Boston), August 1865, 133; Wake County, North Carolina, Minutes of County Court, November term, 1866, NCDAH. Howard N. Rabinowitz has shown that whites routinely used such discriminatory applications of the law to control African Americans living in southern cities during Reconstruction. Race Relations in the Urban South, 1865-1890 (New York: Oxford University Press, 1978), 44-51.

Freedmen's Bureau and agents of the American Missionary Association, some of Raleigh's white residents aided a number of African
Americans in establishing homes. Lewis Peck sold one-acre lots just
west of the city for $50 an acre. With financial help from the National
Freedmen's Savings and Trust Company and local land companies,
many black families purchased lots and began to settle in this new
area. The community quickly became known as Oberlin.[12]

Despite the efforts of so many freedpersons to build a secure
foundation for their families, reports of African-American husbands
or wives deserting their families and the growing number of people
needing government assistance provided the impetus for the North
Carolina legislature to pass a statute that required black couples to
pay a twenty-five cents fee and register their cohabitation or else face
the possibility of a fine. The lawmakers hoped the law would reduce
the number of dependents (both children and adults) burdening the
state's already strained budget. Northern missionaries living in Wake
County also worked to bring the emancipated slaves into legal (as well
as holy) matrimony, believing that "licentiousness . . . undoubtedly
prevails" among the blacks. Even the assistant commissioner of the
Freedmen's Bureau for North Carolina, Col. E. Whittlesey, stepped
in to encourage the nuptials. "Your freedom gives you new privileges.
You can now live in families. The marriage tie is as sacred among you
as among your neighbors."[13]

---

[12]Elizabeth Reid Murray, *Wake: Capital County of North Carolina* (Raleigh: Capital
County Publishing Company, 1983), 642-644. According to Murray, the community was
originally called Peck's Place after the previous landholder, but blacks soon renamed the
village Oberlin—most likely after the town in Ohio which was home to a college which
accepted African American students. Murray also notes that local tradition holds Duncan
Cameron, the largest slaveholder in antebellum North Carolina assisted former slaves in
acquiring land in Oberlin. By 1881, almost all of the community's 750 inhabitants were
black. Rabinowitz, *Race Relations in the Urban South*, 100.

[13]Gutman, *The Black Family*, 414; E. Whittlesey, Circular No. 1 in United States
Congress, House, Report of the Commissioner of the Bureau of Refugees, Freedmen and
Abandoned Lands, by O. O. Howard, March 19, 1866, House Ex. Doc. 70, 1st Sess., 39th
Congress, 1866-1867, 3. Besides discussing marriage and familiar relationships, Whittlesey
also stated that the freed persons also had the right to own homes and to learn to read and
write. This appears to be the limits of his view of freedom for blacks.

Yet the southern legislators and northern clergy had little reason to worry that blacks would not legitimize their marital bonds. During a five-month period from June through October 1866, 659 Wake County couples legally confirmed their marriages under the new cohabitation statute. These reaffirmations of marriage confirm the conclusion reached by Herbert Gutman and Roberta Sue Alexander—that given the choice between dissolving their slave marriages or confirming them, a significant proportion of the freedpersons chose to confirm them. Assuming the number of people in African-American households remained nearly the same between 1866 and 1870, these couples represented households containing an estimated 3,450 people—nearly one-fourth of the black population of Wake County.[14]

Even more telling than the number of confirmations was the eagerness with which freedpersons sought to legalize their bonds. E. H. Leland, a teacher at the freedmen's school, told of "an old gray-headed woman" who visited the school one morning carrying a basket with six eggs in it. The woman wanted to trade the eggs for a "quarter-dollar to buy a 'ticket'" to get her marriage registered. She told Leland she could only spare six eggs at the time, but promised to bring a chicken in the fall. According to Leland, the woman declared: "All 'spectable folks is to be married, and we's 'spectable: me and my

---

[14]Wake County Record of Cohabitation; Francis A. Walker, *Population of the United States in 1870*; Compiled from the Original Returns of the Ninth Census (Washington: Government Printing Office, 1872), 54. Roberta Sue Alexander's study revealed that in North Carolina, almost forty-eight percent of the maximum number of possible slave marriages before emancipation had been registered under the new cohabitation statute. Alexander states that in Wake County, at least thirty-four percent of the possible slave marriages were legalized. Alexander follows Herbert Gutman's method for calculating the maximum possible number of slave marriages. Using the 1860 census, she compared the number of black males over age twenty to the number of black females of the same age in each county. The lower of these two figures would represent the maximum number of people eligible for marriage. It should be noted that by including everyone in a certain age cohort (over 20), this method greatly overestimates the number of slave marriages. Alexander, *North Carolina Faces the Freedmen*, 59-60. The estimated number of people including in the 659 families was derived from a sample of 148 households listed in the cohabitation records. Each household in the sample averaged 5.24 persons, yielding a figure of 3,450 persons when multiplied by all 659 families.

old man has lived together for thirty-five years, and had twelve children." Another woman brought the teacher a quart of wild strawberries to get the twenty-five cents, claiming that her marriage had lasted twenty years. "I's proud the children's all had the same father." Aunt Peggy came to Leland carrying an empty bag and complained that everyone else was getting married but her "old man can't get the money." To these women, marriage to one's mate represented a respectability and freedom that had been denied to African Americans during slavery.[15]

The women who talked with Leland were not alone in having long-lasting marriages. Six hundred-forty couples listed the length of their marriage in the Wake County Record of Cohabitation. Forty percent of these marriages had lasted ten years or longer. Only twelve couples stated they had been married less than two years. One couple, Shaw and Esitra Battle, had already passed their fifty-fifth anniversary when they registered their marriage. Clearly, these people took their marital bonds seriously when given the opportunity.[16]

At the same time the freedpersons worked to construct their families and solemnize their marriage bonds, they also faced what the Raleigh *Journal of Freedom* called the problem of providing "shelter and an honorable subsistence" for themselves and their households. Should they remain with or near their current masters or take a chance at finding better living in another location? For some, their former masters made the choice for them by ejecting them from their homes. Giles Underhill had promised Piety Merritt "a cow and calf, a sow and pigs for what she done for him an' to stay on an' finish de crop." But when fall came Underhill kicked her out without giving her "de wrappin's o' her finger." Piety's husband, George, suffered the same fate on another plantation, even though he had saved two wagon-loads of his owner's meat from Sherman's bummers. On the other hand, Rufus Jones had a reputation for fairness among his

---

[15]E. H. Leland to the *Freedmen's Record*, July 1866, 133. The last name of "Aunt Peggy" remains unknown. Leland and the other reporters for the Freedmen's Record usually referred to the freed persons they described by their first names only.

[16]Wake County Record of Cohabitation, NCDAH.

slaves. When the end of the war came, he told his former slaves they could stay on the plantation. Most remained.[17]

Other blacks, whose owners mistreated them during slavery or who believed a better life lay elsewhere, left "as quick as we could." Some of these found superior conditions on neighboring farms and settled there. Alfred and Bertha Brodie joined others who wandered around from place to place, laboring at various "slave owner's plantations" whenever they could find work. A number of freed-persons, including the Brodies, eventually returned to the homes of former masters, their thoughts of independence overcome by homesickness and miserable living conditions.[18]

For many freedpersons in the Wake County area, as well as from neighboring counties, Raleigh presented an irresistible lure. To them, as well as to African Americans across the South, cities often came to symbolize an opportunity to get away from plantation life. Some looked upon them as places where they could achieve economic success, others came to the cities because they thought the Federal Army would protect them from danger. Some moved to urban areas because cities provided African-Americans a chance to be with significant numbers of their own race, to form churches and benevolent societies, attend school, and participate in politics. One former slave, Henry Bobbitt, walked over thirty miles to Raleigh simply because he had the need "ter find out if I wuz really free."[19]

Many of the African Americans who made Raleigh their home after the war were unmarried females. Economic factors played a large role in their decisions about where to reside. Because white landowners paid lower wages to female farm laborers and preferred to rent land to black men, it became difficult for single women to support

---

[17]*Journal of Freedom* (Raleigh), October 7, 1865; Rawick, *The American Slave*, vol. 14, 294, 419-20, vol. 15, 33. According to Clara Jones, much of the appeal about staying on Rufus Jones' farm stemmed from the fact that he sat around the house and let the blacks run the plantation for the most part.

[18]Rawick, *The American Slave*, vol. 14, 25-26, 316; vol. 15, 181, 361.

[19]Good descriptions of the African American migration to southern cities (and their reasons for doing so) following emancipation can be found in Rabinowitz, *Race Relations in the Urban South*, 18-30, and Leon Litwack, *Been in the Storm So Long*, 310-316.

themselves or their children in the rural areas. Thus, they often chose to move to more populated areas where they might have some chance at steady employment. According to the 1870 census, women headed nearly thirty percent of the African-American households in Raleigh. This number matches the estimates that several other historians have given for other urban areas of the South.[20]

By 1870, over 10,200 (including nearly 5,600 blacks) people lived in the Raleigh township. This was almost double the number of people who had lived there only ten years earlier. The influx of people into the city—many of them arriving with no money and little chance at finding work—made it difficult for a number of people to get adequate food and shelter. When Col. Whittlesey reached Raleigh to take his post as assistant commissioner of the Freedmen's Bureau for the state, he found that "hundreds of white refugees, and thousands of blacks" were collected about the city, "occupying every hovel and shanty, living upon government rations, without employment and without comfort." Many of these refugees died for want of proper food and medical supplies.[21]

Even though the promise of the city proved illusory at times, many freedpersons remained in Raleigh. They found themselves faced with the tasks of locating a place to live and finding work that would support them and their families. Some newly arrived African Americans, such as Lewis and Haley Jones, found small plots of land to farm along the outskirts of the city. Martha Organ recalled that her parents had been fortunate to receive a "little piece o' land" from their former owner following the war. But most blacks had to scramble to find accommodations the best they could.[22]

The 1870 Wake County census reveals that African Americans lived in one of four different types of household structures. The first

[20]Jones, *Labor of Love*, 62, 73-74; 1870 Manuscript Census (Population Schedule), Wake County, North Carolina, NCDAH.

[21]1860 and 1870 Manuscript Censuses (Population and Slave Schedules), Wake County, North Carolina, NCDAH; E. Whittlesey in *Report of the Commissioner of the Bureau of Refugees, Freedmen and Abandoned Lands*, 386.

[22]Rawick, *The American Slave*, vol. 15, 153, 205.

type of household consisted of the nuclear family, made up of a husband and wife along with any children. A second category, the extended household, contained a nuclear family plus other relatives. The third type, the augmented household, included a nuclear family plus anyone not related to members of the family. The final category, the irregular household, could be either one person living alone or where no one was related to the head of the household.[23]

In Raleigh, the nuclear family formed the core of most households headed by African Americans. But only thirty-seven percent of the black households contained only the nuclear family. Nearly half (forty-nine percent) of the households were either extended or augmented. The remaining fourteen percent of the households consisted of people either living by themselves or sharing dwelling space with people to whom they were unrelated.[24]

Three factors explain why so many of the freedpersons in the city lived with people outside their immediate nuclear family. First, housing in Raleigh proved scarce in the first few years following the Civil War. During the 1860s the total population of Raleigh nearly doubled. Although the number of people living in the city grew rapidly, the economic devastation brought on by the war meant that few people could afford to build new houses. So blacks often found themselves losing the competition for dwelling space with new white residents who frequently had better jobs and more money to spend. Second, with the local economy in turmoil, blacks struggled to find employment. Conditions were so bad by 1870, that only 124 (15.5 percent) of the black households surveyed by the census-taker

---

[23]The coding scheme used here is similar to one employed by Orville Vernon Burton in his work on Edgefield County, South Carolina. Burton, *In My Father's Household*, 328-29. The 1870 census did not state the relationship of the members of a household to its head. Therefore, if someone living in a household had a different last name than the head of the household and failed to meet various age requirements, I classified that person as non-related. This means that some household residents who were possibly related to the head of the household were classified as non-related. Thus, the number of augmented households is most likely overstated and the number of extended households understated.

[24]1870 Manuscript Census (Population Schedule), Wake County, North Carolina, NCDAH. See Appendix, Table 2 for breakdown of household types in Raleigh.

possessed property of any economic value. This combination of scarce housing and a poor economy led many African Americans to pool their resources in order to provide some modicum of food and shelter. A third reason some blacks lived with people outside their nuclear family came from the fact that those who resided in Raleigh before emancipation probably had grown accustomed to such living arrangements. The hiring-out and living-out systems found in Raleigh, as well as other antebellum southern cities, resulted in a variety of arrangements for lodging for both slaves and free blacks. While some slaves lived in the homes and outbuildings of their owners, others leased rooms in boarding houses or lived in housing provided by the person renting them.[25]

Because of the poor economic conditions facing most black households in Raleigh, many needed extra income provided by women and children in order to survive. William Scott recalled that his mother worked as a cook, first for northern officers and then for others. Since her additional income proved insufficient to meet the family's needs, she hired William out to whites where he "made jist enough to eat and hardly enough clothes to wear to church." The 1870 census reveals that females in nearly half of the city's black households held occupations other than "keeping house." Most of these women found jobs working mainly for whites (few black households could afford their services) as domestic servants, cooks, seamstresses, or washing clothes. E. H. Leland visited a number of

---

[25]Walker, Population of the United States in 1870, 54. According to Elizabeth Reid Murray, it was not until around 1869-1870 that construction efforts in Raleigh resumed on any significant scale. The local economy began to revive for merchants by late 1865, but this boost did not provide many jobs for African Americans. Wake, 546-573. Although Raleigh's African-American households owned $76,370 of property between them, most of this property rested in the hands of a few. Forty-nine households (four percent of the total) owned over three-fourths of the wealth. However, there appears to be little correlation between wealth and type of household, since these forty-nine households were in roughly the same proportion of nuclear, extended, and augmented as households with little or no wealth. 1860 and 1870 Manuscript Censuses (Population Schedules), Wake County, NCDAH. Elsa Barkley Brown and Gregg D. Kimball provide a good description of the mixed residential arrangements of African Americans (both slave and free) living in antebellum Richmond in "Mapping the Terrain of Black Richmond," Journal of Urban History 21 (March 1995), 302.

African American families in May 1866, and found all the women washing or ironing "except a few sick [women], who were destitute of eatables or money." He felt that such conditions were becoming common in Raleigh.[26]

The large proportion of black households with women in Raleigh's workforce differs significantly from the observations of a number of historians who have noted that overall, African-American women living in the South withdrew from the labor force in great numbers following emancipation. According to Jacqueline Jones and Leon Litwack, the main reason these women remained at home came from a desire to spend more time with their families (especially the children) and avoid contact with white males as much as possible. The reason for this divergence comes from the fact that the focus of most studies has been on rural areas of the South. In the rural areas, women could help the household economy in such ways as growing foodstuffs for the family. But in Raleigh, as in other urban areas throughout the South, the high number of households headed by women (nearly thirty percent) and the scarcity of land for farming meant this option was unavailable for most families. As Jones and Howard Rabinowitz have noted, black women living in the city had to earn wages in some fashion in order to maintain or contribute to the economic survival of their families.[27]

---

[26]Rawick, The American Slave, vol. 14, 119, 406, 453; vol. 15, 119, 262; 1870 Manuscript Census (Population Schedule), Wake County, NCDAH; Freedmen's Record, November 1865, June 1866.

[27]For studies that describe the withdrawal of African-American women from the labor force in rural areas, see: Jones, Labor of Love, 58-60, Kolchin, First Freedom, 62-63; Ransom and Sutch, One Kind of Freedom, 44-45, 55; Litwack, Been in the Storm, 244-245, 341, 434; Gutman, Black Family, 167-168; Burton, In My Father's House, 282. Works describing the participation of black women in the urban labor market include: Rabinowitz, Race Relations in the Urban South, 61-96; Jones, Labor of Love, 73-75; and Claudia Goldin, "Female Labor Force Participation: The Origin of Black and White Differences, 1870 and 1880," Journal of Economic History 37 (March 1977), 92-100. In a study of emancipated blacks in Philadelphia during the 1780s, Gary Nash found that many black families in Philadelphia formed an economic partnership at the lowest end of the spectrum, so the income from both males and females became indispensable. Gary B. Nash, Forging Freedom: The Formation of Philadelphia's Black Community, 1720-1840 (Cambridge, MA: Harvard University Press, 1988), 74.

Looking at households headed by African Americans only tells part of the story. Over 1,300 of the 5,600 blacks in Raleigh lived in households headed by whites. Some of these were freedpersons who chose to continue working for their former masters. But approximately half were minors who found themselves with little choice but to continue working as servants for whites. The economic situation in Raleigh frequently gave the city's black residents few options in choosing where they would reside.[28]

Despite their best efforts, the struggle to create a stable environment for themselves in Raleigh quickly took on a nightmarish quality for many black families. The city's broad avenues, once lined with "abundant trees . . . and rather elegant private residences," now boasted numerous one-room "slab-huts, chinked with yellow mud and rags" as well. After visiting the home of a woman called "Aunt Varney," Miss L. E. Dow wrote a letter to the Freedman's Record describing the conditions she found there. According to Dow, Varney and her family of eleven lived in a "wretched cabin, abundantly ventilated on all sides by great crevices in the wall and so filled up with rubbish and dirt that the appearance [wa]s anything but inviting." Jacob and Lucy Utley were one couple which moved to Raleigh following the Civil War. While living in one of these huts, Lucy found herself being chased by rats. This incident left her terrified and helped solidify her decision to leave Raleigh after being there less than a year.[29]

But problems caused by rats paled compared to the lack of food in the city. When federal troops moved through Wake County in the spring of 1865, they stripped the county of livestock and produce. Crop failures in 1866 and 1867 compounded the problem. As long as the city-dwellers could find work, they could usually purchase food. But when the work stopped, getting sustenance became difficult. At such times blacks (and other refugees) turned to northern sources

---

[28]1870 Manuscript Census (Population Schedule), Wake County, NCDAH. See Appendix, Table 3.

[29]Dennett, *South As It Is*, 148; *Freedmen's Record*, February 1866, March 1866, January 1867; Rawick, *The American Slave*, vol. 14, 119, 407, 456; vol. 15, 195.

such as the army, the Freedmen's Bureau, or missionary organizations for food. Although the fare consisted mainly of hardtack and pickled meat, it kept many people alive during times of scarcity. As late as 1868 the *Raleigh Sentinel* reported that many poor persons, "both white and black, still crowd around the office of the Freedmen's Bureau" seeking food.[30]

Despite the economic hardships suffered by many of Raleigh's black families, a large number continued to reside in the city throughout Reconstruction. Some African-Americans did achieve a modest amount of financial success. *Branson's North Carolina Business Directory* for 1866-1867 shows that nine blacks had opened their own small businesses—six blacksmiths, two grocers, and one cabinet maker—in Raleigh. Of these, only Cameron Perry had operated his blacksmith shop as a free black before the Civil War. From this small beginning, the number of black-owned businesses in Raleigh grew in number (to thirty-five) and scope by the end of Reconstruction. The city directory for 1875 included eleven grocers, nine hotels and boarding houses, six eateries, five butchers, and a variety store among the businesses owned by African Americans. It also showed the formation of a small professional class among the black residents, listing eight ministers, two teachers, and one physician.[31]

Raleigh also offered the freedpersons other benefits. The city boasted four large black churches, led by African American ministers within a few years of the war. These churches functioned not only as religious centers, they also formed the core of Raleigh's black

---

[30]*National Freedman*, October 15, 1865; *Raleigh Sentinel*, June 5, 1868; Nelson A. Miles to unknown, May 9, 1868, James Henry Harrison Papers, NCDAH. Rawick, *The American Slave*, vol. 14, 407, 445; vol. 15, 195. The freed persons occasionally also received clothing from northern sources. William George Hinton remembered that they gave him clothes when he went with his family for food. Rawick, Ibid., 445.

[31]In 1866-1967, Branson listed no blacks among the professional ranks. Levi Branson, *Branson's North Carolina Business Directory, 1866-1867* (Raleigh: Branson and Jones), 106-110. 1860 Manuscript Census (Population Schedule), Wake County, North Carolina, NCDAH; J. H. Chataigne, comp., *Chataigne's Raleigh City Directory, 1875-76* (Np.: 1876).

community and political activities.[32] Freedpersons also felt somewhat safer living in Raleigh. During the first five years of Reconstruction, numerous reports of violence filtered into the city from the counties surrounding the capital. However, the presence of three regiments of Federal troops in Raleigh prevented its black citizens from being harassed by the Ku Klux Klan and other extralegal groups. By the time the army left Raleigh in 1870, the city's police force had become integrated, thus providing a further modicum of protection to black residents.[33] Another advantage Raleigh had over the rural areas of the county in the early years following the war came from the number of schools available to blacks. Northern missionaries and freedmen's societies established six schools that were open in the city during various parts of Reconstruction. In addition, the county school board set aside three of Raleigh's six public schools for the education of African-American students. Two other schools, Shaw Institute and St. Augustine's Normal School and Collegiate Institute (formed in 1865 and 1867 respectively), quickly became the leading colleges in the state for training blacks for careers in teaching and industrial trades. A significant number of Raleigh's black population took as much benefit of the educational opportunities as they could.[34]

Despite the advantages offered by living in the city, most of the African Americans living in Wake County chose to live in the countryside rather than in Raleigh. For many, certainty and familiarity seemed to play a critical role in their decision. A number of former slaves interviewed by WPA workers in the 1930s recalled that their

---

[32]The black congregations in Raleigh worshiped at three Baptist and one African Methodist Episcopal churches. In 1867, Widow's Son Lodge No. 4, a Masonic lodge, was the only other notable African-American social organization in the city during Reconstruction. Murray, *Wake*, 615-618, 622.

[33]Ibid., 543, 595-97, 625; Rabinowitz, *Race Relations in the Urban South*, 42, 266, 278. Although *Chataigne's Raleigh City Directory* for 1875 listed eleven black police officers, Howard Rabinowitz noted that after Reconstruction ended, African Americans no longer served on the force.

[34]Murray, *Wake*, 602, 607-12; Rabinowitz, *Race Relations in the Urban South*, 153-157, 159-163; Rawick, *The American Slave*, vol. 14, 244, 260, 320, 387, 454; *Freedmen's Record*, October 1865, 163; *National Freedmen*, September 1865, July 1866.

families continued to work for their former masters after emancipation. Others reported that freedpersons who had left immediately after the war came back within a year or two, often claiming that they were homesick. For some blacks who remained in the countryside, the certainty that they could find familiar work on farms outweighed the potential economic benefits they could gain from living in the city. A number of those living in the rural areas of Wake County would have liked to take advantage of the social and educational opportunities offered in Raleigh, but were in the same situation as Jennylin Dunn, who noted that "most o' us wuz so busy scramblin' roun' makin' a livin' dat we ain't got no time for schools." For whatever reasons, over two-thirds of the African Americans in the county chose to remain in rural areas rather than the city.[35]

Because most blacks living in the rural portions of Wake County depended on farming to make their living, they too suffered from the scarcity of food that afflicted most the county's residents at one time or another during the first five years of Reconstruction. The first year after emancipation, the harvest fell short of previous years because many of the farm implements and draft animals had been destroyed or taken by Sherman's army. Over the next two years a "combination of causes" almost entirely destroyed a promising harvest. The head of the Freedmen's Bureau in North Carolina stated that the local citizens suffered through widespread "destitution and starvation." He told a correspondent that the current crop promised to be good, but the people needed food immediately if they were to survive until harvest.[36]

---

[35]Rawick, *The American Slave*, vol. 14, 25-26, 90, 244, 277, 281, 294, 316, 430, 445, 448; vol. 15, 361-62; *Freedmen's Record*, February 1866, 27; *National Freedman*, July 1866; U.S. Government, *Ninth Diennial Census of the United States*, vol. 1 (Washington: Government Printing Office, 1872), 53-54. Of the approximately 8,000 school-age black children in Wake County in 1870, only 979 had attended school in the previous year. Ibid., 1870 Manuscript Census (Social Statistics Schedule), Wake County, North Carolina, NCDAH.

[36]Murray, *Wake*, 557; Fannie Graves to *National Freedman*, October 15, 1865, 292; Nelson A. Miles to unknown correspondent, May 9, 1868, James Henry Harris Papers, NCDAH.

Although economic hardships formed a common denominator for the households headed by African Americans in both the rural portions of Wake County and in Raleigh, those in the countryside differed significantly from those in city. The households in four sample census districts—Barton's Creek, Buckhorn, Cedar Fork, and St. Mary's—more closely resembled the black households in other rural portions of the South than their neighbors in Raleigh.

The first noticeable difference between the urban and rural areas of Wake County came from the type of households headed by blacks. In the four rural census districts, seventy-one percent of the African American households contained only the nuclear family. Another fourteen percent included members of the extended family. This presents a sharp contrast to the situation in Raleigh, where barely half of the households contained only family members.[37]

Black households in the countryside also varied from their urban neighbors in who was considered the head of the household. According to the 1870 census, females headed thirty percent of the households in Raleigh, but only twelve percent of those in the rural districts. Occupational differences may explain this disparity. In Raleigh most men worked as unskilled laborers, but those in the countryside mainly worked as farm laborers or tenant farmers. White landowners showed a distinct preference for entering into farm contracts with males. Men were not only likely to receive more land as tenant farmers, they also received more pay than women when doing field work. On one plantation, the labor contract paid adult male laborers an average of nearly $11.00 per month compared to a high of $6.50 per month for adult females. A similar pay scale can be found among the Freedmen's Bureau wage guidelines. Such contracts frequently held males responsible for the actions of all in the household.[38]

---

[37]*1870 Manuscript Census* (Population Schedule), Wake County, NCDAH. See Appendix, Table 2.

[38]Ibid. See Appendix, Table 1. Jones, *Labor of Love,* 62; Labor Contract, January 1, 1867, Alonzo T. and Millard Mial Papers, NCDAH; *National Freedman,* April 1, 1865, 81.

The prevalent acceptance of the male-led family among whites also contributed to their views regarding the head of household among freedpersons. The presumption of male-led households can be seen in the attitudes of representatives of the Freedmen's Bureau and missionary associations and in southern community leaders. In a variety of ways—through land tenures, education, charitable contributions, granting of credit, placing men in local positions of authority (police) or in their correspondence—the view of the male as leader of the family led to the responsibility for the success or failure of the black household being placed on the shoulders of men.[39]

Another area of difference between black households in Raleigh and the four rural districts of the county came from the listed occupations of the women in the households. In seventy-one percent of the rural households, the census takers listed all the women engaged in "keeping house" or staying "at home." It must be noted that staying out of the labor force did not mean women sat around idly. Some used their talents to set up businesses in their homes—sewing, washing and ironing, and midwifery. Most of the women who remained at home worked to increase the household's resources by planting and tending their own garden plots and doing the numerous chores associated with raising a family. The majority of the women who did work outside of their rural households lived in extended or augmented households, and most were not part of the nuclear family.[40]

The final difference between the urban and rural areas of Wake County came from the number of African Americans who lived in black-headed households. As noted earlier, approximately one in four blacks residing in Raleigh dwelled in households headed by whites.

---

[39]1870 *Manuscript Census* (Population Schedule), Wake County, North Carolina, NCDAH; L. E. Dow to *Freedmen's Record*, January 1867, 4; Charles Manly to Basil Manly, August 4, 1868, Charles Manly Papers, NCDAH; Burton, *In My Father's House*, 260-263; Jones, *Labor of Love*, 62-63.

[40]1870 Manuscript Census (Population Schedule), Wake County, North Carolina, NCDAH. See Appendix, Table 4. White, *Ar'n't I a Woman*, 158-59, 163-164; Jones, *Labor of Love*, 58; E. H. Leland to *Freedmen's Record*, June 1866, 121.

But in the four rural districts examined, ninety percent lived in African-American households. The greater availability of land and the higher demand for their labor in the countryside meant that blacks had more control over their living environment than in the city.[41]

This study of African American families in Wake County, North Carolina, reveals that while freedpersons living in rural and urban areas shared some common experiences, in several key areas their lives differed significantly. In all parts of the county, the former slaves showed a strong desire to legitimize and create stable foundations for marriages that had survived the ordeals of bondage. They also shared the common bond of suffering through economic hardships in the years immediately following the Civil War and emancipation. On the other hand, the decision to reside in the city or in the countryside played a significant role in determining the living conditions for a family. For some, such as most single women and persons who had lived as slaves in Raleigh, choosing to reside in the city was their only realistic option. But it could not have been an easy choice for many families, who had to balance the economic and social opportunities offered by Raleigh against the familiarity and certainty of continuing to live in an agrarian setting. Whatever the decision, it affected the type of household in which a family would live, whether women and children worked outside the home, and whether blacks would reside with a household headed by African Americans or whites. The experiences of freedpersons residing in Wake County, North Carolina, point out how differences in economic opportunities and physical landscape between urban and rural areas helped shape the living conditions of black families in the South following emancipation.

---

[41]1870 Manuscript Census (Population Schedule), Wake County, North Carolina, NCDAH, see Appendix, Table 3.

APPENDIX

Table 1: Wake County 1870
Census Sample
Households Headed by African-Americans
Census Districts

		Bar-ton's Creek	Buck-horn	Cedar Fork	St. Mary's	Ra-leigh	Totals
Num-ber of House-holds		.107	120	92	150	804	1,273
Head of House-hold	Male	90	109	85	128	574	986
	Fe-Male	17	11	7	22	230	287
House-hold Type	Nu-clear	79	85	62	108	296	630
	Ex-ten-ded	15	16	18	12	120	630
	Aug-men-ted	6	12	12	29	273	332
	Irreg-ular	7	7	0	1	116	131

Total number in Black headed households		495	628	497	776	4,273	6,669
Avg. Number of persons/ household		4.626	5.233	5.402	5.173	5.315	5.239
Difference from total sample mean of 5.239		-0.613	-0.005	0.163	-0.065	0.076	
Number of African-Americans in District		544	690	549	894	5,589	
% of Blacks living in African-American Households		91.0%	91.0%	90.5%	86.8%	76.5%	

Households with Women Working Outside Household	First-Named Female		6	6	1	20	229
	Any Females		9	17	12	63	353

Table 2: Wake County 1870
Census Sample
Households Headed by African Americans
Census Districts

		Bar-ton's Creek	Buck-horn	Cedar Form	St. Mary's	Ra-leigh
Number of House-holds		107	120	92	150	804
Head of House-hold	% headed by males	84.1%	90.8%	92.4%	85.3%	71.4%
	% head-ed by fe-males	15.9%	9.2%	7.6%	14.7%	28.6%
House-hold Type	Nuclear	73.8%	70.8%	67.4%	72.0%	36.8%
	Extended	14.0%	13.3%	19.6%	8.0%	14.9%
	Augment-ed	5.6%	10.0%	13.0%	19.3%	34.0%
	Irregular	6.5%	5.8%	0.0%	0.7%	14.4%
House-holds with Women Working Outside House-hold	First-Named Female	5.6%	5.0%	1.1%	13.3%	28.5%
	Any Fe-males	8.4%	14.2%	13.0%	42.0%	43.9%

Census Districts

		Bar-ton's Creek	Buck-horn	Cedar Fork	St. Mary's	Ra-leigh	Totals
Num-ber of House-holds		107	120	92	150	804	
Head of House-hold	Nu-clear/Male Head	71	79	58	93	231	532
	Nu-clear/Fe-Male Head	8	6	4	15	65	97
	Ex-ten-ded/Male Head	9	14	16	10	100	149
	Exte nded/Fe-male Head	6	2	2	2	20	32
	Aug-men-ted/Male Head	5	11	11	25	206	258

	Aug-men-ted/Fe-male Head	1	1	1	4	67	74
	Irreg-ular/Male Head	5	5	0	0	37	47
	Irreg-ular/Fe-male Head	2	2	0	1	79	84
Total Male Head		90	109	85	128	574	986
Total Female Head		17	11	7	22	230	287

Table 3: Wake County 1870
Census Sample
Households Headed by African-Americans
Gender of Head of Household
Census Districts

		Barton's Creek	Buck-horn	Cedar Fork	St. Mary's	Raleigh
Nuclear	Male Head	78.9%	72.5%	68.2%	72.7%	40.2%
	Female Head	47.1%	54.5%	57.1%	68.2%	27.8%

Ex-tended	Male Head	10.0%	12.8%	18.8%	7.8%	17.4%
	Female Head	35.3%	18.2%	28.6%	9.1%	8.7%
Aug-mented	Male Head	5.6%	10.1%	12.9%	19.5%	35.9%
	Female Head	5.9%	9.1%	14.3%	18.2%	29.1%
Irregu-lar	Male Head	5.6%	4.6%	0.0%	0.0%	6.4%
	Female Head	11.8%	18.2%	0.0%	4.5%	34.3%

4

"A BITTERNESS OF FEELINGS": BLACK INTRA-RACE RELATIONS IN CIVIL WAR AND EARLY RECONSTRUCTION LOUISIANA

James D. Wilson Jr.

Recent works by several historians have firmly repositioned the contributions and significance of African Americans in the transformation of the American South just after the Civil War and during the period known as Reconstruction; however, the persuasiveness of arguments that a genuine cohesiveness existed among certain segments of the black population has been considerably overestimated. Too often the experiences and attitudes of all segments of the southern black population during this period, as in most other periods as well, have been lumped together as one indecipherable mass. In an essay evaluating the effects of the Civil War on free blacks in New Orleans, historian David Rankin suggested that this historical "neglect has apparently resulted from the assumption that the postwar experiences of free and freed Negroes were similar if not identical. However, a close study of . . . Reconstruction suggests that in viewing all Negroes as members of an undifferentiated mass, historians have exaggerated the unity of the Afro-American population . . . ."[1]

---

[1]David C. Rankin, "The Impact of the Civil War On The Free Colored Community of New Orleans," *Perspectives in American History* 11 (1977-1978): 379; Thomas Holt's *Black Over White: Negro Political Leadership in South Carolina During Reconstruction* (Urbana and Chicago: The University of Illinois Press, 1977) contains similar finding for the state of South

In the case of Louisiana the origins of this "uneasy relationship" between free persons of color (FPC) and slave/freedmen can clearly be traced to the social relations of the colonial and antebellum periods. It has generally been accepted that Louisiana had a three-tier caste structure during the colonial and antebellum periods; yet, it has often been wrongly assumed that the Civil War and emancipation completely destroyed this social system, replacing it with the conventional two-tier, racially based system. In fact, the more than a century and a half of separation between FPC and slave/freedmen in Louisiana would be as difficult to reconcile as it would be for whites and blacks in other places, and black race unity would not become even a remote reality until well into the twentieth century.[2]

Just prior to the end of the Civil War, a government official in New Orleans publicly stated that there had always been "a bitterness of feelings" between free people of color and slaves.[3] A free person of color responded in the *New Orleans Tribune*, the local mouthpiece of the FPC population, that:

> No considerate human being ought to be astonished at there being that feeling among the colored people. The odious Black Code of Louisiana, debarred them from all social intercourse with each other. The slave who had free relatives dared not associate with them, and vice versa. The oppressive laws regulating slavery caused the free colored people and slaves to become estranged of each other. And it is a very poor defense for the authorities to use it as showing the "disunity," of our people—when they themselves have caused the "feelings."[4]

Carolina.

[2] An excellent overview of black-race relations during the late nineteenth century is contained in Joseph Logsdon and Caryn Cosse Bell, "The Americanization of Black New Orleans 1850-1900," in Arnold Hirsch and Joseph Logsdon, eds., *Creole New Orleans: Race and Americanization* (Baton Rouge: Louisiana State University Press, 1992).

[3] Quoted in David C. Rankin, "The Forgotten People: Free People of Color in New Orleans, 1850-1870" (Ph.D. diss., The Johns Hopkins University, 1976), 139.

[4] *New Orleans Tribune*, March 31, 1865.

A short time later, just after the close of the war, a Radical Republican journalist traveling with Chief Justice Salmon P. Chase met with a group of the most prominent FPC in New Orleans. From this meeting the journalist concluded that although the FPC population "held themselves aloof from the slaves, and particularly the plantation negroes" before the war, they no longer held to this contention and in fact as one man candidly told him, "we see that our future is indissolubly bound up with that of the negro race in this country; and we have resolved to make common cause, and rise or fall with them. We have no rights which we can reckon safe while the same are denied to the field-hands on the sugar plantations."[5] These two differing claims, one acknowledging that the animosities still existed and the other claiming that the ill feelings, at least in the minds of FPC, were in the past, suggest a fundamental contradiction and at least two rather obvious questions. First, to what extent, if at all, did previous animosities between FPC and freedmen still exist at the close of the Civil War in Louisiana and, maybe even more importantly, to what extent are generalizations regarding the attitudes of former FPC and freedmen at all adequate or even appropriate when attempting to explain race and/or caste relationships throughout the course of southern history?

Colonial and antebellum Louisiana was dominated by a three-tier caste structure composed of whites, free persons of color, and black slaves. This three-tier structure dates back well into the eighteenth century, the legal foundation for which were first spelled out in the Code Noir of 1724. Although this French code of law that regulated slavery and racial matters in the colony did offer substantial protection of certain rights for slaves, the Code Noir also severely limited the avenues to freedom for bondsmen and thus limited the growth of the FPC caste in Louisiana under the French. The Code Noir also significantly recognized and set out rights and restrictions upon free

---

[5]Whitelaw Reid, *After the War: A Southern Tour*, May 1, 1865 to May 1, 1866, ed. by C. Vann Woodward (New York, 1956), 259-260.

persons of color and in doing so solidified the legal status of FPC in Louisiana.[6] The numerical influence of free blacks in Louisiana expanded greatly under the Spanish regime from 1763 to 1803. There were several reasons for this increase: the implementation of laws more favorable toward the manumission of slaves, the improved economic conditions in the colony, and a greater availability of slaves to replace those emancipated. The number of slaves in the colony also increased during the Spanish regime.[7]

If any one single factor secured the antebellum fate of Louisiana's FPC caste it was the large influx of Saint-Domingue refugees in 1809 and 1810. In this two-year period over 3,100 FPC entered New Orleans alone. This immigration not only enabled FPC to prosper economically, it was also responsible for solidifying the French-Creole culture that came to so dominate and signify their caste. It is this latter French-Creole cultural identity that eventually most distinguished the FPC caste from the slave/freedmen caste, and it is these cultural distinctions and the identities that each engendered that are most responsible for the separation of the two castes for so long despite their shared racial definitions and bound fates.[8]

From the time of their very first appearance in Louisiana, free blacks were consistently manipulated against slaves by the white state authorities. Whenever the white state authorities gave free blacks any rights or privileges it was nearly always at the expense of slaves, whether natives or Africans; however, the most significant way that

---

[6]H. E. Sterkx, *The Free Negro In Ante-Bellum Louisiana* (Cranbury, New Jersey: Associated University Presses, Inc., 1972), 13-17. Also see Carl A. Brasseaux, "The Administration of Slave Regulation in French Louisiana, 1724-1766" *Louisiana History* 21 (Spring 1980): 139-150; and Mathe Allain, "Slave Policies in French Louisiana" *Louisiana History* 21 (Spring 1980): 127-138.

[7]Gwendolyn Midlo Hall, *Africans in Colonial Louisiana: The Development of Afro-Creole Culture in the Eighteenth Century* (Baton Rouge: Louisiana State University, 1992), 278; also see Kimberly S. Hanger, "Avenues to Freedom Open to New Orleans's Black Population, 1769-1779" *Louisiana History* 31 (Summer 1990): 237-264; and Kimberly S. Hanger, *Bound Lives, Bound Places: Free Black Society in Colonial New Orleans, 1769-1803* (Durham, North Carolina: Duke University Press, 1997).

[8]Paul F. Lachance, "The 1809 Immigration of Saint-Domingue Refugees to New Orleans: Reception, Integration, and Impact," *Louisiana History* 29 (Spring 1988): 109-141.

whites manipulated FPC against slaves was by military appointment. While initially both black slaves and FPC were used at times to fight against natives of the region, once the native Indians were no longer a problem this practice evolved into using FPC for protection against possibly unruly slaves, and FPC slave patrols eventually emerged. From 1782 until 1784 the Spanish government actively engaged in organized warfare against maroon slave colonies. The free black militia actively participated in these raids and became targets for retribution from the runaway slaves, who threatened to attack them and their family members.[9] After a little initial apprehension American officials continued the practice of using the free blacks in the militia in Louisiana and in 1811 utilized their services to assist in the suppression of the largest slave revolt in United States history. The Louisiana free black militia was also used against the British at the battle for New Orleans in January 1815. In response to their gallant performance on the battlefield it was alleged that General Andrew Jackson had promised the free men who served full rights of citizenship and for many years to come the descendants of those who fought would repeatedly request that this promise be fulfilled.

Antebellum relations between free blacks and slaves did not differ significantly from the colonial period. FPC remained in a position below whites yet above slaves, and they continued to serve in their role as a buffer between the two. But just as slaves aspired to be free, FPC aspired to be as close to whites as possible. It would be untrue to suggest that FPC were unconcerned with the fate of slaves. More often free blacks cared very much about the fate of slaves, for it was the servile status of slaves that gave FPC their social distinction and unique position in antebellum Louisiana society. FPC realized full well that an end to slavery meant an end to their special status and the limited privileges that came with that status. One "Creole of Louisiana," although his identity and race is unknown he is suspected to be

---

[9]Roland C. McConnell, "Louisiana's Black Military History, 1729-1865" in Robert R. McDonald, John R. Kemp, and Edward F. Haas, eds., *Louisiana's Black Heritage* (New Orleans: Louisiana State Museum, 1979), 34-37; and Ira Berlin, *Slaves Without Masters: The Free Negro in the Antebellum South* (New York: The New Press, 1974), 112-113.

a FPC, wrote to the Governor of Louisiana that free blacks "are able to appreciate the benefits of slavery, very few of them have ever been slaves, they never associate with negroes, their education and good breeding prevented it, they have no sympathy for Abolitionists, knowing that the Abolitionist are the greatest enemies they have."[10] More so than in any other caste system, it was imperative for FPC to encourage and support slavery.

The evidence does not support the notion that FPC somehow supported slaves in their quest for freedom and were allies in their struggle against their southern white oppressors. The best example of the FPC's attitudes toward slavery can be found in a handful of literary materials written by literate free blacks and published during the early to mid 1840s. *L'Album litteraire* was a short-lived literary journal printed at New Orleans in 1843; most of the writers were free blacks, though a few whites did contribute. *Les Cenelles*, which appeared in New Orleans two years later, was the first collection of poetry exclusively by African Americans, in this case free men of color, ever published in the United States. The most interesting quality of these two publications is the resolved contentedness of the authors. As has been pointed out "there is no criticism of slavery, no laments of social injustice, no rancor towards white society who snub them."[11] One critical analysis of the two works concluded that free black authors "felt themselves the equals of their white contemporaries, and wished to become part of the mainstream of white literature, . . . avoiding any outburst which might set them apart as an inferior caste of humanity."[12] Clearly the fact that *L'Album litteraire* and *Les Cenelles* lack even the slightest overt reference to the institution of slavery and antebellum social relations in Louisiana demonstrates the

---

[10]Quoted in Arthur Bergeron Jr., "Louisiana's Free Men of Color In Gray," in *Black Southerners in Gray*, Vol. 11, *Journal of Confederate History Series*, ed. by Richard Rollins (Southern Heritage Press, Murfreesboro, Tenn., 1994), 38.

[11]John Maxwell Jones Jr., *Slavery and Race in Nineteenth-Century Louisiana-French Literature* (Privately Printed, 1978), 46.

[12]Ibid., 48.

contentedness of the FPC authors, both to their and the slaves' stations within the state's three-tier caste system.

While it is true that not every free black was a slave owner, in Louisiana a larger percentage of FPC did own slaves than did whites. The available accounts suggest that in rural areas FPC slave owners were feared and disliked more by slaves than were white slave owners. American slave owners appear to have generally been desired over French, which would support this pattern since most FPC were French Creoles. A traveler through Louisiana in 1803 wrote that when free blacks did "succeed in owning slaves, they treat them with a barbarity that nothing can approach."[13] Nearly a half century later Frederick Law Olmsted reported that one slave in Louisiana had informed him that FPC slave owners were "bad masters, very hard and cruel—hadn't any feelings." The slave went on to say that "You might think, master, dat dey would be good to dar own nation; but dey is not. I will tell you de truth, massa; I know I'se got to answer; and it's a fact, dey is bad masters, sar. I'd rather be a servant to any man in de world, dan to a brack man. If I was sold to a brack man, I'd drown myself. . . . I wouldn't be sold to a coloured master for anything."[14]

On the eve of the Civil War in 1856 the Louisiana State Supreme Court ruled that "in the eyes of the Louisiana law, there is . . . all the difference between a free man of color and a slave, that there is between a white man and a slave."[15] This ruling probably best sums up the relationship of free persons of color and slaves in Louisiana at the time of the outbreak of the Civil War. A century and a half of

---

[13]James A. Robertson, ed. and trans., *Louisiana Under the Rule of Spain, France, and the United States, 1785-1807* (Cleveland, 1911), vol. I, 185.

[14]Frederick Law Olmsted, *The Cotton Kingdom: A Traveler's Observations on Cotton and Slavery in the American Slave States, 1853-1861*, ed. by Arthur M. Schlesinger (New York: Alfred A. Knopf, Inc., 1953; reprint, New York: Da Capo Press, 1996), 262.

[15]This ruling is quoted in Rankin, "The Impact of the Civil War," 386; Ted Tunnell, *Crucible of Reconstruction: War, Radicalism and Race in Louisiana, 1862-1877* (Baton Rouge: Louisiana State University Press, 1984), 67; and Judith Kelleher Schafer, *Slavery, the Civil Law, and the Supreme Court of Louisiana* (Baton Rouge: Louisiana State University Press, 1994), 20-21.

both white-implemented and self-segregation had positioned the free blacks and slaves as far apart as were white and slaves, and, as it was often suggested by the FPC, their interests truly were closer to that of propertied whites than to slaves.

A large portion of the free people of color in Louisiana reacted to the outbreak of the Civil War in a way rather unique among blacks in the South. Many did as they had done some forty-six years earlier when the British attempted to invade New Orleans; these FPC committed themselves to the defense of their homeland. Wealthier free blacks contributed to New Orleans's city defense fund of the Committee on Public Safety, and a large number of free blacks offered their military service to the Confederacy. Whereupon, Confederate Governor Thomas O. Moore authorized the formation of a regiment of free black militia known as "the Native Guard." Almost exclusively from New Orleans, the regiment's numbers quickly grew and numbered over 3,000 in early 1862. One historian has pointed out that "at that time, a considerably larger proportion of the state's free Negroes were under arms for the Confederacy than white Louisianians."[16] Free black planters on the lower parts of Bayou Teche, in the southwest part of the state, reportedly also contributed to the formation of Confederate military units. In addition, slave owning free blacks in several other outlying parishes spread across the state organized into militia units for protection against potential slave revolts and for defense of their home state.[17] While it would be wrong to say that all FPC in Louisiana supported the Confederacy, one historian has gone so far as to say that "at the outbreak of the Civil War, most free persons of color in Louisiana supported the Confederacy".[18]

---

[16]Tunnell, *Crucible of Reconstruction*, 70.

[17]Carl Brasseaux, Keith Fontenot, and Claude Oubre, *Creoles of Color in the Bayou Country* (Jackson: University Press of Mississippi, 1994), 84; Tunnell, *Crucible of Reconstruction*, 69.

[18]Lorans Schlesinger, "Antebellum Free Persons of Color in Postbellum Louisiana," *Louisiana History* 30 (Fall 1989): 353.

It is important to note that with little exception FPC in rural areas reacted to the outbreak of the Civil War in the very same or at least a strikingly similar manner as those in urban New Orleans. This was in keeping with a consistent pattern that seems to have existed before, during, and after the Civil War. In these regards, therefore, it would not be incorrect to suggest that Louisiana's three-tier caste structure played a much stronger role in influencing the actions of FPC than did their environment, i.e. an urban or rural setting.

In areas controlled by southern armies, many prominent FPC remained loyal to the Confederacy throughout the war. In southwest Louisiana for example, Auguste Donato, from one of the most wealthy and prominent FPC families in the state, assisted the Confederate war efforts early on and officially signed up after the Confederate Congress voted in February 1864 to allow blacks to be used in certain limited capacities. Donato offered proof of his service to the Confederacy after the war in civil district court, where he requested a sum of $5,000 for property that had been seized from him.[19] Other free black Confederate supporters simply signed up with white regiments from their area and reportedly fought throughout the war right along side their white neighbors. This was the case for a group of several FPC from St. Landry Parish who saw action for the Confederacy at Shiloh, Fredericksburg, and Vicksburg.[20] In the case of Louis Lefort, a free person of color from Ascension Parish who joined a Confederate artillery regiment from the area, it was later alleged that he was buried with Confederate military honors.[21] Since FPC in Confederate-occupied territories were able to avoid conscription until early in 1864, they were able to profit enormously from the illegal export of cotton in particular. Once the Confederacy did attempt to draft these men into service, several—particularly in the

---

[19]Brasseaux, Fontenot, and Oubre, *Creoles of Color in the Bayou Country*, 50-52.
[20]Schlesinger, "Antebellum Free Persons of Color," 353.
[21]Unaddressed Louis Lefort letter, December 10, 1884, Dunn-Landry Family Paper, Amistad Research Center, New Orleans, La.

southwestern prairie regions of the state—organized themselves in jayhawking operations in order to protect their illegal trade.[22]

White Confederates quickly abandoned the city of New Orleans after Union troops arrived in April 1862. The free black Confederate unit organized in 1860, the Native Guard, remained in the city, however, and many of the city's FPC eventually offered their service to General Benjamin Butler once the Union army had firmly established its control. These FPC were accepted into the Union Army and fought at several battles during the war, including the siege of Port Hudson, Louisiana. This group of former FPC would be the most vocal during the immediate post-war period and would consistently point to their strong military showing during the Civil War as evidence of their capabilities and desire to have all the rights of full citizenship.[23]

These varied and constantly shifting alliances offer excellent proof that even more so than the state's white citizens, Louisiana's FPC population dramatically demonstrated their capacities to act toward their own best self-interest during the Civil War. As the tide of the various war campaigns shifted, so did the FPC's alliances, some allied with Confederates, some allied with the Union, some simply jayhawking for their own sake. Most importantly Louisiana FPC's actions during the Civil War uphold their consistent pattern of acting in their own propertied self-interest, with very little, if any, thought given to altruistic motives. One historian has concluded that blacks in Louisiana seem to have been motivated to join the Confederacy by "the desire to protect their standing which kept them above blacks in slavery. . . . There is no evidence that anyone forced them to take that step. Rather, it seems that they followed the dictates of their consciences. . . ."[24]

---

[22]Brasseaux, Fontenot, and Oubre, *Creoles of Color in the Bayou Country*, 85-87.

[23]The complete history of the FPC regiment is contained in James Hollandsworth Jr, *The Louisiana Native Guard: The Black Military Experience During the Civil War* (Baton Rouge: Louisiana State University Press, 1995).

[24]Bergeron, "Louisiana's Free Men of Color In Gray," 50.

Some historians have suggested other factors to explain the FPC joining the Confederate cause.[25] This group asserts that the FPC were forced by social pressures from whites to join with the Confederate forces, then when given the opportunity acted on their true feelings and led the fight to end slavery by joining the Union Army. This suggestion substantially ignores the attitudes of the rural FPC population. Confusion also seems to have arisen out of these historians' insistence on treating the attitudes of all New Orleans FPC as one indecipherable whole. It appears that the individual free men of color who joined the Confederate state militia may not have even been the same individuals who later joined the Union ranks. One historian's calculations indicate that only 108 (out of over 3000) former Confederate militiamen joined the primary FPC Union regiment.[26] Furthermore, evidence indicates that the blacks who fought in other Union regiments were not in fact former free men of color but slaves recently emancipated by Union forces.[27] Clearly a large portion of the Louisiana antebellum FPC population did not actively join the fight against slavery and did see themselves on a level well above other blacks, particularly slaves and recently freed slaves.

Even prior to the Civil War, free people of color in New Orleans and Louisiana had sought political suffrage for themselves and continuously been denied. The war had greatly upset the old social order in the entire South, and FPC in Louisiana realized that their wish was as close at hand as it might ever be. Demands for suffrage by those FPC loyal to the Union steadily intensified during the initial years of the war and culminated in a meeting of FPC held on November 5, 1863. The meeting was a heated one, in which it was suggested by one free black speaker that "if we cannot succeed with

---

[25]Caryn Cosse Bell's *Revolution, Romanticism, and the Afro-Creole Protest Tradition in Louisiana, 1718-1868* (Baton Rouge: Louisiana State University Press, 1997) provides a good general discussion of this debate, 2-6; Bell is also very representative of the social pressure theory for FPC Confederate service, 231-232 and 236-237.

[26]Hollandsworth, *The Louisiana Native Guard*, 18, 25. Subsequently investigation has led Hollandsworth to believe that the number of FPC who served in both the Confederate state militia and the Union Army might be higher than he initially indicated.

[27]Ibid., 18.

the authorities here we will . . . go to President Lincoln." The black leader stated that "they did not ask for social equality, and did not expect it, but they demanded political rights—they wanted to be men."[28]

True to their threats, when continuous inquiries to the local military authorities received no definitive resolution, a delegation of the most prominent FPC in the state set out in March 1864 to Washington, D.C., and eventually met with President Lincoln. Although Lincoln candidly told the men that he could not at that time act upon their demands, he did acknowledge them as citizens and suggested that when the time was right he would lend them and their cause his support.[29]

The free state constitution that was drafted for Louisiana in 1864 insured that the fate of former FPC and freedmen would be forever bound together. The convention that drafted the constitution went so far as to adopt a provision that stated that "the Legislature shall never pass any act authorizing free Negroes to vote, or to immigrate into this state under any pretense whatever."[30] One white delegate to the convention observed that former FPC were "in an infinitely worse position than they were under any of the antecedent pro-slavery constitutions" and strongly objected to the provisions that limited the rights of former FPC.[31]

The adoption of the Louisiana state constitution of 1864 caused an abrupt change in the attitudes and expressed opinions of the former free black community. Up until this point all suffrage demands by FPC were intended only for free blacks of the most prestigious standing. Few, if any, FPC favored, much less ever suggested, political suffrage for freedmen. It was not until the FPC finally realized that

---

[28]Quoted from the *New Orleans Times*, November 6, 1863, in Donald E. Everett, "Demands of the New Orleans Free Colored Population for Political Equality, 1862-1865," *Louisiana Historical Quarterly* (April 1955): 45.

[29]Tunnell, *Crucible of Reconstruction*, 78-81; Everett, "Demands of New Orleans Free Colored," 47-51.

[30]Quoted in Everett, "Demands of New Orleans Free Colored," 51-52.

[31]Ibid.

their fates truly were bound with that of freedmen and that all hope of special privileges and social standing were lost, that a significant number of FPC began to push for universal black male suffrage. This shift is best represented by the fact that *L'Union*, the radical FPC newspaper founded during the war, stopped publication just before the constitutional convention adjourned and was replaced twelve days later by the *New Orleans Tribune*.[32] Although published by and in the interest of former FPC the *Tribune* was allegedly dedicated to black race unity and seeking a reconciliation of the two castes; however, far from being a genuinely enlightened publication, the *Tribune*'s efforts were most often dedicated to the promotion of former FPC as the natural leaders and spokesmen of all blacks. Sensing that the freedmen would one day "hold the controlling political influence in Louisiana," the *Tribune* advised that former FPC and freedmen, "equally rejected and deprived of their rights, cannot be well estranged from one another."[33]

In the course of the Civil War a new group of individuals gradually entered onto the scene in Louisiana and by the end of the war had established themselves as a significant new player in the battle for postwar political control of the state. Most "carpetbaggers" initially entered the South as Union soldiers and would go on to hold prominent positions in all of the state Republican parties in the South. Many of these carpetbaggers were pre-war abolitionists who Louisiana FPC allegedly feared as "the greatest enemies."[34] Carpetbaggers were tremendously important to the political history of Louisiana during Reconstruction because of their large numbers and the disproportionate influence that they wielded in the state. The fact

---

[32]The *New Orleans Tribune* was edited by a white Belgian scientist, Jean-Charles Houzeau. The shift in attitudes expressed in the *Tribune* were largely the result of his influence; however, a free black, Louis Charles Roudanez, remained the owner of the newspaper and oversaw all of its operation. See Jean-Charles Houzeau, *My Passage at the New Orleans Tribune*, ed. by David C. Rankin (Baton Rouge: Louisiana State University Press, 1984).

[33]Tunnell, *Crucible of Reconstruction*, 78-80; Rankin, "The Impact of the Civil War," 391- 393.

[34]Bergeron, "Louisiana's Free Men of Color in Gray," 38.

that Louisiana's FPC population also exhibited large numbers and a disproportional influence given their large property holdings only added to the intensity of the approaching friction between the two groups.

Carpetbaggers had their most dramatic effects on southern blacks through the activities of the Freedmen's Bureau and the schools their agents operated. It was in their capacities with the Freedmen's Bureau that carpetbaggers were best able to secure the support of freedmen, particularly in the rural areas. It is also here in the schools conducted by northerners for blacks that friction between Louisiana's FPC and carpetbaggers first appeared. One reason for this friction was simply because the FPC could see no need for the Freedmen's school. One northern visitor to the Pointe Coupee region of central Louisiana observed in 1866, "out of nearly two hundred colored families who were free before the war, only one family is unable to read and write while among the white people from twenty to twenty-five percent are in ignorance." He also informed that FPC "have little to do with the Freedmen's Bureau, and do not recognize it as having any application to themselves. They object to being placed in the same class with freedmen just released from bondage, and seem to feel that they are a superior race. . . ."[35] The superintendent of education for the Freedmen's Bureau in Louisiana even went so far as to write that "perhaps the white population, as a class, would send their children to freedmen schools much more willingly, than this 'Creole Aristocracy' so slightly bleached from the veritable black,"[36] clearly referring to former free blacks. Given the willful disdain for association with the freedmen expressed by FPC it took only a little time before northern carpetbaggers began seeing themselves as the natural leaders of the recently emancipated slaves.

Much like the former FPC at the *Tribune*, carpetbaggers dedicated much energy to promoting themselves as the true leaders and

---

[35]Nathan Willey, "Education of the Colored Population of Louisiana," *Harper's New Monthly Magazine* 33 (1866): 247.

[36]Howard Ashley White, *The Freedmen's Bureau in Louisiana* (Baton Rouge: Louisiana State University Press, 1970), 7.

spokesmen of freedmen and went out of their way to portray former FPC as insincere and inevitably opposed to the best interest of freedmen. One northern agent with the Freedmen's Bureau wrote that "the free born colored people seem to be as great an enemy to the freedmen as some of the whites . . . ."[37] A principal of a Freedmen's Bureau school and native New Yorker wrote in 1866 that FPC "do not feel in the least identified with the freedmen or their interest. Nor need we wonder, when we remember that many of them were formerly slave holders. You know the peculiar institution cared little for the ethnology of its supporters."[38] And yet another northerner noted in the same year that the FPC were "entirely above all intercourse with the freedmen. There is far more distance between them and the freedmen so far as pride is concerned than between the [white] Southerner and his [black] servant."[39] All of these statements are clear testimony to the extraordinary lengths that carpetbaggers went to in order, if not to exaggerate, to at least illuminate the disunity that still existed between the former FPC and freedmen.

The conflicting agendas of the former FPC and carpetbaggers finally came to a head in the late spring of 1867. First, in April of that year the carpetbaggers formed into political organizations called Ben Butler clubs, initially excluding blacks from membership. The *New Orleans Republican* then appeared around the same time. The *Republican* was to be the carpetbagger's mouthpiece and a counter to the FPC's *Tribune*. The growing antagonism between the former FPC and the carpetbaggers erupted into open conflict at the Republican state convention in June 1867. After weeks of heated debate, just before the convention adjourned the carpetbag delegation hurriedly passed a last–minute measure that added a large number of new members to the powerful state central committee of the Republican party. It was not until after the adjournment that the former FPC delegates realized that the carpetbaggers had packed the committee

---

[37]Quoted in Rankin, "The Impact of the Civil War," 392.
[38]Ibid.
[39]Ibid.

with their members and in turn now controlled the state Republican party.[40]

The next battleground for the two Republican factions was the constitutional convention that met in the early fall of 1867. The convention was made up of several different factions that represented all of Louisiana's political interests at the time. The convention was, however, dominated by the carpetbaggers and the former FPC. The carpetbaggers, as had long been charged by former FPC, began to cooperate openly with conservatives and Democrats on certain issues. Also, for the first time freedmen from rural areas served as delegates in the state political process and, as something of a surprise to the former FPC delegation, most often sided with the white carpetbaggers. The pure radicals, as the former FPC delegates were known, did achieve many of their goals. The most coveted of these goals seems to have been the securing of the state printing contract for the *Tribune* over the *Republican* by the slim margin of 46 votes to 45. More important, however, was a battle that pure radicals lost. The compromisers, as the carpetbagger faction was known, proposed that the age limit to be governor be lowered from thirty-five to twenty-five, in a clear attempt to secure the election of their most prominent leader, the twenty-five-year-old Henry Clay Warmoth. One pure radical leader tauntingly proposed that the limit be lowered, but only to twenty-eight, thus disqualifying Warmoth. The delegates eventually decided to make American citizenship and two years residence in the state the only requirements to be governor, and hence the carpetbaggers had scored what would eventually be one of their most significant victories.[41]

The carpetbaggers' next political coup came at the Republican nominating convention in January 1868. In the contest for the endorsement of the Republican party in the governor's race, former free man of color and respected statesman, Francis E. Dumas, led on

---

[40]F. Wayne Binning, "Carpetbaggers' Triumph: The Louisiana State Election of 1868," *Louisiana History* 16 (Winter 1973): 26-28.
[41]Ibid., 27-34.

the first ballot with forty-one votes and was closely followed by Henry Clay Warmoth who received thirty-seven votes. On the next ballot Warmoth received forty-five votes, the minimum needed for the nomination, and Dumas received forty-three votes. Dumas easily secured the endorsement for lieutenant governor but was forced by the embittered former FPC leadership to decline it.[42]

The pure radicals, led by the former FPC faction, wasted no time in organizing a rival ticket. A white Unionist and former slaveholder, James G. Taliaferro was selected to run as governor and Dumas, also a former slaveholder, as lieutenant governor. Warmoth and the carpetbaggers responded by using the Republican party's state central committee to repudiate the *Tribune* as the official organ of the party and subsequently appointed the *Republican* in its place. The committee also expelled from the Republican party those "disorganizers" who were responsible for the rival ticket. The showdown between the carpetbaggers and former FPC was set for April 16 and 17 and would be the final act in the long battle for the support of the freedmen and ultimate control over Louisiana state government.[43]

The gubernatorial election of April 1868 was in many ways the most important event ever in the history of Louisiana race relations. The impact of this election on relations between former free people of color and freedmen is particularly significant; however, the general importance of the election to white-black relations is also overwhelming. The April 1868 election was more than a simple struggle for political control of the state; it was in many ways the defining moment in regard to the relationship between former FPC and freedmen. It was both the culmination of antebellum and Civil War animosities and the beginning of a whole new era of resentment between the two groups. The roles of the two groups had largely reversed, whereas FPC were the more powerful of the two castes during the antebellum period and the slave masses had in general felt abandoned by them, the freedmen given their newly established rights

---

[42]Ibid., 34.
[43]Ibid., 35-36.

and numerical majority were now in the more powerful position and the former FPC were the ones feeling abandoned.

As the *Tribune* had accurately assumed in 1864, the controlling political influence in Louisiana now rested in the hands of the recently emancipated freedmen, and they would in fact determine which group, the recently arrived white carpetbaggers or their newly sympathetic racial brothers, the former FPC, could best be trusted with control of state government and the job of reconstructing the state. The Democrats had been shut out of the election procedure and had no chance at political control of the state. The former FPC faction did ultimately draw support from conservatives and the Democrats, who would have much rather seen Taliaferro as governor than Warmoth. Thus the former FPC population had returned to the alliance which best represented their true propertied interest. They had tied their fates not to that of the freedmen, as they so often publicly pledged, but to that of their white Democrat associates, much like the alliance to the Confederacy that they had initially entered into with the very same men at the outbreak of the war. It was alleged that Louis Roudanez, owner of the *New Orleans Tribune* and outspoken leader of the former FPC faction, said a month prior to the election that "he would rather join hands with the old white citizens of New Orleans than support the Warmoth ticket."[44] Furthermore the *Republican* quoted Roudanez as declaring that "I'd rather see Beauregard or Jeff Davis governor of Louisiana than Warmoth."[45]

Former FPC in rural sections of the Louisiana also aligned themselves with the Taliaferro faction. In St. Landry Parish for example there existed a Republican newspaper originally founded by four whites and about fifteen former FPC, the *St. Landry Progress.* Once a carpetbagger by the name of Emerson Bentley obtained a controlling interest in the newspaper, and as editor came out in support of the Warmoth ticket, the free black owners liquidated their

---

[44]Ibid., 36-39; Quote from the *New Orleans Republican*, March 1, 1868, and included in ibid., 38.

[45]Quote from the *New Orleans Republican*, March 28, 1868, and included in Houzeau, *My Passage at the New Orleans Tribune*, 53.

interest in the paper, and their support faded.[46] This St. Landry Parish group contained the most vocal rural FPC supporters of Taliaferro in the state. The leadership of the St. Landry Parish Republican party was, like the state party, dominated by two factions: one former FPC and one carpetbagger. The former FPC faction was controlled by former Confederate solider Auguste Donato and his brother Gustave. Along with their support of Taliaferro, the Donato brothers ran an entire ticket of candidates, composedly largely of former FPC, for local political offices in direct competition with Warmoth's Regular Republicans. The mere candidacy of these former FPC clearly demonstrates where the alliances of Louisiana's rural former FPC lay during the April election of 1868.[47]

Many newly emerged black leaders not of Creole FPC origin, who had at times supported the efforts of the *Tribune* group, supported Warmoth from the very time of his nomination; P. B. S. Pinchback, James H. Ingraham, Oscar Dunn, and C. C. Antoine being the most influential of the group. These four black leaders commanded a tremendous amount of respect and exerted enormous influence with the freedmen population. This defection would have a tremendous effect on the eventual election outcome. Somewhat surprisingly, several of the most outspoken Creole FPC leaders refused to join the pure radical faction and eventually supported Warmoth and the regular Republican ticket. Jean-Charles Houzeau, the white editor of the *Tribune* and the architect of many of the conciliatory FPC efforts prior to 1868, refused to support the pure radical ticket, abruptly resigned his post, and left New Orleans shortly after the election. Before his departure Houzeau noted that "the old aristocratic spirit of the mulatto [FPC faction] has reawakened," and just a few days before the election Houzeau predicted that "among the blacks [freedmen], the influence of the *Tribune* is naturally lost forever."

---

[46]Geraldine Mary McTigue, "Forms of Racial Interaction in Louisiana, 1860-1880," (Ph.D. diss., Yale University, 1975), 174-175.

[47]Ibid., 250-290.

The freedmen voters ultimately repudiated the former FPC's pure radical ticket and helped sweep Warmoth and the carpetbaggers into office by a two to one margin. Ten days later the *New Orleans Tribune* closed its doors and stopped publication. The former FPC leaders attempted on several occasions during Reconstruction to reenter the Louisiana political scene but failed in nearly every effort. Even after several years under Warmoth and the most corrupt administration ever seen in Louisiana, a state known for its political corruption, freedmen still did not trust the former FPC leadership and would continuously reject black race unity, much like the FPC population had done for the previous century and a half.[48]

Given the historical tension between the two groups it is easy to understand why the freedmen rejected the former FPC leadership in April 1868. The interest of former FPC were closer to that of the white southerners at the time of the outbreak of the Civil War, and the FPC's efforts to reconcile their differences with the freedmen during and immediately after the war were clearly not completely sincere. Whereas the FPC had consistently done everything in their power to suppress slaves and uphold slavery, once on the scene in Louisiana, carpetbaggers appeared like Lincoln or Garrison, or even Moses himself, and were in turn chiefly, in the minds of the slaves, the ones responsible for bringing about the Civil War, the liberation of the slave masses, and the ultimate obliteration of the dark shadow of the peculiar institution. Whereas the former FPC were devout Roman Catholics, the carpetbaggers were generally Protestant and played key roles in the expansion of Protestant churches in the immediate postwar South. Whereas FPC refused to associate or participate with the Freedmen's Bureau, carpetbaggers led the fight for educational and economic reform for freedmen. All of these factors were barriers to black race unity in Civil War and Reconstruction Louisiana and surely were in part responsible for the freedmen's rejection of former FPC leadership. Clearly the carpetbaggers were at least at this point the better representatives of the freedmen's interest.

---

[48]Binning, "Carpetbaggers' Triumph," 36-39.

Many former free men of color did succeed in winning elected office in Louisiana during Reconstruction; however, no organized former FPC faction ever succeeded as a unified group element. Former FPC always succeeded as single individuals judged on their individual accomplishments. Many of these men had served in the Union Army during the Civil War, and few were Confederate sympathizers. Additionally, few if any black political leaders during Reconstruction were affiliated with the *New Orleans Tribune* in 1868. Many suffered the same fate as Francis E. Dumas, who was clearly one of the most educated, articulate, and cultured men in Louisiana before the Civil War. He did not join the Confederate state militia, and in fact fought gallantly for the Union Army. His affiliation with the pure radical faction during 1868, however, permanently tarnished his reputation with many blacks. Before running unsuccessfully for secretary of state in 1872, Dumas's only Reconstruction office was a rather insignificant federal appointment as an engineer on a project to rebuild the Mississippi River levees in 1871.[49]

Contrary to what some historians have suggested, it would seem that most of the prominent African American political officials to serve in Louisiana during Reconstruction were not derived from the former free black French Creole elite. Of the most prominent former FPC members of the *Tribune* faction in 1868 (Louis Roudanez, Aristide Mary, and Paul Trivigne), none ever succeeded in securing any elected political office during Reconstruction. The most comprehensive study of black leadership in New Orleans during Reconstruction lists "the Bonseigneurs and the Glaudins, the Roudanezes and the Saulays, the Boisdores and Esteves, the Canelles and the Adolphes, the Raynals and the Belots" as families who provided black leadership during this period.[50] Of the ten families listed, however, only members of three (the Adolphes, the Bonseigneurs and the

---

[49]Eric Foner, *Freedom's Lawmakers: A Directory of Black Officeholders During Reconstruction* (Baton Rouge: Louisiana State University Press, 1996); additional information on Francis Dumas is in Hollandsworth, *The Louisiana Native Guard*, 26-27.

[50]David Rankin, "The Origins of Black Leadership in New Orleans During Reconstruction," *Journal of Southern History* 60 (August 1974): 425.

Belots) every served in significant political positions in Louisiana during Reconstruction, and all but two of the families (the Roudanezes and the Adolphes) contributed to the Confederate state militia.[51]

The three most prominent black elected officials in Louisiana during Reconstruction (P. B. S. Pinchback, Oscar Dunn, and C. C. Antoine) did not come from the former free black aristocracy, but were of more humble origins. Although free before the war, two of these men were barbers and the other a largely unknown Mississippi river boat pilot. None of the men ever assisted the Confederates, and two of the three raised black Union regiments during the Civil War. Certainly two of three, excepting Antoine, did not have any French Creole family connections. Most importantly, all three of these men opposed the pure radical, FPC-led faction in 1868. Dunn was elected Lieutenant Governor on the Warmoth ticket, an office to which Pinchback subsequently rose after Dunn's untimely death in 1871. Antoine also sided with the Warmoth faction in 1868 and was even an associate editor of the *New Orleans Black Republican*, a short-lived newspaper established in direct opposition to the FPC faction controlling the *New Orleans Tribune*. These examples clearly support the idea that in Louisiana a certain amount of animosity still existed between former elite free persons of color and freedmen well into the period of Reconstruction and probably much longer. These examples also demonstrate that because of these animosities the former free person of color elite were very disconnected from the black population at large during Reconstruction, and most were unsuccessful in obtaining significant political offices.[52]

These animosities between former FPC and freedmen would continue for many generations and are still largely evident in both rural and urban sections of Louisiana's black community. The FPC's

---

[51]For Reconstruction officials see Foner, *Freedom's Lawmakers*, 249-251; Confederate state militia information obtained from copy of a muster roll provided by historian James G. Hollandsworth.

[52]Foner, *Freedom's Lawmakers*, 171-172, 67-68, 8-9 (entries on Pinchback, Dunn, and Antoine).

reaction to the ultimate failure of black race unity that occurred in Louisiana during the immediate postwar and Reconstruction periods is remarkably similar in both rural areas and New Orleans. A study of the former FPC population of New Orleans during the period beginning in the 1880s concludes that "instead of establishing a closer relationship with the city's larger Negro population, they [former FPC] withdrew further into a world of their own and created a community that accentuated the differences between themselves and Afro-Americans. . . . Creoles of Color [former FPC] in New Orleans avoided extensive and intimate contact with other Negros in the city."[53] In one dramatic example a large portion of the former FPC membership of the St. James AME church splintered from their congregation to form the Central Congregational Church rather than be part of a denomination that allowed freedmen as regular members.[54] Similarly a study of former free blacks in the rural areas of Southwest Louisiana found that "even more than before they looked inward."[55] These rural former FPC also isolated themselves from interaction with others and because of their rural setting it was even possible for these former FPC to establish complete, separate communities. By avoiding interaction with whites, and more importantly with freedmen, Louisiana's former FPC population held on to many of the cultural and social distinctions that it had exhibited in the antebellum period and thus greatly impaired social relations within the black race in Louisiana for many years.[56]

While the Civil War and the resulting emancipation of four million slaves was certainly a revolutionary event in American history,

---

[53]Willard B. Gatewood, *Aristocrats of Color: The Black Elite, 1880-1920* (Bloomington and Indianapolis: Indiana University Press, 1990), 84.

[54]William E. Montgomery, *Under Their Own Vine and Fig Tree: The African-American Church in the South, 1865-1900* (Baton Rouge: Louisiana State University Press, 1993), 103, 260.

[55]Loren Schweninger, "Socioeconomic Dynamics among the Gulf Creole Populations: The Antebellum and Civil War Years," in James H. Dormon, ed., *Creoles of Color of the Gulf South* (Knoxville: University of Tennessee Press, 1996), 62.

[56]See Gatewood, *Aristocrats of Color*; Schweninger, "Socioeconomic Dynamics" and Brasseaux, Fontenot, and Oubre, *Creoles of Color in the Bayou County*.

it had the unforeseen and unintended effect of obliterating the special status and social privileges that free persons of color in Louisiana had historically enjoyed. In addition, despite the fact that the fates of former free persons of color and freedmen were now unequivocally tied together, the war did not reconcile the century and a half of separation and ill feelings between the two groups and as a result did not produce black race unity. Instead, it only heightened tensions and renewed century-old animosities. The state of Louisiana is possibly the best example of the truly complex nature of southern race relations. The relationship between former free people of color and freedmen in Civil War and early Reconstruction Louisiana well demonstrates this fact and clearly shows how historical treatments have often failed adequately to explain these complexities.

III.

ETHNICITY, GENDER, AND VIOLENCE IN THE SOUTH

5

THE SOCIAL ACCEPTABILITY OF NINETEENTH-CENTURY DOMESTIC VIOLENCE

Angela Boswell

On May 19, 1871, Anton went to the bed of Wilhelmine

and with his fist struck [her] in the face on the head and in the breast with repeated blows and when [she] succeeded in getting away from the bed and was escaping from the room [he] violently kicked [her] into the yard and [he] pursued [her] and continued beating her with his fist and [she] and the children sought refuge with a neighbor for two days . . . .[1]

This was not the first time Anton had assaulted Wilhelmine. In 1869,

Anton being in a rage threw at her a china cup and cut her head so badly that she bled profusely and pieces of the cup were afterwards picked from the wound. . . [He] knocked her down and stomped her, [and] about the first of August last past he beat her. . . .[2]

---

[1]Amended Petition, Wilhelmine Burttschell vs. Anton Burttschell, June 6, 1871, Docket File No. 2554, Colorado County District Clerk's Office (hereinafter referred to as CCDC).

[2]Petition, Wilhelmine Burttschell vs. Anton Burttschell, September 20, 1870, Docket File No. 2554, CCDC.

Despite the violent attacks, Anton Burttschell, like most abusive nineteenth-century husbands, never faced trial for assaulting his wife. The details of her suffering do not appear in a criminal indictment but in a divorce petition. Even the divorce petition was never heard by a court or a jury. Wilhelmine Burttschell dropped her suit in June 1871, renewed it again later that month, and allowed it to be dismissed the next year.[3]

Historians will not be surprised that the "epidemic" of family violence, highlighted by such cases as the recent trial of O. J. Simpson, did not begin in this, the last, decade of the twentieth century. Nor did it necessarily reach its peak of frequency or violence in this century. The collection of statistics on family violence, showing it to be the number one cause of injury to women in the United States and affecting one out of every four households, has only heightened our awareness of the situation and demanded a social, not just personal response.[4] No such statistical analysis can be provided for the nineteenth-century South or United States. If, with the contemporary heightened awareness of the problem, domestic violence is still one of the most under-reported crimes in the United States, then nineteenth-century southern society certainly did not encourage the reporting or keeping of such statistics. Texas law specifically granted a husband the right to physically restrain and correct his wife in order to control her actions, granting him immunity from prosecution for such actions.[5]

In the nineteenth-century, women, who depended even more upon marriage for their support and social position, had even more compelling reasons to stay in abusive marriages, and as a result most did so. This does not mean, however, that nineteenth-century

---

[3]Wilhelmine Burttschell vs. Anton Burttschell, June 7, 1871, June 26, 1871, and June 17, 1872, District Court Minutes, Book E, 16, 70, and 324, CCDC.

[4]C. Everett Koop, M.D., U.S. Surgeon General's Report, U.S. Public Health Service, 1988, as cited by the Domestic Violence Statistics in Texas, prepared June 1995 by the Texas Council of Family Violence.

[5]Williamson S. Oldham and George W. White, comps., *A Digest of the General Statute Laws of the State of Texas*. . . (Austin, Texas: John Marshall & Co., 1859), 517.

southern society completely ignored the plight of an assaulted and abused wife. Even in a patriarchal society that recognized the right of the husband to physically control and punish his wife, his children, and his slaves, he could not have unchecked power over any of these parties. Antebellum proslavery arguments denied that masters had unrestrained power over slaves; their power was limited by moral restraints and social pressure as well as weak laws that could punish the most flagrant abuses.[6] Husbands, likewise, though rarely criminally culpable, faced the same moral and social pressures to avoid the most extreme abuses of their wives.

This essay studies domestic violence and the social response as revealed in the legal sources of one rural southern county from 1837-1873. These dates represent the beginning of the county and follow the records for a period of over thirty-five years through many changes in the South and the country as a whole: the civilizing of the frontier, the establishment of antebellum culture, civil war, and Reconstruction. The end of Reconstruction is a convenient cut-off point for this study because it traditionally signals the beginning of a new era for the South, although it is likely that any significant changes in attitudes toward domestic violence in this county as in the South as a whole took place only very gradually in the latter part of the nineteenth century. Colorado County, Texas (located about one hour west of present-day Houston), much like the rest of the nineteenth-century South, was a predominantly rural area populated mostly by farmers and planters who grew cotton on land tracts of various size. The very small population of about 1700 in 1848 burgeoned to 7,885 by 1860. By 1870, the white population had risen to 8,324. Between ten and fifteen percent of adult white males owned slaves with slaves comprising thirty-two percent of the total population of the county in 1850, and forty-five percent of the population in 1860.[7] A large portion of the residents also raised cattle, a pattern

---

[6]Peter J. Parish, *Slavery: History and Historians* (New York: Harper and Row Publishers, 1989), 140.

[7]Based on "1850 Slave Holders" compiled by Bill Stein, Archivist, Nesbitt Memorial Library, Columbus, Texas.

that was not atypical for the South, but much more common in western Texas.[8] The vast majority of the Anglo and African American population had their origins in other southern states.

Yet many of the county's settlers and inhabitants came from German-speaking countries. Germans made up nearly half the county's population in 1850, and forty percent in 1860.[9] Many Germans lived in the predominantly Anglo county seat of Columbus or in other Anglo areas. Most, however, settled in separate areas such as Bernardo and Frelsburg. Even while maintaining much of their cultural distinctiveness in these communities, Germans in Colorado County associated more frequently with the Anglo southerners than those Germans who settled in west Texas. They quickly adopted southern agriculture and commercial practices that forced them into the matrix of southern society. A few of the wealthier Germans not only grew cotton, but also owned slaves.[10]

No one county can "typify" the South as a whole. However, because most information about nineteenth-century domestic violence comes from divorce petitions filed in the District Court, studying a single county in Texas can show how these particular southerners dealt with not only violence against women but how these questions were modified by questions of race and ethnicity. Forty-seven out of sixty-seven divorce petitions (seventy percent) filed by wives in Colorado County cited some instance of abuse or cruelty, many as graphic as Wilhelmine Burttschell's description above. Another five women claimed cruelty in their cross-petitions for divorce. Forty-one of these detailed physical acts of violence or threats of violence. A much higher percentage of nineteenth-century women sought divorces on the grounds of physical cruelty because

---

[8]Based on Probate Records, Deed Records, and Bond and Mortgage Records in Colorado County Clerk's Office.

[9]Schedule 1 (Free Inhabitants), Seventh and Eighth Census of the United States (1850 and 1860), Texas, Colorado County.

[10]Glen E. Lich, *The German Texans* (San Antonio: University of Texas Institute of Texan Cultures, 1981), 68-73; Terry G. Jordan, *German Seed in Texas Soil: Immigrant Farmers in Nineteenth-Century Texas* (Austin: University of Texas Press, 1966), especially 8 and 194.

divorce was the primary source of legal relief for abused wives provided by southern states, and cruelty was one of the very few grounds on which a wife could obtain a divorce.[11]

Southern legislators and lawmakers in the first half of the nineteenth century had moved to provide greater access to divorce in order to relieve victimized and wronged wives. Changing assumptions about gender roles and the rising ideal of companionate marriage highlighted the injustice of virtuous women forever tied to abusive, deserting, or otherwise degenerate husbands.[12] Southern states, which had previously required an act of the legislature to obtain a divorce, offered relief to women by moving the divorce process to the less intimidating local judicial level and out of the legislative level. At this time, many southern states added or enlarged the scope of cruelty clauses giving abused women the option to end the violence by leaving the marriage. Texas passed its divorce statute in 1841 in the midst of the southern trend liberalizing divorces and as a result had one of the most liberal of the southern divorce statutes. Local district courts granted divorce, and the cruelty clause was one of the broadest available.[13]

---

[11]Docket Files and District Court Minutes, CCDC. In the 1990s, "a third of all divorces are sought by women on grounds of physical cruelty." Alisa Deltufo, *Domestic Violence for Beginners* (New York: Writers and Readers Publishing, Inc., 1995), 129. Domestic Violence Statistics in Texas, Texas Council on Family Violence (June 1995).

[12]Jane Tuner Censer, " 'Smiling Through Her Tears': Ante-Bellum Southern Women and Divorce," *American Journal of Legal History* 25 (January 1981), 27; Lawrence B. Goodheart, Neil Hanks, and Elizabeth Johnson, "An Act for the Relief of Females. . .': Divorce and the Changing Legal Status of Women in Tennessee, 1796-1860, Part I," *Tennessee Historical Quarterly* 44 (# 3, 1985): 322-23; Sally McMillen, *Southern Women: Black and White in the Old South* (Arlington Heights, Ill.: Harlan Davidson, Inc., 1992); Robert L. Griswold, "The Evolution of the Doctrine of Mental Cruelty in Victorian American Divorce, 1790-1900," *Journal of Social History* 20 (Fall 1986), 127; Norma Basch, "Relief in the Premises: Divorce as a Woman's Remedy in New York and Indiana, 1815-1870," *Law and History Review* 8 (Spring 1990), 1-24. For the importance of the ideal of companionate marriage in the South, see Jane Turner Censer, *North Carolina Planters and Their Children: 1800-1860* (Baton Rouge: Louisiana State University Press, 1984), 72-73.

[13]Goodheart, Hanks, and Johnson, "An Act for the Relief of Females," 323, 404-405. Also see Christopher Lasch, "Divorce and the 'Decline of the Family'" in *The World of Nations* (New York, 1973), 39; and Censer, "Smiling Through Her Tears," 46-47; Richard H. Chused, *Private Acts in Public Places: A Social History of Divorce in the Formative Era of*

In Colorado County, the grounds of cruel treatment did not at first primarily benefit abused women as most southern legislators had assumed it would. During the frontier era of the county (1837-1852), men used cruelty as a means of obtaining a divorce with more success than women. Jesse Robinson won a divorce from his wife Sally when she refused to live up to the nineteenth-century ideal of true womanhood and its basic tenets: piety, purity, domesticity, and submissiveness.[14] In addition to being a "scold and termagant," he alleged that "she conducted herself towards other men with the most unjustifiable familiarity," and abandoned her husband and one of her children.[15] John Hope complained that his wife Rusha "invariably wreaked her incorrigible temper & disposition upon [him] whenever in her reach . . . in a manner unbecoming her sex, a wife or a mother and disgraceful to humanity."[16] James Dickson's primary complaint of his wife Hetty was "that she was in the habit when in company of using the most obscene and vulgar language such as the rule of society forbid. . . ." He procured the depositions of two witnesses who swore that they "heard Hetty use vulgar and very unbecoming language to

---

American Family Law (Philadelphia: University of Pennsylvania Press, 1944) 7-11. Frontier southern states such as Tennessee and North Carolina generally had more liberal divorce laws than the older established southern states. McMillen, Southern Women, 46; Goodheart, Hanks, and Johnson, "An Act for the Relief of Females," 320; Mary Somerville Jones, An Historical Geography of the Changing Divorce Law in the United States (New York and London: Garland Publishing, Inc., 1987), 30-31. Jones shows in a later period in the western United States that the more liberal laws and frontier regions did not necessarily lead to an increase in divorce. Jones, 166-71.

[14]Barbara Welter, "The Cult of True Womanhood: 1820-1860," American Quarterly 18 (Summer 1966), 151-174; Goodheart, Hanks, and Johnson, "An Act for the Relief of Females," 332.

[15]Petition and Jury Finding, Jesse Robinson vs. Sarah alias Sally Robinson, February 1, 1843, and March 8, 1843, Docket No. 220, CCDC; District Court Minutes, Book A & B, March 8, 1843, 161-62.

[16]Amended Petition, John Hope vs. Rusha Hope, April 28, 1841, Docket No. 137, CCDC.

her husband and in fact talk more than any woman I ever did hear talk to her husband. . . ."[17]

Four of the five frontier husbands who sought divorces on the grounds of cruel treatment received those divorces. Women cited cruel treatment in divorce petitions more often than men (ten women compared to five men), but enjoyed a lower success rate than the husbands in actually obtaining the divorce. While men claimed small matters such as mean tempers and abusive language as "cruelty," women had to prove a higher degree of cruel treatment. Only five of the ten frontier cases filed by wives citing cruelty resulted in a divorce. Two cases were voluntarily withdrawn after a year or two of protracted legal opposition. Three petitioners who did not demonstrate physical cruelty or at least the threats of such cruelty did not get a chance to take their case to the jury. Virgillia Woolsey claimed her husband was "guilty of great excesses, cruel treatment, and outrages," but she did not claim he was dangerous to her health. The judge dismissed her case and ordered her to pay the court costs, even though there was no evidence her husband Abner contested the divorce.[18] Another unhappily married woman, Susan Bostick, brought suit against her husband Sion in 1851, charging that he "refused to recognize or speak to her" for over a month, and that "he drove her from his house and home, and has repeatedly declared since that he will never speak to nor live with her again. . . ." Sion evidently wanted the divorce as much as Susan did, since after Susan's case was dismissed, he later filed actions twice to obtain it. However, a great deal of property was involved and guilt would greatly influence its

---

[17]Petition and Interrogatories, James Dickson vs. Hetty Dickson, May 8, 1843, May 16 and August 1, 1843, Docket No. 227; District Court Minutes, Book A & B, September 5, 1843, 176, all in CCDC; H. P. N. Gammel comp., The Laws of Texas, 1822-1897, Vol. 7 (Austin: Gammel Book Company, 1898)483-86.

[18]Petition, Virgillia Woolsey vs. Abner W. Woolsey, May 22, 1845, Docket No. 381, CCDC.

distribution, so Sion fought Susan's divorce action. At the next term of the court, the judge dismissed the case entirely.[19]

The double standard in cruelty cases worked against women only during the frontier era of Colorado County. Three of the four men who won divorces on the grounds of cruelty all did so before 1848, when the Texas Supreme Court handed down a decision stating that only threats to the life or health of the victim should be considered cruelty.[20] The fourth male to divorce on the grounds of excesses and outrages after 1848 somewhat vaguely and unconvincingly claimed that his wife "did curse, swear at, and threaten to beat and maltreat your petitioner and other wrongs and outrages. . . ."[21] Only two other men received a divorce under the cruelty clause before the end of Reconstruction: both charged that their wives abused not them, but the children from the husbands' previous marriages.[22] Women, however, continued to rely on cruel treatment as the number one grounds for divorce, and to demonstrate that the cruelty inflicted upon them was physical abuse.

By the antebellum period in Colorado County, the cruelty clause began to resemble what contemporaries and historians assumed it was meant to be: a modification "favoring women" and an opportunity for

---

[19]Petition, Susan Bostick vs. Sion Bostick, October 17, 1851, Docket No. 709; District Court Minutes, Book C, March 30, 1852, 878, both in CCDC. The court records do not specifically state why these cases were dismissed. When a plaintiff would decide to no longer pursue case, a notation to that effect would be made. When the parties reached agreements, this would also be noted in the records.

[20]Griswold, "Evolution of Mental Cruelty," *Journal of Social History* 20 (Fall 1986): 130; Censer, "Smiling Through Her Tears," 28-29, 34-35. Griswold maintains that in the 1840s cruelty was considered by judges to mean just physical cruelty and that thereafter it gradually came under attack. In Texas, lower courts had the ability to interpret cruelty as mental suffering until the Supreme Court guided them to do so no longer, which it did in 1848. Later, cruelty was broadened by the Texas Supreme Court in a way which favored women much more than the local district court did, i.e. by allowing a false charge of adultery to be considered cruelty.

[21]Petition, Reuben Bonds vs. Darcas Bonds, April 1, 1850, Docket No. 650, CCDC.

[22]Petition, Moses Townsend vs. Rebecca C. Townsend, September 26, 1857, Docket No. 1267; Petition, Thadeus W. Hunter vs. Tempie J. Hunter, September 16, 1873, Docket No. 2995, CCDC.

abused women to escape the situation.[23] Based on the failure of those who did not cite specific instances of physical harm or fear of physical harm, as well as on the success of those petitioners who did, attorneys for wives seeking divorce encouraged descriptions of the violence that they suffered. Two frontier cases filed by women even included rewritten petitions. After their first appearance in court, these wives submitted new petitions placing more emphasis upon the physical and threatening nature of their relationship. Both cases received continuances, allowing the plaintiffs to amend their petitions.[24] Margaret Pinchback's first petition had alleged only generic "divers acts of unkindness and ill treatment." According to her amended petition, her husband James "without cause or any provocation whatever, unlawfully beat and bruised" her and drove her from their home "with the marks of the rod upon her body inflicted by his cruelty and abuse."[25] Mary Dresler's petition included a description of her husband striking her with a chair.[26] After filing for divorce, her husband made an "attack upon her person with a drawn knife in his hand threatening to take her life and inflicted severe blows and bruises on her body with his fist and with a large club" and attacked their daughter also. All of which her attorney hastened to present in an amended petition.[27]

Although women who wanted a divorce needed to cite physical violence, the detailed descriptions of many of the assaults in divorce petitions substantiates the veracity of these claims. The petitions also often refer to other parties who either witnessed the assault(s) or

---

[23]Censer, "Smiling Through Her Tears," 46; Griswold, "Law, Sex, Cruelty, and Divorce," 730-731.

[24]Margaret Pinchback vs. James Pinchback, District Court Minutes, Book A & B, 191, 202 and 232; Mary Dressler vs. Henry Dressler, District Court Minutes, Book C, 881 and 934, CCDC.

[25]Amended petition, Margaret Pinchback vs James Pinchback, August 24, 1844, Docket No. 322, CCDC.

[26]Petition, Margaret Pinchback vs James Pinchback, August 4, 1843, Docket No. 322; Petition, Mary Dresler vs. Henry Dresler, October 23, 1850, Docket No. 739, both in CCDC.

[27]Amended Petition, Mary Dresler vs. Henry Dresler, April 16, 1852, Docket No. 739, CCDC.

protected them from further harm. This, of course, lent credibility to the allegations in the eyes of judges and juries. The court sometimes called these witnesses to testify or, in the case of female witnesses, to give their depositions.[28] Colina Hoff in one such deposition described an assault: Emil Wichman pushed his wife Caroline "and struck her three very severe blows in the face. . . ."[29]

Witnesses had no choice, of course, but to come to court or give their depositions regarding the violence in a family. Although these people described the assaults upon women, it is conceivable that they still saw nothing legally wrong with a man beating his wife. The petitions, however, describe another group of people who obviously saw the danger of violent domestic situations: those who interfered and protected her.

The "interposition" of others saved the lives of many wives or at least protected them from serious injury. Often it was a relative who stepped in to help. William Dunford "drew his knife . . . and made an assault" upon his wife Sarah "intending to take her life, and would probably have succeeded in doing so had it not been for the timely interference of her mother."[30] Fanny Smith's son Ben interfered several times to prevent Fanny's husband James "from inflicting serious bodily harm."[31]

Not just relatives, however, felt the responsibility to interfere between a husband and wife when the abuse was potentially serious. The "interposition of third persons" prevented Hubert Albrecht from continuing the "severe and cruel beating" he gave his wife Marie. Some bystander prevented Adam Peltzer from hitting Catherine with a water keg. Another prevented Thomas Bateman from killing his

---

[28]See Subpoenas, Polly Reels vs. Patrick Reels, Docket File No. 245; Margaret Pinchback vs. James Pinchback, Docket File No. 322; and Wilhelmine Burttschell vs. Anton Burttschell, Docket File No. 2554, CCDC, for example.

[29]Deposition of Colina Hoff, Caroline Louise Elise Henrica Wichman vs. Emil W. Wichmann, February 7, 1874, Docket File No. 2971, CCDC.

[30]Petition, Sarah Dunford vs. William Dunford, June 13, 1857, Docket File No. 1240, CCDC.

[31]Petition, Fanny Smith vs. James Smith and J. N. Binkley, August 13, 1872, Docket File No. 2871, CCDC.

wife Elizabeth when he saw that Thomas "was choking her severely and threatened to kill her."[32] Caroline Wichman believed if only she "would call for help" she would receive assistance when her husband beat and whipped her "as she was in familie [sic] way." Her husband Emil, however, "was strong enough to prevent her from so doing" by pinching her jaws and cheeks to keep her from yelling.[33]

According to the divorce petitions, third parties most often stepped to the defense of women who were in the most serious danger. However, community members also protected women in other ways. Ellen Lacey recounted that on one night "to escape bodily harm she fled to her nearest neighbor who received her in her house." Other petitioners speak of seeking shelter at neighbors', friends', and relatives' houses when the violence became too severe.[34] Jennie Naill and Cornelia Binkley described how they would try to defuse tense situations between H. A. and Jane Tatum who sometimes boarded at their house, especially when Jane "seemed frightened." Immediately after the birth of their child, H. A. told Jane that she would have to leave the boardinghouse where she was staying. He threatened her with homelessness claiming "it will be impossible for you to get board in any decent family in town." Cornelia Binkley recounts in her deposition that she came to Jane's defense: "I then said you are mistaken Mr. Tatum[;] I will board Mrs. Tatum."[35]

---

[32]Petition, Marie Albrecht vs. Hubert Albrecht, September 8, 1855, Docket File No. 1065; Petition, Catherine Peltzer vs. Adam Peltzer, September 24, 1860, Docket File No. 1554; Petition, Elizabeth Bateman vs. Thomas Bateman, August 24, 1853, Docket File No. 802, CCDC. See also Petition, Caroline Kahnd vs. Jacob Kahnd, October 15, 1848, Docket File No. 541, CCDC.

[33]Petition, Caroline Louise Elise Henrica Wichman vs. Emil W. Wichmann, July 28, 1873, Docket File No. 2971, CCDC.

[34]Petition, Ellenora Lacey vs. Beverly M. Lacey, September 13, 1869, Docket File No. 2374; Petition, Catherina Zainik vs. Jos Zainik, April 24, 1871, Docket File No. 2649; Petition, Elizabeth Hahn vs. Jacob Hahn, August 30, 1859, Docket File No. 1459; Petition, Margaret Zimmerschitte vs. Fredrich Zimmerschitte, May 24, 1848, Docket File No. 538; Petition, Wilhelmine Burttschell vs. Anton Burttschell, September 20, 1870, Docket File No. 2554, CCDC.

[35]Deposition of Jennie Naill, H. A. Tatum vs. Jane Tatum, April 29, 1865, Docket File No. 1790 (first quote); Deposition of Cornelia N. Binkley, H. A. Tatum vs. Jane Tatum, April 29, 1865, Docket File No. 1790 (second and third quotes), CCDC.

No matter what legal right husbands had to physically punish or coerce their wives, at least some community members exerted moral—and physical—pressure to protect wives from the worst abuses. When members of the community, in the form of a jury, were given the opportunity to free a woman from an abusive marriage, they overwhelmingly chose to do so. Twenty-two divorce cases filed by women citing physical cruelty as grounds for divorce reached a jury. All but three of those women were granted a divorce. Two of the four women sued for divorce by their husbands who cross-petitioned citing physical cruelty had the divorces granted to them instead of to their husbands.[36]

Women who pursued a divorce and convinced the judge to allow juries to hear their trials were liberated from their abusive husbands by those members of the community. However bad the abuse, women, were much less likely to pursue the divorce to its end than a jury was to grant the divorce. Fifteen of the thirty-seven women who filed for divorce describing physical threats or acts of violence did not make it to a jury trial. Only two of these were dismissed by the judge; the other thirteen either dropped their cases or came to an agreement with their husbands. Margaret Zimmerschitte's husband abused her often, threatening to shoot her at one time and to kill her with an axe at another. On one drunken occasion, Frederick did assault her with the axe and "struck her on the hand thereby inflicting a severe wound [on her hand] and permanently disabling her. . . ."[37] Margaret apparently endured her husband's abuse because she was afraid of the financial consequences of leaving. When Frederick's constant inebriation threatened that financial stability anyway, Margaret filed for divorce. She charged in her petition that Frederick " has been and still is waisting [sic] away in intoxication and dissipation all the

---

[36]In the other two cross-petitions citing cruelty, the jury did not grant a divorce to either party. Jacob Illg vs. Sophia Illg, Docket File No. 1466, and *Sion R. Bostick vs. Susan Bostick*, Docket File No. 1064, CCDC. Both husbands filed again for divorce until they received divorces from their wives on the grounds of adultery.

[37]Petition, Margaret Zimmerschitte vs. Fredrich Zimmerschitte, May 24, 1848, Docket No. 538, CCDC.

property that he can possibly so dispose of and that to no advantage to himself or family . . . ." When Frederick agreed to transfer the bulk of the property to more reliable relatives, thus securing them financially, she dropped the divorce suit and returned to live with her abusive husband.[38] Margaret faced not only social and financial pressures to remain married but familial pressures as well. Nine years later, after her husband's death, Margaret wrote to her daughter:

> I know well if murderers had shot me, my family would shed few tears. Why—I know it and many know it unfortunately. . . . If I had let my husband do as he wanted, I would have had no quarrels and would have had none with you either. Then you would not have had a foot of land nor would I either.[39]

Margaret Zimmerschitte was not unusual in returning to her abusive husband even after taking the drastic step of filing for divorce. Wilhelmine Burttschell filed for divorce in September 1870. Her husband Anton soon thereafter "pretending to repent of his outrages to pltff [sic] sought a reconciliation" and Wilhelmine "too fondly trusting to his false and deceitful promises agreed to live with him as his wife" again. Her lawyer dropped her suit during the Spring court session, but before summer Anton "began and continued his brutal outrages to her person and has far exceed in cruelty his former conduct as complained of in the original petition."[40] Her case was reinstated on the docket, but again she agreed to return to her husband. One year later, the case was finally dismissed by agreement at Anton's costs.[41]

---

[38]Margaret Zimmerschitte vs. Fredrich Zimmerschitte, District Court Minutes, Book C, April 6, 1850, 782.

[39]January 1, 1857, anonymous translation, Leyendecker Family Papers, University of Texas Archives.

[40]Petition, Amended Petition, Wilhelmine Burttschell vs. Anton Burttschell, September 20, 1870, June 6, 1871, Docket File No. 2554, CCDC.

[41]Wilhelmine Burttschell vs. Anton Burttschell, June 26, 1871 and June 17, 1872, District Court Minutes, Book E, 70 and 324, CCDC.

Mary Dressler continually returned to her husband's abuse. In her first petition to the court for divorce she described how several times she was forced to flee her home. She would return, sometimes months later, hoping for a reconciliation "but instead of that he committed other and greater outrages." After her first divorce petition was dismissed by the judge, she tried reconciling yet again before suing for divorce a second time.[42] Likewise, Ellen Lacey filed for divorce three times before finally pursuing it to the jury. She filed first in September 1865, but less than two months later agreed that the suit be dropped, when her husband Beverly "had apparently reformed his habits [and] made such protestations of affection for petitioner and their two children . . . ." Ellen "soon found to her sorrow that the intentions of the Defendant [Beverly] were still of the most base character and that his object was only to deceive [her] and if possible more deeply to degrade her." Four years later she filed for divorce again, and again when Beverly "pretending to be penitent and promising [her] to reform his life and do better in the future," asked for a reconciliation, "she was induced for the sake of her children to withdraw her suit and try still to live with him in the marital state." Two years later, Ellen sued for divorce one last time. The jury found her allegations of abuse to be true and the judge granted her divorce, more than seven years after her initial filing.[43]

Some wives tried to make arrangements to escape their violent husbands short of filing for divorce. Sophia and Jacob Illg signed an agreement dividing their property stating that "there is no prospect or desire upon either side for a reconciliation." Jacob officially registered the agreement with the county clerk the day before he filed for divorce from Sophia. When Margaret and Charles Giesecke "sepa-

---

[42]Petition, Mary Dresler vs. Henry Dresler, October 23, 1850, Docket File No. 667; November 6, 1851, District Court Minutes, Book C, 863; Petition, April 16, 1852, Docket File No. 739, CCDC.

[43]Petition, Ellen Lacy vs. Beverly M. Lacy, September 7, 1865, Docket File No. 1813; November 3, 1865, District Court Minutes, Book C2, 452; Petition, Ellenora Lacey vs. Beverly M. Lacey, September 13, 1869, Docket File No. 2374; October 11, 1870, District Court Minutes, Book D, 346; Petition, Ellen Lacy vs. Beverly M. Lacy, December 20, 1872, Docket File No. 2906; February 24, 1873, District Court Minutes, Book E, 509, CCDC.

rated and f[ou]nd they cannot live together," they also signed an agreement dividing their property. Two months later Margaret sued for divorce anyway, describing how Charles had "assaulted, bruised, maimed and beat her with a cow hide until she was so disfigured and disabled that the marks remained on her body for several weeks. . . ."[44] Elizabeth Bateman also signed an agreement one month after she filed for divorce from Thomas Bateman. She decided to pursue the divorce anyway and the agreement became an exhibit in their trial.[45] There is no record of an agreement between a married couple involved in domestic violence in which the parties did not eventually obtain a divorce.

Of those women who filed for divorce charging their husbands with physical cruelty, German women were the least likely to win. Anglo women and African American women (after emancipation) pursued divorces and received favorable jury verdicts sixty percent of the time. Juries granted German women only thirty-five percent of the divorces they filed. This is partially explained by the slightly higher percentage of German women who dropped their cases—forty-seven percent of German female petitioners never pursued their case to the jury trial, while only forty percent of Anglo women dropped their cases. German women, however, were also more likely to lose their cases once in jury trial.

The jury heard Margaret Giesecke's case against her husband Charles, but decided that the continual and specific accounts of abuse she recited in her petition were not justification for divorce. They did find Charles's allegation of Margaret's adultery to be true and so the couple was divorced to Margaret's extreme financial disadvantage.[46] Marie Albrecht's husband did not answer his wife's petition or defend

---

[44]Petition, Jacob Illg vs. Sophia Illg, September 15, 1859, Docket File No. 1466; Petition, Margaret Schlopar (alias Giesecke) vs. Charles Giesecke, October 20, 1851, Docket File No. 710, CCDC. Bond and Mortgage Records, Book E, 359, September 14, 1859; Deed Records Transcribed, Book G, 556, August 23, 1851, CCCC.

[45]Article of agreement, Elizabeth Bateman vs. Thomas Bateman, September 3, 1853, Docket File No. 802, CCDC.

[46]Margaret Giesecke vs. Charles H. Giesecke, April 6, 1852, District Court Minutes, Book C, 890, CCDC.

against the divorce proceedings. Marie's attorney even produced witnesses to the abuse and fights that she had with her husband Hubert, but the jury found "the allegations set forth in the petition are not proven and give our verdict for the defendant. . . ." Her motion for a new trial was denied.[47] Finally, Meta Frels alleged Fredrich Frels abused her to the degree that she deserved a divorce, and the jury agreed. The judge, however, chose to set the verdict aside, "because the same is not supported by the testimony." When Meta Frels' cause came up again before the judge, her attorney moved for a change of venue, and she received her divorce in Lavaca County.[48]

The judges and juries in Colorado County left no historical evidence why they were less sympathetic to German women's claims of abuse. The German women who lost their cases all did so after 1852, in the midst of growing anti-immigrant feeling throughout the United States. Nativist organizations, such as the Know-Nothings in the North and South disdained immigrants and the growing influence they had on American culture and population. Nativist organizations underwent a surge of interest and greater participation beginning in 1845, much of it directed against Irish filling northern cities. However, beginning in 1848 political upheavals in Europe brought many conspicuous German intellectuals to the United States who spoke, wrote, and published defenses of German thought and criticized American institutions. Throughout the United States, these outspoken individuals highlighted what many Americans felt to be the irreconcilable differences between the German immigrants and American culture. In particular, the German intellectuals' highly publicized criticism of slavery at a time when sectional issues consumed much public attention, caused southerners to increase their

---

[47]Petition and Motion for new trial, Marie Albrecht vs. Hubert Albrecht, September 8, 1855 and April 5, 1856, Docket No. 1065; April 4 and 7, 1856, District Court Minutes, Book C, 1195 and 1208, CCDC.

[48]Meta Frels vs. Fredrich Frels, November 11, 1857, District Court Minutes, Book C, 1305, CCDC.

suspicion of the Germans already in their midst who had more quietly resisted adopting the institution.[49]

Nativists increasingly pointed out the threat that immigrants posed to the United States because of the immigrants' failure to assimilate. Describing them as immoral and wedded to old ideas of Europe, nativists attempted to decrease the unassimilated immigrants' power in politics by extending the naturalization period from five years to twenty-one. There is little doubt that Texans also imbibed the belief that immigrants posed a danger until they assimilated to American culture and embraced American ideals including temperance, republicanism, and hopefully Protestantism. Additionally, the widespread assumption that immigrants were the primary cause of rising crime and moral decay in the United States contributed to a growing suspicion of Germans who might not be adopting American ideals by judges and juries in Colorado County. These judges and juries in turn most likely held Germans to a higher standard of moral behavior when it came to divorce in hopes of convincing the German population to assimilate to American ideals of marriage.[50]

Citizens of Colorado County in the midst of growing antagonism toward immigrants would have less trouble seeing Germans as having distinctive characteristics that set them apart, particularly their fondness for alcohol. German-Americans reacted in solidarity against only a few political issues as they did against the temperance movement. The Germans' fondness for and defense of their right to drink alcohol, particularly beer, led many to associate Germans and

---

[49]Tyler Anbinder, *Nativism and Slavery: The Northern Know Nothings and the Politics of the 1850s* (New York and Oxford: Oxford University Press, 1992), 106-107 and 120-121; Richard O'Connor, *The German-Americans: An Informal History* (Boston and Toronto: Little, Brown, and Company, 1968), 113, 120-127; LaVern J. Rippley, *The German-Americans* (Boston: Twayne Publishers, 1976), 56-57; Robert Henry Billigmeier, *Americans From Germany: A Study in Cultural Diversity* (Belmont, Ca.: Wadsworth Publishing Company, 1974), 56-57; Joe B. Frantz, "Ethnicity and Politics in Texas," in Glen E. Lich and Dona B. Reeves, eds., *German Culture in Texas: A Free Earth, Essays from the 1978 Southwest Symposium*, (Boston: Twayne Publishers, 1980), 194-95.

[50]Anbinder, *Nativism and Slavery*, 120-121; O'Connor, *The German-Americans*, 113; Frantz, "Ethnicity and Politics in Texas," 194-195.

drunkenness. At the same time, the national temperance movement was increasingly connecting drunkenness to violence in the minds of many in the mid-nineteenth century.[51]

Following this logic, German women were therefore daily accustomed to a higher degree of violence than Anglo women. This assumption did play a part in accepting what constituted cruelty. The Chief Justice of the Texas Supreme Court had summed up the views of many when he issued an 1857 opinion that "no exact definition of legal cruelty can be given." In some instances, women should be allowed to divorce on the grounds of cruelty even when no violence had occurred. But "there may be cases in which mere blows should not be so considered" as cruelty: "Among persons of coarse habits they may pass for little more than rudeness of language or manner. They might occasion no apprehension and be productive of but slight unhappiness."[52]

Justice Hemphill, of course, referred primarily to women of lower classes in this opinion, and the German women who lost their divorces in Colorado County were not necessarily of a lower class. The families of Margaret Giesecke and Meta Frels owned enough property to place them in the top half of the population in terms of wealth. However, the cultural perception that Germans were as a group more violent perhaps led members of the Colorado County juries to require a higher level of physical cruelty in order to release a German woman from marriage. Following Chief Justice Hemphill's line of reasoning, German women accustomed to their husbands'

---

[51]Mack Walker, "The Old Homeland and the New," in Lich and Reeves, *German Culture in Texas*, 78 and 197; Ruth Bordin, *Woman and Temperance: The Quest for Power and Liberty, 1873-1900* (Philadelphia: Temple University Press, 1981), 6-7; Elizabeth Pleck, *Domestic Tyranny: The Making of Social Policy against Family Violence from Colonial Times to the Present* (Oxford University Press, 1987), 49; Danelle L. Moon, "Marital Rape, Incest and Intemperance: A Nineteenth Century Perspective," given at the Southwest Social Science Association, March 24, 1995. Dallas, Texas (paper in possession of author); Anbinder, *Nativism and Slavery*, 120-121; O'Connor, *The German-Americans*, 113; Frantz, "Ethnicity and Politics in Texas," 194-195.

[52]Taylor vs. Taylor, 18 Tex. 574 (1857) cited in Censer, "Smiling Through Her Tears," 35.

drinking and the violence that results from drunkenness were not suffering from cruelty meriting a divorce.

Of the four African American women who pursued their divorces to a jury trial, one was also denied a divorce. Charles Virginia assaulted Rachel on numerous occasions, beating, choking, and hitting her with a chair. He knocked her down "and stamped upon her with heavy boots and dislocated her jaw-bone." Charles answered that none of the allegations were true and that Rachel had brought the suit for "no other purpose" than to leave him penniless. The jury came to the verdict that Rachel had lied in the petition. Rachel made a motion for a new trial because the verdict was "contrary to law, and to evidence," but the judge denied this as well.[53] Only three other African American women charged their husbands with cruelty and continued with the divorce proceedings to a jury trial. None of their husbands answered the petition and defended themselves; the juries returned verdicts in their favor in all three cases.[54]

In contrast to German and African American women, the nine Anglo women who took their cases of cruel treatment to the jury all received favorable verdicts. Four of the nine husbands did not contest the allegations. Five, however, did contest the divorce, and a few of these did so very vehemently, drawing out the procedures for years.

Individuals in the community provided sanctuary to abused wives and sometimes physically stepped in to protect them. The members of the community serving on juries and as judges, although more skeptical of German and African American women's claims of abuse, still overwhelmingly allowed abused wives the outlet of a divorce. The community might look the other way at some level of wife abuse, and even joke about in the newspaper, but excessive assaults were not

---

[53]Petition, Answer, Amended Petition, Jury Verdict, and Motion for new trial, Rachel Virginia vs. Charles Virginia et al, April 24, 1873, June 6, 1873, June 14, 1873, October 8, 1873, and October 9, 1873, Docket File No. 2939, CCDC.

[54]Petition, Cornelia Johnson vs. Jack Johnson, May 18, 1871, Docket File No. 2668; Petition, Charity Whitley vs. Dennis Whitley, September 28, 1871, Docket File No. 2746; Petition, Mary Susan Tatum vs. Frank Tatum, January 21, 1873, Docket File No. 2917, CCDC.

socially acceptable.[55] The community stopped short, however, of allowing any but the most horrendous assaults by husbands against wives to be considered criminal.

One-third of all indictments in Colorado County from 1837-1873 for violent crimes against white women were crimes perpetrated by a family member, much lower than contemporary statistics. Part of that reason is that only four husbands were ever indicted for assaulting their wives.[56] These four indictments give some indication as to why more husbands were not indicted for their abusive behavior.

A month after Catherine Peltzer filed for divorce from her husband, the grand jury returned an indictment against Adam for assault. Adam had often beaten and abused her throughout the marriage, but in 1860 he drew a knife and a gun and threatened to kill her. A third party interposed to save her, but Adam continued to threaten her life and the district attorney pressed forward with criminal charges. Adam saved the courts the trouble of a trial by dying a few months later in Comal County.[57]

The district attorney did not or could not pursue all criminal indictments with vigor. "Nolle Prosequi," the formal entry in a case that the state no longer chooses to prosecute, occurred much more frequently in the criminal minutes than guilty. Thirty-one of the fifty-three criminal cases involving women never made it to trial. However, once a husband was indicted for assaulting his wife, whether she had filed for divorce or not, the district attorney did pursue the case to its conclusion.

Jacob Illg's indictment came for an aggravated assault he committed a month after he filed for divorce from his wife Sophia and several

---

[55]"Cases of cruel treatment of wives by husbands are becoming more and more common daily. The last and most shocking one recorded in the papers is that of a man named Marten, who lately married a woman named Martin, and in that way knocked out her I on the very day of their marriage." *Colorado Citizen*, August 29, 1857, 1.

[56]In Texas in 1993, murders alone resulted in 38 percent being charged to a husband, ex-husband, or boyfriend. Texas Department of Public Safety, 1993, as cited in Domestic Violence Statistics in Texas, Texas Council on Family Violence (June 1995).

[57]State of Texas vs. Adam Peltzer, October 30, 1860, Criminal Docket File No. 343, CCDC.

months after they agreed to no longer live together. According to Sophia Illg, Jacob broke into their house "struck, beat, battered and drew [her] blood . . . and threatened to take her life."[58] The jury finally heard the criminal case a year later, after Jacob had won his second attempt to prove Sophia had committed adultery and obtain a divorce. The judge charged the jury that an assault became aggravated when committed by an adult male upon an adult female, the punishment for which was $100 to $1000 and up to two years in jail. The jury decided that Jacob had indeed assaulted Sophia, but apparently a minimum $100 fine was too great a punishment for a man whose wife had committed adultery. Giving no legal reasoning, the jury found Jacob guilty of only a simple assault and assessed a five dollar fine. The judge upheld the verdict.[59]

Lewis Brooks was the only husband indicted for assaulting his wife not involved in a divorce suit. The Grand Jury handed down three indictments against Brooks for aggravated assault, for inducing an abortion in his wife by beating her, and for assault with intent to kill. According to the indictments, in August 1872, Lewis beat his wife Lucy so badly "that her life was greatly despaired of by reason whereof she the said Lucy afterwards . . . [did] have an abortion. . . ." In October, he attacked Lucy again with a knife cutting and wounding her "with malice aforethought to murder."[60] The indictment for inducing an abortion was quashed because it alleged no crime against the State of Texas.[61] The judge again explained to the jury the meaning of an aggravated assault. Then the charge continued:

---

[58]Answer, Jacob Illg vs. Sophia Illg, November 4, 1859, Docket File No. 1466; Indictment, State of Texas vs. Jacob Illg, November 2, 1859, Criminal Docket File No. 286, CCDC.

[59]Charge and Verdict, State of Texas vs. Jacob Illg, November 3, 1860, Criminal Docket File No. 286, CCDC.

[60]Indictments, State of Texas vs. Lewis Brooks, October 1, 1872, Docket File Nos. 1027, 1028, and 1029, CCDC.

[61]State of Texas vs. Lewis Brooks, February 15, 1873, District Court Minutes, Book E, 487.

But the Court charges the jury, that it is not unlawful violence of a husband to control the conduct and actions of his wife, provided he only uses such force as will restrain and control her, without doing her any serious bodily injury. . . . If therefore, the jury believe from the evidence the defendant did use such violence towards his wife, as to inflict upon her serious bodily injury; then he was guilty of an aggravated assault. But if the jury believe that he used no more force than he lawfully might as above defined, then he is not guilty.[62]

The jury found Lewis Brooks not guilty. Juries might be willing to grant divorces to abused wives, but some violence during marriage was not to be criminally punishable.

Only one jury truly punished a husband for assaulting his wife. In this case, Thomas Bateman, in the midst of a very messy divorce suit, made an "assault with intent to kill Elizabeth Bateman." The exact nature of the September 10, 1853, assault was not stated by the indictment, only that it was to "the great damage of her the said Elizabeth Bateman."[63] Previous assaults as described in Elizabeth's divorce petition had been extremely brutal. The charge to the jury in this case gave them an option of finding Thomas guilty of an aggravated assault or an assault and battery. A conviction for aggravated assault in 1855 carried a maximum fine of two hundred dollars and a maximum term of six months in jail. For assault and battery, the fine and jail time were left to the discretion of the jury. The jurors found him guilty of assault and battery sentencing him to six months in jail and a five hundred dollar fine.[64]

With the one exception judges and juries did not want to criminally judge a husband's actions against his wife too harshly. In

---

[62]Charge of Court, State of Texas vs. Lewis Brooks, February 15, 1873, Criminal Docket File No. 1027, CCDC.

[63]Indictment, States of Texas vs. Thomas Bateman, October 27, 1853, Docket File No. 140, CCDC.

[64]Charge and Verdict, State of Texas vs. Thomas Bateman, October 24, 1855, Criminal Docket File No. 140, CCDC.

Colorado County, the right of the husband to control his wife physically, even to the point of assault and abuse, was not to be lightly challenged. However, when the abuse became too flagrant, when a husband seriously attempted to murder his wife, the jurors in this southern county were willing to insert law between a husband and wife.

Despite the evidence that domestic violence was widespread, southern society as it was exemplified in Colorado County was not prepared to challenge the unbalanced power hierarchy of marriage that encouraged the violence. Laws, judges, juries, and society continued to uphold the patriarchal privilege of the husband, as they did that of the master. However, this does not mean that southern society believed the men should beat their wives. People in Colorado County showed their moral and social disapproval of abusive husbands by sheltering abused wives, physically defending them, and by allowing them the choice of leaving an abusive marriage. The options for abused wives remained minimal at best, discouraging many women from pursuing even divorces from their husbands. The courts' willingness to punish the most flagrant abuses by the husband, through criminal action for the worst crimes and with divorce for less serious incidents, protected a few women from violence and indicated general social repugnance for the abusers. These rare legal solutions also protected the system under which domestic violence was mostly tolerated.

6

"A THING SO ILLOGICAL" IN GEORGIA: RECONSIDERING RACE, MYTH, AND THE LYNCHING OF LEO FRANK

Stephen A. Brown

I have watched the trial of L. M. Frank all the way down the line and if a man ever had a fair trial he had one. . . . I have a few good Jew friends and I believe there is some good Jews. But if you watch them you will find there is two things most of them will do. One is that they will steal or make or have money and the other is that they will do everything possible all through life to seduce Gentile girls and women. Watch and see if I am not right.[1]

—M. M. Parker to Georgia Prison Commission

From April 1913 to August 1915, there occurred a series of controversial events that shook both Atlanta, Georgia and the entire nation. In cities and towns throughout the United States, people of many cultural and socioeconomic backgrounds openly discussed the vicious murder of Mary Phagan, the trial and eventual lynching of Leo Frank, and the shameful state of racial and ethnic relations in the American South. Almost two years

---

[1]M. M. Parker to Georgia Prison Commission, May 31, 1915, box 35, folder 4, John Marshall Slaton Collection, Georgia Department of Archives and History.

before he was lynched, Leo Frank had been found guilty of the murder of Mary Phagan, an employee at the National Pencil Factory which Frank managed. The case ultimately rested on the suspect testimony of the factory's black sweeper, James Conley. Disregarding Conley's prison record—one filled with minor incarcerations for public drunkenness and disorderly conduct—as well as the color of his skin, a jury of southern whites accepted his testimony without pause or concern. Besides the evidence Conley offered, the jury was also influenced by a series of anti-Semitic outbursts from mobs of curious Atlantans positioned just outside the courthouse. Not surprisingly, the jury deliberated for less than four hours before finding Frank guilty as charged.

Until the day he was lynched, Frank and his legal counsel worked tirelessly to appeal his verdict. All told, they spent over a year and a half petitioning Fulton County Judge Leonard S. Roan, the Georgia State Supreme Court, and the United States Supreme Court. Their appeals for redress, however, proved fruitless. After the Georgia Prison Commission refused to commute Frank's death sentence, Governor John Marshall Slaton investigated the incident, convened those closest to the case, and commuted Frank's sentence to life imprisonment. Approximately one month after his commutation, Leo Frank wrote that the trial against him, and the public outcry it caused, had been "a thing so illogical, so unstable, and so subverting of all principles of basic human rights" as to be almost dumbfounding.[2] Slaton's act of equanimity almost cost him his own life when mobs of frustrated Georgians met and threatened to storm Slaton's estate. After these anxious moments were quelled, the leaders of a vigilante mob decided to seek their own brand of retribution. On August 17, 1915, Leo Frank's plight came to an abrupt end when more than twenty-five of Marietta, Georgia's "best citizens," calling themselves the "Knights of Mary Phagan," avenged the murder of their namesake by lynching Frank.

---

[2]Leo M. Frank to Colonel Yoemans, July 9, 1915, box 6, folder 13, Leo Frank Collections, Atlanta Historical Society.

On the day Governor John Marshall Slaton commuted the death sentence of Leo Frank from death by hanging to life imprisonment, the governor's office was inundated with hundreds of letters both congratulating and vilifying Slaton for his actions. The murder of Mary Phagan, a thirteen–year-old working girl from the hinterlands surrounding Atlanta, had captured the attention of most Atlantans. Few were without an opinion as to who had murdered Phagan and why. The combination of several elements, including the brutality of Phagan's death, her youthful age, and the possibility that a sexual violation had occurred, frustrated many people of Atlanta. A few Atlantans, including the editor of the city's leading newspaper, chose to blame the city's poorly staffed police department; some bemoaned the effects of modernization, industrialization, and commercialism on their growing city; and others chose to cling to a mythic past and blame the influence of "Jewish money," "Jewish avarice," or a "foreign presence" for the murder of "little Mary Phagan." This work examines how those important myths were shaped and why they proved to be so influential to Leo Frank's plight.

In the weeks and months following Mary Phagan's murder, the propagation of certain myths about Jews and their proliferation throughout the Georgia countryside began to have a noticeable effect on those observing the developments in Atlanta. Rhetoric that linked the "Jewish race" to white slavery and savagery against white women was especially potent. Its impact could be seen in the way many Georgians wrote and spoke of Leo Frank and his ancestry. However, the supposed presence and impact of "foreign money" on the outcome of the Frank case was equally important to residents of the country-side. Despondent over the recent turn of events, for instance, Mrs. Henry L. Ozburn wrote to Governor Slaton hoping to make him aware of how she and many other Georgians viewed the situation. "When this Frank case rested with our Governor . . . I felt no uneasiness. One of my neighbors remarked she was afraid. I told her no. [D]on't fear[,] our Gov[ernor] is the son of a noble man, a friend to the working class. [L]ittle did I think you would betr[a]y the trust of the Georgia people. It was money against honor and 'money' weighed heavier. . . . May our Father forgive you for I don't believe the Georgia people ever will." Later she articulated what many Georgians secretly feared when she suggested that "money would keep [Frank] from punishment[,] and it has."[3]

The myths that surfaced during the Leo Frank case had been part of southern rural culture for many decades. These myths developed gradually over time and remained mostly dormant until an event of unquestioned importance, like the discovery of Mary Phagan's corpse, stirred them from their slumber. Examining the significance of these myths will shed light on the reasons why many Georgians reacted as they did and why a few chose to lynch Leo Frank. Until they were loudly voiced, these myths remained understood but unstated, assumed but unspoken.

The anti-Semitic tirades directed at Frank, and the mob action against Georgia's Jews which followed his lynching, were not concomitant parts of a linear progression. Anti–Semitism surfaced sporadically and as a response to various events and episodes, particularly the agitation voiced by southern patriarchal figures like Tom Watson. Along with outright anti–Semitism, however, rural Georgians also showed a great deal of disdain toward Frank and, more specifically, his Jewish upbringing. I refer to attitudes of this nature as Judaeophobia, a fear of or anxiety over Jews that rarely led to political, economic, or violent acts of intimidation but which, when ignited, often paved the way for more anti-Semitic activities. The distinction between Judaeophobia and anti–Semitism—and its connection to the myths spread about Jews—has been noticeably absent from the literature. Placing these myths in their proper cultural context will help us better understand the reasons why Leo Frank was initially made the scapegoat, and eventually lynched, for the murder of Mary Phagan. The role of these myths has yet to be thoroughly investigated by those, be they professional historians or otherwise, interested in the complexities of the Leo Frank case.

---

[3]Mrs. Henry L. Ozburn to John M. Slaton, June 22, 1915, box 4, reel 2, Leo Frank Correspondence, Special Collections, Brandeis University.

A great deal, however, has been written about the case and its tragic conclusion. Over the last eighty years, many contemporary commentators and journalists, legal scholars, amateur and professional historians alike have delved into the particulars of this case. Most have sought to explain how and why belief in Frank's guilt spread so quickly throughout Georgia and, ultimately, why the lynching of Leo Frank occurred. Some, like Leonard Dinnerstein and Albert Lindemann, have suggested that the "persecution" of Frank was little more than a manifestation of virulent anti–Semitism. They see the Frank case as an outpouring of irrational, emotional venom similar in its ferocity to the "Dreyfus affair" which occurred in France in the late nineteenth century or the Beiliss "ritual murder" case which led to popular outbreaks of hysteria throughout Russia in the early twentieth century. Others have posited tensions developing between the agrarian, provincial countryside and the commercially expanding, market-oriented urban center of Atlanta as the cause for mob action. Still others, attempting to explain the causes and consequences of the Leo Frank case, have shown how particular southern rhetoric—like that pertaining to "home rule," the sanctity of white womanhood, or the protection of southern females—was related to Frank's troubles. More recently, Nancy MacLean posed questions concerning gender, changing sexual mores among southern white working girls, and the rise of what she terms "reactionary populism."[4]

---

[4]Contemporary accounts of the Leo Frank case include C.P. Connolly, *The Truth About the Frank Case* (New York: Vail-Balliu Co., 1915); C.P. Connolly, *The Frank Case: Inside Story of Georgia's Greatest Murder Mystery* (Atlanta: Atlanta Publishing Co., 1914); W. E. Thompson, *A Short Review of the Frank Case* (Atlanta, n.p., 1914); "Why Was Frank Lynched?" *Forum* 56 (December 1916): 677-692; Henry S. Woods, "The Crime at Marietta," *America* 13 (September 11, 1915): 535-537. Legal scholars contemporaneous to the trial and lynching have offered their own insight into the case. See "Due Process of Law in the Frank Case," *Harvard Law Review* 28 (1915): 793-795; "The Last Legal Stage of the Frank Case," *The Outlook* 109 (April 28, 1915): 958-959; Harry Schofield, "Federal Courts and Mob Domination of State Courts: Leo Frank's Case," *Illinois Law Review* 10 (1916): 479-506; John W. Curran, "The Leo Frank Case Again," *Journal of Criminal Law and Criminology* 34 (1944): 363-364. Popular accounts of the case include Charles and Louise Samuels, *Night Fell on Georgia* (New York: Dell Publishing Company, 1956); David Schwartz, "The Leo Frank

In contrast to the scholarship that deals solely with the Leo Frank case, that concerned primarily with the study of Jews and "race" is more difficult to delineate. When historians of the South have discussed race, they have typically focused their studies on the trials and sacrifices of particular African Americans, the interaction between whites and blacks (especially the political, economic, and social attempts by whites to segregate blacks from white society), or some similar topic.[5] However, throughout the New South era and

---

Case," *Congress Weekly* 10 (December 24, 1943): 6-7; Mary Phagan, *The Murder of Little Mary Phagan* (Far Hills, New Jersey: New Horizon Press, 1987); Robert Seitz Frey and Nancy Thompson-Frey, *The Murder of Mary Phagan and the Lynching of Leo Frank* (Lanham, Md.: Madison Books, 1988). The most lasting scholarly work on the subject continues to be Leonard Dinnerstein, *The Leo Frank Case* (Athens: University of Georgia Press, 1968). Other significant contributions include Albert Lindemann, *The Jew Accused: Three Anti-Semitic Affairs* (New York: Cambridge University Press, 1991); Steven Hertzberg, *Strangers Within the Gate: The Jews of Atlanta, 1845-1915* (Philadelphia: Jewish Publication Society of America, 1978); Leonard Dinnerstein, "Atlanta in the Progressive Era: A Dreyfus Affair in Georgia," in *The Age of Industrialism in America: Essays in Social Structure and Cultural Values.* Edited by Frederic Cople Jahar (New York: The Free Press, 1968); Harry Golden, *A Little Girl is Dead* (Cleveland: The World Publishing Company, 1965); Clement Carlton Mosely, "The Case of Leo M. Frank, 1913-1915," *Georgia Historical Quarterly* 51(March 1967): 42-62; Robert Seitz Frey, "Christian Responses to the Trial and Eventual Lynching of Leo Frank: Ministers, Theologians, and Laymen," *Georgia Historical Quarterly* 71(Fall 1987): 461-76; Nancy MacLean, "The Leo Frank Case Reconsidered: Gender and Sexual Politics in the Making of Reactionary Populism," *Journal of American History* 78(December 1991): 917-948.

[5]Southern historians have almost always associated the study of "race" with the study of the region's African American population. Recent studies include Osha Gray Davidson, *The Best of Enemies: Race and Redemption in the New South* (New York: Scribner, 1996); Edward J. Larson, *Sex, Race, and Science: Eugenics in the Deep South* (Baltimore: Johns Hopkins University Press, 1995); Diane Roberts, *The Myth of Aunt Jemima: Representations of Race and Region* (New York: Routledge, 1994); Melvyn Stokes and Rick Halpern, eds., *Race and Class in the American South Since 1890* (Providence, R.I.: Berg, 1994); Hans A. Baer and Yvonne Jones, eds., *African Americans in the South: Issues of Race, Class, and Gender* (Athens: University of Georgia Press, 1991); Cynthia Neverdon-Morton, *Afro-American Women of the South and the Advancement of the Race, 1895-1925* (Knoxville: University of Tennessee Press, 1991). Southern Jews have received much less attention from scholars. Few have examined how Jews have been historically perceived by their white neighbors as an alien race. Exceptions to this observation include Eugene Levy, " 'Is the Jew a White Man?': Press Reaction to the Leo Frank Case, 1913-1915," *Phylon* 35 (June 1974): 212-222; Harry Golden, "Jew and Gentile in the New South: Segregation at Sundown," *Commentary* 20 (November 1955): 403-412.

continuing well into the early decades of the twentieth century, theories of racial (not religious) analysis were utilized by many southerners to explain the formation of southern Jewish cultural traits. These theories were applied in much the same way as they had been to describe the distinctive characteristics of the South's black population. These analyses, and the beliefs they engendered, enabled southerners to regard Jews as a foreign and distinguishable "race" with customs and values wholly separate from those of the dominant white southern society. In reconsidering the Leo Frank case of 1913-1915, it is important to remember that the assumptions held by Georgia's whites regarding Jews as an alien race in the South helped lead to the lynching of Leo Frank. A better understanding of and appreciation for the power of such views will help clarify why, in the case of Leo Frank, southerners leaned toward extralegal violence to solve their most pressing concerns. Furthermore, if we are to gain additional insight into southern culture we need to understand how white southerners constructed Leo Frank's race, paying special attention to the nuances central to that construction.

Leo Frank considered himself a well-adjusted, college educated, white middle-class factory manager. In Atlanta, his home by choice, not by birth, these attributes could actually work against him. An ambitious factory manager was, in many ways, anathema to most southerners. He was the opposite of that most southern of icons—the southern gentleman. Unlike the middle-class manager, whose professional training, education, and affiliation with any number of professional associations distinguished him from most others in society, the southern gentleman commanded the respect of most rural people because of his traditional position within a culture of honor. That culture bred traditional values linked closely to the South's older conception of landownership, power, prestige, and position. Leo Frank possessed none of these characteristics—except perhaps the limited sense of position and power that came with his duties as manager of a factory. Georgia's indigenous people rarely neglected to consider Leo Frank's tentative status within their culture of honor when they elaborated upon Frank's role in the murder of Mary Phagan or Frank's racial makeup.[6]

Aside from his middle-class status, Leo Frank was also a Jew. He was born in Cuero, Texas, but had been reared in Brooklyn, New York. He was raised to speak both English and Yiddish, and his family observed the traditional fasting accorded to the Yom Kippur high holy days. When he moved to Atlanta in 1907, Frank not only joined the B'nai B'rith Gate City Lodge, but became its president in 1912. Denied entrance to many of Atlanta's most prestigious social clubs, Frank maintained memberships with organizations like the Hebrew Benevolent Congregation, the Jewish National Fund Bureau, the Jewish Publication Society of America, and the Progress Club.[7] He respected his past, but he also understood its basic irrelevance in a nation where middle-class principles, particularly those based on a thorough understanding and appreciation of the English language and its communicative powers, meant the difference between "getting ahead" in the world of business or languishing behind in mediocrity and anonymity. Regardless of the fact that he was rarely admitted into Atlanta's "Christian" social enclaves, Frank continued to think of himself as part of Atlanta's white elite.

In correspondence to and from Frank, family members, and friends, there were subtle reminders that Frank was generally perceived to be a "white" man. After reading these letters it becomes clear that it was far more important to the Franks that they be considered "white" than either Jewish or ethnic. Leo Frank's parents, who made allusions to various sub-cultural religious practices and used choice Yiddish slang in many of their letters to their son, still understood what it meant to be white Americans in the early twentieth century. For example, when recounting a wedding she had recently attended, Rhea Frank, Leo Frank's mother, described the bride, Ada Maud Soper, as "of the Gibson type[:] tall and thin and

---

[6]For the best explanation of the honor culture in the South, see Bertram Wyatt-Brown, *Honor and Violence in the Old South* (New York: Oxford University Press, 1986).

[7]Atlanta Miscellany, box 6, folder 7, Leo Frank Collections, Atlanta Historical Society.

stylish looking." Her use of the term "Gibson type" was a direct reference to the Gibson Girl, a popular advertising icon used to help show early twentieth-century women what to wear and how to be more stylish. Had Rhea Frank not been introduced to this "white" world of the Gibson Girl, she would never have alluded to such a powerful cultural symbol. Rhea Frank also wrote about venturing to a "Church in [the] Midwood section of Brooklyn," where there occurred "a real impressive wedding and no [money] was spared to make it a thoro [sic] success."[8] She did not see how attending such a "gentile" event could be misinterpreted as improper or unacceptable; she had simply received an invitation from a family friend and had decided to be present.

Leo Frank rarely showed any hesitance in describing himself as a white man. He relayed as much by implication when he wrote a return letter to Dr. David Hawkins, an inquisitive scribe who had requested that Frank send him a copy of some information pertinent to his legal case. Frank was only too willing to oblige. "Beg to state that the negro Conley is short, stout and coffee colored; the reverse of the negro described in the notes," wrote Frank. "He first denied his ability to write; then after it was known that he could write, he stated that he did not write the notes. Subsequently he said he wrote one of the notes at my dictation and I wrote the other one, and then finally stated that he wrote both of them at my dictation. Of Course, you will readily see that it is preposterous for any *white man* of average common sense to leave anything behind any crime."[9] Only a criminal

---

[8]Rhea Frank to Leo M. Frank, October 21, 1914, box 1, folder 3, Leo Frank Collections, Atlanta Historical Society. On the Gibson Girl, see William E. Leuchtenburg, *The Perils of Prosperity, 1914-1932* (Chicago: University of Chicago Press, 1993), 173. On the importance of changing tastes and styles in dress, and the influence of those tastes on the purchasing habits of working-class American women, see Kathy Peiss, *Cheap Amusements: Leisure in Turn-of-the-Century New York* (Philadelphia: Temple University Press, 1986), 64. Also see Paula S. Fass, *The Damned and the Beautiful: American Youth in the 1920s* (New York: Oxford University Press, 1977), 21-22.

[9]Leo M. Frank to Dr. David B. Hawkins, May 18, 1915, box 1, reel 1, Leo Frank Correspondence, Special Collections, Brandeis University, (emphasis added). On Frank's "whiteness," see Leo M. Frank to Colonel Yoemans, July 9, 1915, box 6, folder 13, Leo Frank Collections, Atlanta Historical Society, in which he writes: "The Warden and his staff have

black, he implied, would be as foolish as to have left behind such essentially damaging evidence. The notion that black criminal behavior could be distinguished from white illegal activity is an important one here. Throughout society—especially southern society—it was presupposed that blacks were by nature criminal. When, for example, Luther Rosser, Leo Frank's defense attorney, referred to Conley as a "drunken criminal negro," he assumed quite naturally that the jury would understand these remarks and consider them both legitimate and plausible.[10] In using "whiteness" to distinguish Conley's criminal behavior from his own, Leo Frank was intentionally drawing attention to the color of his skin. In a society where race mattered, it was Frank's only proper recourse.

In a telling letter from his father, Rudolf Frank mentioned his son's "whiteness" and its importance to his defense. Rudolf Frank wrote that "in all the annals of jurisprudence in the South, there never was the word of such an unaccount[able] roustabound [sic] and criminal [individual] as J. C. [James Conley], taken in preference to that of a *clean and honorable white man* as in our case. It seems too ridiculous to consider even for a moment. . . ."[11] To many interested observers throughout the country it did seem ridiculous. The deeper question, however, and the one Rudolf Frank never broached, was whether or not those in the South thought Leo Frank—the Jewish, Northern-bred, factory manager—was as clean, honorable, and preferred to his black accuser as did his father. This is certainly not clear. Many in southern society failed to share Rudolf Frank's confidence in his son, especially when the safety and well-being of

---

treated me white."

[10]On Rosser's cross-examination of James Conley, see Dinnerstein, *The Leo Frank Case*, 45-48; also see letter from Gustave Haas to Georgia Prison Commission, May 29, 1915, box 35, folder 8, John Marshall Slaton Collection, Georgia Department of Archives and History.

[11]Rudolf Frank to Leo M. Frank, October 8, 1914, box 1, folder 3, Leo Frank Collections, Atlanta Historical Society, (emphasis added). Recently a paper was delivered at the 1997 Annual Meeting of the Organization of American Historians that dealt with Jews and "whiteness." See Eric L. Goldstein, "'A White Race of Another Kind': Immigrant Jews and Whiteness in the Urban North, 1914-1945," paper given at the Organization of American Historians, April 1997, San Francisco, California.

their daughters was at stake. Indeed, if this "Jew" was viewed as no better than and perhaps similar to the black, then the issue of whiteness was clearly important to all those involved. This is because ultimately southern whites saw themselves as inherently trustworthy, honorable, and dignified while they attached every denigrating characteristic to blackness or dark skin. One's race, along with the color of his or her skin, was a significant determining factor in a society that valued "whiteness" above almost anything else.[12]

The question of race is crucial when contemplating the Leo Frank case. The case—occurring as it did in the South—represents perhaps the first recorded instance when the testimony of a black factory hand, James Conley, was manipulated by a southern prosecutor in order to make such a dramatic impact on a southern jury in a case against a white man. However, if the white man were a Jew, as Leo Frank was, would we expect him to receive the same treatment accorded to virtually all other white southerners? The answer is intrinsically tied to the dissemination of various important myths about Jews. If, in the eyes of the typical rural southerner, for instance, the Jew could be made to assume the physical and mental characteristics of the typical black male, then the association between "black" and "Jew" and "criminal" (or, in this case, "defiler" of white womanhood) could be made with relative ease. This, I argue, is exactly what took place throughout the two–year interim between the discovery of Mary Phagan's corpse and the lynching of Leo Frank. Many socially accepted and generally benign myths about Jews were transformed into racially motivated hate. This dramatic shift ultimately led to the extralegal violence used by the Knights of Mary Phagan, and was spread by the reprehensible words and actions of southerners like Tom Watson. Indeed, the mostly harmless Judaeophobic views held by southerners did not much concern the likes of Leo Frank until they became outwardly visible and fashionable to proclaim. The development of this shift startled and frightened Leo Frank because as an

---

[12]On the cultural construction of race in the South, see Grace Elizabeth Hale, *Making Whiteness: The Culture of Segregation, 1890-1950* (New York: Pantheon Books, 1998).

individual who saw himself as a "white man," Frank could not believe he would be racially targeted by and distinguished from other whites. Indeed, Frank not only thought of himself as a white man, but he had no qualms about using racially charged language and casually accepted the validity of certain widely shared beliefs about blacks.

Significantly, many southern Jews like Leo Frank held several of the same beliefs about southern blacks as did their white neighbors. Middle-class Jewish Atlantans like Leo Frank generally advocated social and political segregation of the races. Frank assumed that there existed an unspoken racial hierarchy in the South and, if not at the apex, he certainly thought he was close to the top. Frank had no reservations whatsoever in believing that the average black southern man posed a threat to society, was an inveterate liar, and was ultimately a brutish and bestial individual. It was also assumed by most white southerners, Leo Frank included, that the black man was inherently capable of perpetrating crimes whites were thought incapable of committing—such as the gruesome and bloody slaying of Mary Phagan. The language used by men like Leo Frank to designate such racial justifications mirrored that of most other white southerners, especially the language that reflected the common perception held by almost every white man that he was superior to his black neighbor. The use of racial epithets and prejudicial language to describe blacks was widespread throughout the nation. The word "nigger," for example, was so widely used in American English throughout the nineteenth and early twentieth centuries that the *Oxford English Dictionary* devotes several pages to its use as slang alone. As a prefix, the word had numerous meanings and connotations and, as such, could evoke passionate emotions. Those in southern society, for example, white or black, rich or poor, fully understood what it meant to do "nigger-work," or be "nigger-rich." These were terms of cultural importance and they rarely obscured one's meaning. Furthermore, there is no indication that words like "nigger," or the meanings they conveyed, were foreign to Leo Frank, or that they disturbed him in the least. Indeed, such terminology was less powerful than it was commonplace. Leo Frank might not have been considered a "nigger" by most southerners, but his tentative status as a so-called foreign-bred Jew undeniably caused much tension and concern among rural southerners.

As a group in southern society, Jews were considered a "race" well before they were thought of as a religious denomination. As such, Jews were often perceived by many southerners as an alien, even mongrel race. In contrast to Leo Frank's belief in his own inherent whiteness, few rural Georgians believed that Jews were part of the "white race." That designation was reserved for gentiles only. Ultimately, one must ask how southerners defined Jews as a race? A letter from Elsie Tinnell, a poor, rural teenage girl, to the Georgia Prison Commission begins to answer this perplexing question. After asking how the state of Georgia could hang a man she believed to be innocent, she wrote: "If you knew for sure he was guilty it would be different, but you have no evidence but that of a *black negro*, and that [Frank] is a *Jew*." She concluded by asking "Men[,] would you rather believe a negro than a Jew?"[13] Tinnell had already drawn her own conclusions concerning the innocence of the accused. However, the terminology she applied to her query is more important and telling for the purposes of our discussion. Tinnell distinguished between the "black" Negro and the "Jew" without mentioning Frank's "whiteness." Indeed, it is probable that Tinnell, like most others in her lowly social station, did not regard Frank as a southern white man. He was, as she wrote, a "Jew," not a white man, and thus his tenuous position in society was distinct from her own.

Elsie Tinnell was employing a coded language based entirely on racial considerations that described a social hierarchy widely familiar to most southerners. In a society based on racial distinctions, southern whites assumed the mantle of authority and superiority. Divisions across class and gender lines may have complicated southern white society, but not enough to impact the importance of "herrenvolk" democratic traditions. Although southerners were a more diverse lot

---

[13]Miss Elsie Tinnell to the Georgia Prison Commission, May 17, 1915, box 2, reel 1, Leo Frank Correspondence, Special Collections, Brandeis University, (emphasis added).

than some have suggested, virtually all continued to believe in their innate superiority over non-whites. Among southern women, a division along class lines also played a role in developing a late nineteenth-century southern social hierarchy. Despite these various fissures, however, southern whites believed in a racially constructed unity among themselves. Furthermore, most believed that their superiority atop such a pyramid remained a truth few could openly challenge.[14]

The central predicament facing Frank was whether southerners would view him as a white man, with all the privileges and exemptions normally afforded to one of such color in the South. If he was not considered "white" by those of the dominant culture, would Frank's "Jewishness" negate his obviously white skin? To most southerners Jews were not quite "white," though in cultural and social terms they were generally regarded above the region's black population.[15] By 1915, however, after Frank had spent over a year seeking official exoneration from the highest tribunals in Georgia as well as the United States Supreme Court, the majority of Georgians were simply not ready to confer the blessings of southern whiteness upon Leo Frank, nor were they ready to accept his word over that of his black accuser.

Tom Watson helped clarify questions of this nature for rural Georgians when he wrote of a secret language spoken and shared by the culprit Leo Frank and his accuser and accomplice James Conley. "[T]he Jew was talking in a secretive, confidential manner with the negro, on the sidewalk, where he thought he was unobserved—and this negro had been his trusty for two years!"[16] According to Watson,

---

[14]On herrenvolk democracy, see Pierre L. van den Berghe, *Race and Racism: A Comparative Approach* (New York: Wiley, 1967).

[15]The position of southern Jewry within a well-constructed and socially acceptable racial hierarchy in the South is discussed in Eugene Levy, "'Is the Jew a White Man?': Press Reaction to the Leo Frank Case, 1913-1915."

[16]Thomas E. Watson, "The Celebrated Case of the State of Georgia vs. Leo Frank," *Watson's Magazine* 21 (August 1915): 187, in box 3, folder 2, Leo Frank Collections, Atlanta Historical Society. On the transformation of Tom Watson from Populist spokesman of the rural dispossessed to virulent racialist, see C. Vann Woodward, *Tom Watson: Agrarian Rebel*

these two unwanted elements in white society shared a deep perversity. Both the "mongrel" black and the "libertine" Jew sought to seduce gentile girls and mock the traditions of white society. Frank's presumed access to wealth only made his presence more unacceptable. "Frank," wrote Watson, "belonged to the Jewish aristocracy, and it was determined by the rich Jews that no aristocrat of their race should die for the death of a working-class Gentile—'nothing but a factory girl.'"[17]

Watson's essays were based on little more than unsubstantiated rumors. To the average resident of Georgia's hinterlands, however, Watson was the sole voice of reason; in many cases, his publications were the only source of information and the basis for the opinions formed by those residents. In light of the evidence Watson presented, did these people need further proof of Leo Frank's guilt? Who else but a Jew, they reasoned (and by imputation a treacherous, deceitful, and lust-crazed one at that), would take a black man as his confidant? The message was clear: no self-respecting southerner, with any notion of personal dignity or respect for southern traditions, would take part in such a shameful episode with such a shiftless individual as Conley. Only a Jew, who's status as an outsider accorded him the opportunity to take such a risk, would make such a mistake.

In letters to Georgia's governor, many southerners explained why they believed Jews like Frank would purposely challenge the South's racial hierarchy and other socially acceptable norms. Men like R.W. Daniel, for example, could inquire in all seriousness, "have you ever studied [sic] the Jew[?] [H]ave you ever known why Russia kills the Jews [?] [H]ave you ever known why England banishes the Jew[?] [S]ee with your own eyes then you will know why."[18] By taking into consideration the "Jewish character," with its propensity for "low-

---

(New York: Oxford University Press, 1977), especially 396-450; Fred D. Regan, "Obscenity or Politics? Tom Watson, Anti-Catholicism, and the Department of Justice," *Georgia Historical Quarterly* 70 (Spring 1986): 17-46.

[17]Watson, "The Celebrated Case of the State of Georgia vs. Leo Frank," 222.

[18]R. W. Daniel to R. E. Davison, May 22, 1915, box 35, folder 4, John Marshall Slaton Collection, Georgia Department of Archives and History.

ness," many native southerners discovered answers to the questions posed above. In this tradition, southerners assumed that Jews, being so "low" themselves, would naturally befriend the lowliest of southern persons—the African American man. In essence, as "marked" races, they were allowed to interact with one another and perhaps even commingle. Only those who lived in a society based so thoroughly on racial distinctions could justify such a conclusion.

In the same way black males were reviled as oversexed brutes, so too were Jews like Leo Frank. Numerous newspaper stories appeared monthly detailing violence perpetrated by blacks against white women. These stories almost always correlated black violence against their white victims with a black lust for white women.[19] Many Atlantans who read the city's daily papers, and freely associated racial similarities between "lowly" types like blacks and Jews, often assumed that the latter were capable of similar episodes of gross sexual impropriety. Many southern rural parents and protectors emphasized their fear of Jewish sexual interaction with southern white girls and women. The potential for "miscegenation" between these two "races" galvanized white southerners and resulted in their intense desire to protect their daughters and wives. "What will become of the wives and daughters of the State of Georgia?" asked W. S. Lancaster. "The people are not appealing to you for sympathy but for justice. Dear Gov[ernor,] our wives and daughters are at stake and it lies with you in the end [to protect them]."[20] In Atlanta during the decade of the 1910s, rural fathers and mothers worried aloud about the welfare of their daughters. Southern girls between the ages of ten and twenty had been migrating to mill towns and cities like Atlanta in search of gainful employment since the last quarter of the nineteenth century.

---

[19]At least four stories appeared during the month of January 1913, for example, involving crimes committed by blacks against white women. On January 18, two front-page stories appeared, one entitled "Mob hangs black who killed girl," and the other entitled "Woman attacked by five Negroes." See *Atlanta Constitution*, January 18, 1913, 1. For other similar stories see *Atlanta Constitution*, January 8, 10, and January 9, 2.

[20]W. S. Lancaster to John M. Slaton, December 29, 1914, box 45, folder 10, John Marshall Slaton Collection, Georgia Department of Archives and History.

In Atlanta, working girls were introduced to many new forms of entertainment, recreation, and vice. They were also introduced to the relaxed sexual attitudes found in the cities. Many of their rural protectors found it disturbing to learn that Jewish managers like Leo Frank held positions of authority and power of their womenfolk. These people had heard stories about treacherous managers and sexual episodes. Thus, in their own minds, their concerns were entirely grounded.

Rural Georgians commonly believed that cities were thriving dens of iniquity. They had been told as much by countless evangelical ministers and itinerant preachers. Their fears stemmed in part from a growing awareness among them that for years white slave traffic had been on the rise.[21] A story describing how forty-one girls had been "lured to ruin" appeared in the *Atlanta Constitution* on April 22, 1913, only a week before Mary Phagan's death. Readers were told of a California residence "known as 'The Jonquil,' where many young girls, gathered from [the city's] department stores, restaurants, and other places of employment, were alleged to have been lured to meet wealthy men." At this "den," millionaires and prominent residents of the city cavorted with underage girls. One young girl acknowledged a gentleman who had been nicknamed "the 'Black Pearl,' because of a setting of a scarf pin he always wore. At times, however, he was said to have been known simply as 'Mr. King,' a tribute, it was declared, to his majestic disregard of money." The article concluded by telling how "the millionaires involved had a complete organization."[22]

That such people, often considered "foreign elements," could run such an "organization" and, in the process, manipulate and exploit

---

[21]On Jews and the white slave traffic, see contemporary articles like Burton J. Hendrick, "The Great Jewish Invasion," *McClure's Magazine* 28 (January 1907): 307-321. Jews often found themselves trying frantically to refute the claim that they were deeply involved with such illegal trafficking. See Maurice Fishberg, "White Slave Traffic and Jews," *American Monthly Jewish Review* 4 (December 1909): 4, 23; "Jews in the White Slave Traffic," *The Temple* 2 (February 25, 1910): 176. For a historical interpretation of this problem, see Edward J. Bristow, *Prostitution and Prejudice: The Jewish Fight Against White Slavery, 1870-1939* (New York: Schocken Books, 1983).

[22]*Atlanta Constitution*, April 22, 1913, 1.

working girls and women adrift appalled those who read the article. Some believed that similar circumstances could develop in Atlanta as the city prospered and grew. These were important considerations to rural southerners, especially when they contemplated sending their daughters to Atlanta for work; according to some rural protectors, unattended girls in the city risked being surrounded by an indiscriminate number of "foreign elements." The expression "foreign elements" was a euphemism for immigrants, ethnics, and outsiders, many of whom included Jews. A recurrent theme throughout southern rural enclaves was the belief that women who ventured to the cities risked being imprisoned by "foreign elements" in a world of forbidden lust and illicit sex. It was commonly feared that Jews in particular yearned for the forbidden fruit and were especially attracted to gentile girls. These fears were crystallized at Leo Frank's murder trial when James Conley took the stand and astounded his white audience with his fantastic testimony.

James Conley's testimony told in stark detail the sexual exploits of his employer, Leo Frank. He told the jury how in exchange for a few dollars for beer money he would stand guard for Frank while the superintendent entertained female visitors in the pencil plant. Many Georgians who observed the case made an easy connection between these illicit trysts and the intimate role shared by the "black" and the "Jew." Their provincial social world allowed them to justify such a conclusion. Thus, Conley's testimony failed to shock most rural Georgians; in fact, most found it very easy to believe. "Well you are a little early to do what I wanted you to do for me, I want you to watch for me like you have been doing the rest of the Saturdays." These were the words Conley said Frank used when speaking to him on the morning of Mary Phagan's murder. Conley continued: "I always stayed on the first floor like I stayed the 26th of April and watched [for] Mr. Frank, while he and a young lady would be upon the second floor chatting, I don't know what they were doing. He only told me they wanted to chat. When young ladies come there, I would sit down at the first floor and watch the door for him."

Later Conley described the sexual indiscretions which presumably had been taking place in Frank's office for quite some time. " 'I wanted to be with the little girl,' " said Frank, according to Conley, "'and she refused me, and I struck her too hard and she fell and hit her head against something, and I don't know how bad she got hurt. Of course you know I ain't built like other men.' " At this point Conley began to explain what Frank had apparently meant by his last statement. "The reason he said that was, I had seen him in a position I haven't seen any other man that has got children. I have seen him in the office two or three times before Thanksgiving and a lady was in his office, and she was sitting down in a chair (and she had her clothes up to here, and he was down on his knees, and she had her hands on Mr. Frank. I have seen him another time there in the packing room with a young lady lying on the table, she was on the edge of the table when I saw her)." The parenthetical testimony was delivered after women and children, deemed too innocent for such sensitive material, had been escorted out of the courtroom.[23]

This was the first instance when "Jewish sexuality" was presented to the court and its white on lookers. Conley had described how Frank had engaged in cunnilingus and, perhaps, sodomy. To many observers, these were unnatural forms of sexual expression. Testimony of this nature, however, also titillated southern readers. It gave them the opportunity to eavesdrop on a world of forbidden passions which they had been taught to resist. According to many rural dwellers, only a deviant—a "foreign element"—with bizarre sexual habits could overstep the bounds of traditional courtship and good taste. The myth of the virtuous southern white female and the uncontrollable black or Jewish male brute was clearly influential throughout the countryside. When many southerners heard that Frank "wasn't built like other men," they became even more convinced that his body—the "Jewish body"—was that of a brute's. Many assumed that it was somehow

---

[23]Brief of Evidence at 52, 53, 55, *Leo M. Frank v. State of Georgia*, Fulton County Superior Court at the July Term, 1913, Atlanta Miscellany, Special Collections, Robert W. Woodruff Library, Emory University.

anatomically distinct from the gentile body. Many southern Christians presumed that the Jewish body was vulgar and unclean. Accordingly, in order to blend into the dominant culture, Jews were thought to desire equality through sexual interaction with gentile females.[24] It hardly mattered that Frank had been happily married to Lucille Selig for almost three years. As a Jew, his contentment could only be secured with the seduction of white women. The myth of "Jewish sexuality" was too significant in southern society, and its role throughout Frank's trial and the two years he spent appealing its verdict would haunt Frank until his final days. It is important to remember that the testimony proving Frank's licentiousness was offered by a black man. To most southerners, blacks were presumed to be in touch with the world of the transgressive; Conley's supposed relationship to Frank only added weight to his testimony's plausibility.

According to Thomas Nelson Page, an early twentieth-century southern editor and social critic, blacks were not to be trusted around white women. In his view, blacks were by nature sexually motivated. Their lustful appetites appeared insatiable. Accordingly, Page believed that without white supervision blacks would take liberties with white women whenever possible. Page warned that interracial sexual activity, even the slightest potential or hint of such activity, should be dealt with seriously and swiftly.[25] The discovery of a number of letters written by James Conley to his would-be wife, Annie Maud Carter, solidified Page's fears. They convinced those who read or heard about them that as far as Conley was concerned, Page's assessment of the black man had been quite correct.

Conley's letters were as perverse, replete with utterances of uncontrollable passion, and lascivious as most people feared, and his connection with Leo Frank, another presumed pervert, seemed only

---

[24]On the myths associated with Jewish physical features, see Sander Gilman, *The Jew's Body* (New York: Routledge, 1991); Frank Felsenstein, *Anti-semitic Stereotypes: A Paradigm of Otherness in English Popular Culture, 1660-1830* (Baltimore: Johns Hopkins University Press, 1995).

[25]On Thomas Nelson Page, see Lawrence J. Friedman, *The White Savage: Racial Fantasies in the Postbellum South* (Englewood Cliffs, N.J.: Prentice-Hall, Inc., 1970), 68.

natural. Most southerners never had the opportunity to view those letters, though. They were thought too lewd to present in public. Local newspapers refused to print Conley's correspondence because many editors believed that the language in the letters was too shocking. Yet, when rural southerners read of the lewd quality of the letters, many again assumed an understanding of their contents and meaning. Consequently, those already inclined to believe that blacks were naturally perverse, and that Conley specifically was a deviant, had no need to read any of Conley's letters. If they had, they would have encountered the following vulgar mélange:

> Baby, you ought not never said anything to me about your hipped, why my dick went clean across my cell, and I read it all night, your letter. I could not sleep. Honey, you was right when you said that you had up there what I wants. You know that I could not be mad with you, when you said you could make me call you mama, well Baby, if you do, Papa will give you what it takes to bring the bacon home. . . .[26]

Conley was a barely literate, uneducated, working man who had spent various years of his life on the chain gang. His employer, Leo Frank, was a college graduate from a prestigious eastern institution, a prominent member of the city's Jewish community, and the manager of a successful business in Atlanta. Aside from their individual obligations at the pencil factory, what possible common interests could these two quite different men share?[27] Yet, as different as these

---

[26]James Conley to Annie Maud Carter, letter 1, undated, box 35, folder 4, John Marshall Slaton Collection, Georgia Department of Archives and History.

[27]One need only examine the letters Frank wrote to his betrothed, which embody a loving and subtle nature. See, for example, his correspondence of June 14, 1909, in which he writes "I am not much on the sentimental letter writing. Read between the lines and see if you can feel the warmth of the writer's feelings for you!" In another letter he wrote "Was carried 'transcendentally' to the seventh heaven of happiness and joy by the receipt of your letter of the 14th. . . ." See Leo M. Frank to Lucille Selig, June 14, 1909, box 2, reel 1, Leo Frank Correspondence, Special Collections, Brandeis University; Leo M. Frank to Lucille Selig, June 16, 1909, ibid.

two men appeared to be, many Atlantans assumed that a partnership existed between them. Much of that assumption was based on a set of myths associated with racial-sexual fantasies and fears of miscegenation. Many southerners simply took it for granted that a connection between the Jewish superintendent and his black sweeper clearly existed; if nothing else, it was what most white rural Georgians wanted to believe.

Thus, it became relatively easy for most Georgians to identify Leo Frank as a sexual deviant. It hardly mattered that Frank's demeanor, as recounted by virtually all those questioned, was that of a composed, educated, timorous, and respectable member of Atlanta's growing middle class. Jews were believed to be capable of committing the most outrageous acts of sexual perversity. In part, Jews were held accountable to these beliefs because of the common perception that they were the ultimate outsiders; that wherever Jews went and established communities, they were ultimately little more than nomadic visitors—those without a homeland. What stake, asked many gentiles of their Jewish neighbors, did they have in their community? How much of their apparent ability to assimilate themselves to the cultural practices and standards of any society was legitimate or could be trusted and accepted? Late nineteenth-century European anti-Semitic views—which included the prescribed interrelated role of "blood" and "race," questions concerning nomadic migratory patterns and permanent settlement, and the transparency of cultural assimilation—had gradually made their way to the United States.[28] They were not lost on many Americans who viewed Jews, and certainly other immigrant groups as well, with mistrust and fear. Indeed, these views were allowed to seep into the very social fabric of many American communities, particularly those in the South.

---

[28]On the development of European anti-Semitic thought, see Richard S. Levy, *Antisemitism in the Modern World: An Anthology of Texts* (Lexington: D.C. Heath and Company, 1991); on the influence of these ideological beliefs on the development of American antisemitism, see David A. Gerber, *Anti-Semitism in American History* (Urbana: University of Illinois Press, 1986).

Belief in the "foreign" nature of Jews helped to justify the need to investigate Leo Frank's physical and mental character for signs of weakness or deficiency. Frank was literally probed by a panel of expert physicians who were searching for any indication that he was physically awkward or abnormal. A committee of prominent physicians and psychologists examined Frank's "potential" for perversion in an effort to qualify the extent to which Frank was "abnormally perverse." Hoping to determine whether Frank "was, or had ever been, *addicted* to perversion, or had any traits of a pervert," this panel of physicians found he bore no such outward signs. They further stated unconditionally that a series of examinations proved Frank "a strictly normal, healthy man, with not a single sign or trace of degeneracy or perversion. . . . [H]e possessed a clean, well-balanced mind, without any trace or taint of anything common in degenerates or perverts. . . . [He] is in no sense a pervert, and has never been addicted to, or practiced, perversion."[29] The conclusions drawn by such a distinguished body of medical scientists could not mollify or temper the views held by most rural Georgians. Their assumptions as to Frank's perverse nature were too deep-seated. Besides, most rural dwellers viewed the findings of these "experts" with suspicion and apprehension. As such, most continued to believe that Frank was a perverse brute who had sexually assaulted Mary Phagan before murdering her in a fit of uncontrollable passion. The myth of Jewish sexuality, with its connection to a "Jewish lust" for gentile girls, was simply too strong.

Another important myth that played a dominant role throughout the Leo Frank case focused on the mythical interplay between Jews and money. Unlike the myth of Jewish sexuality, in which white southerners based many of their assumptions on their own interaction with blacks, the connection between Jews and money was constructed free from such an influence. Jews had historically been associated with

---

[29]Medical communique to Georgia Fulton County, May 20, 1915, box 35, folder 16, John Marshall Slaton Collection, Georgia Department of Archives and History, (emphasis added).

money lenders and middlemen; in the South, Jewish peddlers, with their vast assortment of goods and wares, became symbolic of the region's limited consumer and commercial growth throughout the nineteenth century. Consequently, popular images of Jewish petty shysters, floaters, lenders, thieves, and hustlers flourished in the minds of many rural southerners. At times, these beliefs caused great resentment among southern agrarians and hostility toward Jews. However, they rarely led to any outbreaks of physical violence directed specifically against Jews. Typically, the impact of such imagery led to the proliferation of certain Judaeophobic assumptions. When ignited by events like those surrounding Mary Phagan's murder, they resulted in widespread anti-Semitic outbursts. Indeed, prior to the lynching of Leo Frank, there is only one recorded instance of the lynching of a Jewish man by a southern mob. In 1868, S. A. Bierfield, a Jewish dry-goods store operator, was lynched in Franklin, Tennessee. The reasons for this instance of extralegal violence are not clear. However, considering that many southern gentiles often accused Jewish merchants and peddlers of participating in exploitative purchasing and selling practices during the Civil War, it is probable that many residents of Franklin believed that Bierfield had been guilty of similar exploits. With the rise and influence of the Knights of the White Camellia and the Ku Klux Klan during the era of Reconstruction, undoubtedly there arose in the minds of the vigilantes who murdered Bierfield a correlation between his business dealings and the depressed state of the area's economy; a correlation, in their view, that warranted mob retribution.[30]

Several memoir accounts by other nineteenth-century southern Jewish peddlers relate similar episodes of bigotry. It is important to note that many southern Jews, especially those who resided in the region during the antebellum period, clung tenaciously to their religious practices and cultural ways. "I must state," wrote Philip Sartorius, that "when I came to Vicksburg, the Jews all lived Kosher,

---

[30]On the lynching of S. A. Bierfield, see Anti-Defamation League Bulletin, June 1958, Leo Frank Folder, Anti-Defamation League, New York, New York.

had a chasan (cantor) and shochet (slaughterer of cattle) [and] had services Rosh Hashana (New Year) two days and Yom Kippur (the Day of Atonement)." The apparent refusal by these disparate groups of southern Jews to relinquish their cultural traditions and assimilate into southern Christian society often made them easy prey for southern chauvinists. Consequently, many rural southerners chose to believe that since Jews *in their vicinity* maintained a certain religious and cultural identity, then the same most hold true for *all* Jews. Sartorious would later add that "we had an uphill battle when we started there. A great deal of prejudice prevailed towards foreigners." Oscar Solomon Straus, another peddler, explained both the extent to which cultural assumptions were embedded in the minds of a majority of southern whites and how those assumptions spread due to the provincialism of the countryside. "We were the only Jewish family in the town. This at first aroused some curiosity among those who had never met [Jews] before. I remember hearing someone doubt that we were Jews and remarking to my father, who had very blond hair and blue eyes, that he thought all Jews had black hair and dark complexion."[31] As this evidence shows, Jews were thought to have certain physical features which could easily distinguish them from others in society.

Southerners often condemned the Jews who lived among them when conditions seemed out of control. In so doing, many relied on numerous assumptions about Jews like those suggested above. Throughout the Civil War years, for example, as the South's economy plummeted and goods became especially difficult to attain, southerners began blaming their troubles on the influence of "outsiders." Isidor Straus, yet another southern Jewish peddler, described how merchants, Jews and gentiles alike, "who were engaged in this perfectly legitimate enterprise [the cotton trade] were denounced as extortionists, speculating on the necessities of the people while many of their

---

[31]The comments from different southern Jewish peddlers are found in Jacob Rader Marcus, *Memoirs of American Jews, 1775-1865* (Philadelphia: The Jewish Publication Society of America, 1955), 24, 29, 294.

breadwinners were at the front, risking their lives on the altar of their country. . . ." In the heat of the moment some southerners argued that while Confederate soldiers, stationed on the battlefields, were fighting for an honorable cause, merchants and peddlers, concerned only with the flow of capital, remained hidden in the background. By suggesting that "the Jews were singled out as if they alone were the perpetrators of what was termed iniquitous practices," Straus described a subtle and significant shift in blame that was then taking place. He concluded by telling how "a prejudice against the Jewish merchants was inaugurated that found utterance in official and semi-official quarters. So it occurred that a great jury of Talbot County, in winding up its session and making its presentations to the court, as was the custom, referred to the evil and unpatriotic conduct of the representatives of Jewish houses who had engaged in this nefarious business."[32] Here we have an instance of blatant anti–Semitism: it was a dramatic change that, unlike socialized Judaeophobia, was based entirely on religious preference and resulted in a form of political discrimination against Jews.[33]

Considering the frequency of anti-Semitic or Judaeophobic acts in the South, it is ironic that certain southerners occasionally spoke enviously of Jews who were thought to control and amass wealth. In accordance with the rhetoric of the New South, which sought northern commercial investment at virtually any price, some southern leaders actually hoped to entice northern Jews to migrate to the South. If Jews had some type of imaginary access to reserves of wealth, as these leaders often contended, and the South was "money poor," then Jewish aid in promoting a consumer-driven economy was viewed as essential. Historian Louis Schmier has written how "economic considerations were an added inducement for the Gentiles to accept the Jewish arrival, for in the period after the war, when merchants and commodities were scarce, [various Jewish merchant families] and

---

[32]Ibid., 303-304.

[33]On the distinction between Judaeophobic social assumptions and anti-Semitic economic and political acts, I am indebted to Richard S. Levy, who discussed these issues with me at length.

their 'connections' were greeted as significant contributors to the revival of the town."[34] This is an important consideration, and one which works especially well when we remember that most southerners presumed that there already existed a Jewish predisposition to accumulating wealth and assets.

During the Leo Frank case and its aftermath, it was a commonly held belief that Frank had invisible connections to northern monied interests and, by implication, an international banking consortium. Leo Frank fought hard to denounce rumors of this kind. Many southerners, however, were reluctant to believe otherwise and refused even to consider Frank's word as truth. Just the hint of denunciation by Frank, his counsel, or his allies, provoked terse replies from rural southerners and led to increased tension between southern gentiles and Jews. "There is a very strong feeling among the country people, that is almost prevalent to a man," wrote F. N. Reeves, a cashier at the Bank of Cherokee, "that outside influences and big money are trying to dictate to our State and brow-beat our courts. The masses of the people resent very strongly this effort to influence our officials from the outside people by other states who know nothing of the official records of the case. . . ."[35] That New York City Jews appeared willing and ready to subsidize Leo Frank's mounting legal fees, especially those he accrued during his year and a half long appeals process, was further proof for many southerners that an insidious conspiracy had developed among wealthy Jews. Some southerners suggested that the intention of such a conspiracy was to bend and, if necessary, re-write the laws or re-create the customs of established southern white society.

When James Conley had told the jury that Leo Frank had said "why should I hang [for Mary Phagan's murder], I have wealthy

---

[34]Louis Schmier, "Jews and Gentiles in a South Georgia Town," in *The Jews of the South.* Edited by Samuel Proctor, Louis Schmier, and Malcolm Stern (Macon, Ga.: Mercer University Press, 1984), 2.

[35]F. N. Reeves to John M. Slaton, June 4, 1915, box 45, folder 10, John Marshall Slaton Collection, Georgia Department of Archives and History.

people in Brooklyn," most observers believed his testimony.[36] Most had assumed all along that a wealthy Jewish elite existed in the North and that, indeed, they oversaw the litigation of transgressions like the one then surrounding Frank. It hardly mattered to most observers that Frank's own mother had testified under oath to her family's limited resources. Many southerners continued to believe that when Jews applied economic or political pressure, they always received the compensation they intended to collect from their "victims." Countless rural people have left behind evidence of this nature. In letters to Governor Slaton and the Georgia Prison Commission, many of Georgia's rural constituents described what they believed was the extent to which "Jewish money" exerted its unwanted influence. "Should Jew money be allowed against Georgia virtue," asked H. J. Sandlin, "will we of the good old state of Georgia who represent the very best element of southern manhood submit[?]" T. B. Hogan, another correspondent, wrote "I hear that Frank had his millions at his back. Should money cut any ice when it comes to justice[?] If Frank killed the girl after doing his dirty work[,] he should be burned at the stake."[37] Sandlin and Hogan both reasoned that the unwanted influence of money had gone too far. According to many rural Georgians, no one—from individual members of the print media to southern political officeholders—was safe from such an influence.

"The maddening thing to the people of Georgia," wrote Tom Watson after Leo Frank's death sentence had been commuted, "is, not that one man's life has been spared, but that Jew Money has done for a foul Sodomite and murderer, a thing that shatters all precedents, nullifies the highest law, sinks juries and courts into contempt, brings upon us a sickening consciousness that our public men and our newspapers are for sale, weakens the defenses of every poor man's

---

[36]Conley's statement is found in Dinnerstein, *The Leo Frank Case*, 44.

[37]H. J. Sandlin to Georgia Prison Commission, June 2, 1915, box 35, folder 14, John Marshall Slaton Collection, Georgia Department of Archives and History; T. B. Hogan to John M. Slaton, May 25, 1915, box 35, folder 1, John Marshall Slaton Collection, Georgia Department of Archives and History.

home, and adds to the perils that beset every poor man's child."[38]
Watson's incendiary comments touched Georgia's rural constituency.
For them, perhaps the most disconcerting aspect of "Jewish money"
was the invidious way it crept into Georgia's political infrastructure
and corrupted its most honored individuals. The belief that Governor
Slaton had been "bought off" by greedy manipulators was shared by
countless rural Georgians. It was, by all accounts, an abomination of
their culture of honor.

Rural southerners often used words like "scoundrel," "dishonorable," "disreputable," and "criminal" to describe Governor Slaton.
According to these people honor was not for sale. Moreover, many
southerners considered money and personal ambition incongruous
parts of their culture of honor. Those who have studied the southern
honor culture, however, know this was typically not the case.
Patronage, largesse, and political "gift-giving" were important, even
essential, components of the culture. For example, the number of
personal pleas to Slaton for government positions and titles is
astonishing and illuminates the true meaning of the honor culture.
Ordinary people, however, witnessed none of these excesses. They
saw only the public rituals and pageantry and they considered them
the most important features of their culture. They saw the bows and
curtsies, the clothing of the gentleman class, the leisure and, most of
all, the deference shown to those considered gentlemen. These
outward appearances far outweighed the gamesmanship and
deal-making that were ultimately the most significant parts of this
particular culture.[39]

Accordingly, several rural southerners responded to the prospect
that Slaton had "sold them out" by reminding various correspondents
that other public officials would never have committed such acts of

---

[38]Watson, "The Celebrated Case of the State of Georgia vs. Leo Frank," 230.

[39]For requests made to Governor Slaton for political patronage, see Governor Joseph M.
Brown to John M. Slaton, June 12, 1913, box 6, folder 2, Joseph Mackey Brown Papers,
Atlanta Historical Society; H. F. Martin to John M. Slaton, June 16, 1915, box 45, folder 4,
John Marshall Slaton Collection, Georgia Department of Archives and History; J. P. Berrong
to John M. Slaton, May 15, 1915, ibid.

perfidy. "I [know in] my mind," wrote "A Friend of the Just," "I don't believe rich Jews could have bought over Joseph M. Brown [the governor who preceded Slaton]. Thank God your term of Govoner [*sic*] is at a close. May we be blessed with a Gov[ernor] that money can not [*sic*] bribe to pardoning Frank[,] which will be the next step of your brutes." Another Georgian, writing only days before Slaton would commute Frank's sentence, listed "lawyers, technicalities of the law, News papers [*sic*] for hire, officers for sale: these are the withering curse of our land." He then added that "this does not apply to honest lawyers, nor honest papers, for they are the exceptions to the rule, and I refuse to believe that you belong to the class who serve for hire." If Slaton needed an example of one such honest lawyer, wrote J. P. Berrong, he need look no further than his own Fulton County Solicitor. "I still hope there is [*sic*] plenty of good men that [*sic*] cannot be bought with Jewish *money*. Hugh M. Dorsey has made a reputation that will elevate him to any office he may ask [for] in Ga. [H]e is certainly one man that can't be bought." Reputation, integrity, and character—to the typical southerner, more faith would be given a man who possessed such qualities than one who possessed mere wealth.[40]

The role money played in the development of hostilities between indigenous Georgians and their "dishonorable" countrymen led ultimately to an outbreak of vigilante justice. As H. O. Durham explained in a letter to Governor Slaton, when all other action proved ineffective, extralegal violence appeared the only appropriate recourse. "Now to set this judgement aside at the request of big Hebrew money and Political pressure will be to invite lynchings and to establish a precedent of a law for the wealthy criminal Jew and another for the Gentile." Indeed, violence was intimately tied to the role of money, the loss of honor, and the desire to vindicate the death

---

[40]The quoted passages include "A Friend of the Just" to John M. Slaton, June 22, 1915, box 4, reel 2, Leo Frank Correspondence, Special Collections, Brandeis University; P.A.B. to John M. Slaton, June 15, 1915, box 45, folder 10, John Marshall Slaton Collection, Georgia Department of Archives and History; J. P. Berrong to John M. Slaton, May 15, 1915, ibid.

of "little" Mary Phagan. J. H. Christian sent Slaton the following letter: "The blood of the poor little outraged and murdered Phagan Girl will haunt you to your dying day for your failing to uphold the law—by doing as you did. You will realize the enormity of your crime when some night you awake and see her poor little blood stained body standing at your bedside with the little finger pointing to you, her face asking for justice." And justice is what an "American Citizen" had in mind when he wrote Slaton the following passage: "I want to be fair with you. There [sic] is five of us who have sworn to never stop till we stop your heart from beating and it fell on me to notify you. . . ." For many southerners, "justice" could only be had with the hanging of Frank, and, indeed, the hanging of anyone who attempted to prevent this execution of "justice."[41] Men like J. H. Christian undoubtedly believed that the use of violence was honorable and acceptable when that use would help preserve the memory of a girl like Mary Phagan who, as most had been told, died protecting her virtue. In fact, few southerners could resist such an "honorable" cause.

At his murder trial, Leo Frank was given the opportunity to deliver a prepared statement. As per his constitutional rights, he had chosen not to take the witness stand, believing that the public opprobrium against him was too strong. Instead of testifying, Frank was granted time to read a four–hour statement he had personally composed. It was both a passionate plea for acquittal and a well-constructed argument against his accusers. Frank painstakingly challenged the mass of evidence weighed against him. He carefully scrutinized every detail pertinent to the case. When it came to clarifying the testimony of James Conley, Frank's words revealed a man both disgusted and incredulous. "The statement of the negro Conley is a tissue of lies from first to last. . . . The story as to women coming into the factory with me for immoral purposes is a base lie and

---

[41]H. O. Durham to R. E. Davison, Georgia Prison Commission, June 1, 1915, box 35, folder 1, John Marshall Slaton Collection, Georgia Department of Archives and History; J. H. Christian to John M. Slaton, n.d., box 4, reel 2, Leo Frank Correspondence, Special Collections, Brandeis University; An "American Citizen" to John M. Slaton, n.d., ibid.

the few occasions that he claims to have seen me in indecent positions with women is a lie so vile that I have no language with which to fitly denounce it."[42]

By many accounts his impassioned plea was affecting. Some observers who had initially been convinced of Frank's guilt, set about to publicly pronounce him an innocent man.[43] Most, however, were not moved to quite this extent. Indeed, the influence of the many myths associated with southern Jews like Leo Frank—such as Frank's supposedly rapacious sexual appetite, the corrupting influence Jewish monied interests had on southern institutions, and the Judaeophobic assumptions held by most southerners with regard to Jews as an alien race—was too strong. These myths were too deeply rooted in the culture of Georgia's poor whites, just as they were with the state's political and landed elites as well. These same myths, which had worked together to initially implicate, then prosecute, and finally convict Leo Frank, were also used to justify the extralegal violence of the Knights of Mary Phagan. The potency of these ingrained beliefs, their role within a culture of honor, and their connection to Frank's violent demise, significantly contributed to the trail of events which were to become known as the "Leo Frank case."

---

[42]Brief of Evidence at 219, 220, *Leo M. Frank v. State of Georgia.*

[43]One such individual was Tom Loyless, the editor of the *Augusta Chronicle*, whose reading of the evidence persuaded him that Frank was an innocent man and,further, that Tom Watson was a dangerous one. Loyless eventually became not only Leo Frank's ally, but a friend to his wife, Lucille. See the editorial in the *Augusta Chronicle*, September 13, 1915, n.p., in box 7, folder 2, Leo Frank Collections, Atlanta Historical Society; also see Lucille Frank to Thomas Loyless, September 20, 1915, box 1, reel 1, Leo Frank Correspondence, Special Collections, Brandeis University.

IV.

THE ENDURING SIGNIFICANCE OF RACE AND ETHNICITY IN THE MODERN SOUTH

7

THE CITY IT ALWAYS WANTED TO BE: THE CHILD MURDERS AND THE COMING OF AGE OF ATLANTA

Nancy Lopez

During the 1960s, urban areas throughout the United States experienced a host of problems ranging from "white flight" to an increased crime rate. A consensus that America's cities were in serious trouble soon gripped the country, talk of "urban blight" increased, and as one commentator asserted, "[c]ataloguing the ills of America's urban areas [became] something of a national sport."[1] But though the rest of the country was reeling under the weight of the inner city malaise, Atlanta, Georgia appeared to avoid this fate. Where other metropolitan areas lapsed into stagnation, Atlanta's businesses and industries prospered. Moreover, Atlanta, the heart of the Confederacy, had pursued a policy of racial moderation since the 1940s. In 1973, voters elected an African American mayor, outwardly becoming a model of racial harmony. By the end of the 1970s, however, Atlanta proved susceptible to urban ills. Despite the African American political power structure, at times because of it, racial resentments within the city escalated. A skyrock-

---

[1]Dick Netzer, "The Problems: An Overview," in *Exploring Urban Problems*, ed. Melvin R. Levin (Boston: The Urban Press, 1971), 635, quoted in John D. Hutcheson Jr., *Racial Attitudes in Atlanta* (Atlanta: Center for Research in Social Change, Emory University, 1973), 1.

eting crime rate at the end of the decade also increased tensions. Throughout the period, however, Atlanta, ever image-conscious, fought to maintain the guise of a biracial, urban success story.

As the problems multiplied, in the summer of 1979 a new crisis confronted the city. The bodies of children, most of them teenagers, all but two of them male, and all of them black and poor, began surfacing in weed-choked vacant lots along the banks of the Chatahoochee River and in the dense woods surrounding Atlanta. Under intense local pressure and national scrutiny, the city administration and the law enforcement community searched desperately for a killer while attempting to maintain a sometimes tenuous hold on public order. Twenty-eight bodies would be found before the authorities made an arrest.[2] The race and socio-economic backgrounds of the victims kindled fears among Atlanta's African American population. The subsequent arrest of a black man, Wayne Williams, prompted a spate of conspiracy theories accusing city authorities of engaging in a frame-up followed by a cover-up. Regardless of the efforts of the business-political elite to present Atlanta as a model of racial moderation, and the presence of a black power structure, decades of latent racial tensions came spilling out onto the public stage during the crisis. The child murders exposed the gap between the self-consciously adopted image of "the city too busy to hate" and an urban reality of race and social issues that was not far removed from the problems experienced by other southern cities.

Since the end of the Second World War, Atlanta's political and business elite carefully cultivated an image of a progressive city on the move. Economic growth would likely have been impossible, however,

---

[2]The number of dead is reported alternately as twenty-eight and as thirty. The original list of victims, including the last two recovered, Nathanial Cater and Billy Ray Payne, numbered twenty-eight. The final number of murders investigated by the Missing and Murdered Children Task Force was thirty. To the original list, the Task Force later added one missing person and one victim, John Harold Porter, originally excluded because he was an adult. FBI Report, Special Agent Harold Deadman, June 11, 1981, Trial Record, State of Georgia v. Wayne Bertram Williams, Criminal Action File No. A-56186, Book 2963, 433-437 (Hereafter citations to the trial record will include the title of the document followed by Book __, __).

had the city been unable to dispel regional stereotypes by convincing the nation that provincial attitudes, in particular racism, had been eradicated from Atlanta. William B. Hartsfield, Atlanta's mayor from 1936 through 1961, maintained a strong relationship with the city's business interests, including Coca Cola president Robert Woodruff. This civic-business alliance had long supported racial moderation as a means of encouraging economic growth. "[T]he people of Atlanta don't want Atlanta growth and prosperity to be stopped by racial controversy," Hartsfield explained, "our aim in life is to make no business, no industry, no educational or social organization ashamed of the dateline 'Atlanta.' "[3] To this end, Hartsfield coined the term "the city too busy to hate," oversaw the hiring of Atlanta's first African American police officers in 1947, removed the "white" and "colored" signs from the restrooms in the city airport, negotiated land deals between white and African American homeowners, and shepherded the desegregation of golf courses and buses during the 1950s. Many commentators suggest that although these changes were mostly symbolic and prompted by the self-serving interests of the business elite, the "negotiated gradualism" of Hartsfield's policies made Atlanta appear to be "an isle of reasonableness in a sea of die-hard resistance."[4]

Beginning with elections in 1949, Hartsfield's racial moderation and pro-business stance enabled him to cobble together a voting bloc consisting of middle-class whites and African Americans. Hartsfield held onto this bloc until the election of 1961, during which he passed

---

[3]William B. Hartsfield, quoted in Ronald Bayor, *Race and the Shaping of Twentieth Century Atlanta*. (Chapel Hill: University of North Carolina Press, 1966), 31.

[4]The assertion that integration in Atlanta was motivated by business interests rather than concern over racial equality has been the subject of much commentary. See Virginia P. Hein, "The Image of 'A City Too Busy to Hate': Atlanta in the 1960's," *Phylon* 23 (1972): 205-221; Ronald Bayor, "A City Too Busy to Hate: Atlanta's Business Community and Civil Rights," *Business and Its Environment*, ed. Harold I. Sharlin (Connecticut: Greenwood Press, 1983), 145-159; Bayor, *Race and the Shaping of Twentieth Century Atlanta*, 26-31; Clarence N. Stone, *Regime Politics Governing Atlanta, 1946-1988* (Lawrence: University Press of Kansas, 1989), 28-32; David Andrew Harmon, *Beneath the Image of the Civil Rights Movement and Race Relations: Atlanta, Georgia, 1946-1981* (New York: Garland Publishing, 1996).

the torch to his successor, Chamber of Commerce president Ivan Allen Jr. Allen not only maintained the close relationship between city government and business elites, he also continued the policy of racial moderation: "I could promise all I wanted to about Atlanta's bright, booming economic future, but none of it would come about if Atlanta failed to cope with the racial issue. That[,] I knew, was the real issue in this campaign: was Atlanta going to be another Little Rock, or was Atlanta going to set the pace for the New South."[5]

Although Atlanta tried to foster its image as a prosperous, progressive city, all was not as it seemed. Despite the efforts of the Hartsfield and Allen administrations, the city remained essentially segregated. "Pretty much the culture and ethos of Atlanta was that it was better than the rest of the South—it was more progressive than the rest of the South," observed Central Atlanta Progress[6] vice president Larry Fonts. But, he added, "it was still Southern, still segregationist at heart." Even the highly praised peaceful school desegregation of 1961 involved only nine students. The following year, this number increased by forty-four, after which the process ground almost to a halt. "Segregation still was king," Fonts insisted, "and that went deep into the genes of a lot of people."[7] Economic successes in the 1960s also exhibited a downside. The impressive increase in new jobs was actually unable to keep pace with the number of people entering the job market. African American unemployment rates were double those of whites throughout the 1960s. Moreover, these highly touted economic gains benefited the suburbs at the expense of the city. The suburban population surged as a result of white flight, while the population of the incorporated

---

[5]Ivan Allen Jr. quoted in Bayor, *Race and the Shaping of Twentieth Century Atlanta*, 37

[6]Central Atlanta Progress is a corporation comprised of the CEO's of the top one hundred businesses located within downtown Atlanta. It was an active participant in city politics, having emerged as an important player after the Atlanta Chamber of Commerce began focusing its activities on reaching out to the suburban population. City Hall perceived the Chamber to have deserted downtown, and Central Atlanta Progress stepped into the breach. Larry Fonts, interview by author, tape recording, Dallas, Texas, March 13, 1997.

[7]Fonts, interview; Peter K. Eisinger, *The Politics of Displacement* (New York: Academic Press, 1980), 59.

city remained stagnant. The percentage of African Americans living within the incorporated part of the city grew from thirty-eight to fifty-one percent. From 1960 to 1970, 60,000 people moved to the suburbs, resulting in a twenty percent decline in the white population of the city and a suburban population that was ninety-four percent white. Atlanta had become, as one African American resident stated, a city "too busy moving to hate." Competition between the incorporated city and the surrounding suburbs emerged along racial lines as the tension that failed to materialize during Atlanta's efforts to desegregate began to manifest itself in battles over public housing and annexation.[8]

White flight, however, resulted in an unexpected benefit for the African American community. The city's racial composition became forty-nine percent black, and blacks comprised forty-one percent of its registered voters. The result was a shift in the city's political power away from the Ivan Allen Jr.-led civic-business alliance and toward African Americans, who soon occupied seats on the Board of Aldermen and in the state senate. When Allen did not seek a third term in 1969, the city elected Sam Massell. Although white, Massell won office on the strength of ninety-three percent of the African American vote. In addition, Maynard Jackson, an African American, was elected vice-mayor. Finally, in the mayoral race of 1973, blacks deserted Massell, handing the victory to Jackson. Atlanta had elected its first African American mayor. In addition, African Americans also won half the seats on the Board of Aldermen and five of nine seats on the school board. Now, while the white business elite remained in control of the city's economic life, Atlanta's political structure was predominantly African American.[9]

Although he once considered becoming a pastor like his father, Maynard Jackson instead followed his maternal grandfather, John

---

[8]Harmon, *Beneath the Image*, 177-178; Hutcheson, *Racial Attitudes in Atlanta*, 6-7, 55-59; Arnold Fleischman, "Atlanta: Urban Coalitions in a Suburban Sea," *Big City Politics in Transition*, eds. H. V. Savitch and John Clayton Thomas (Newbury Park: Sage Publications, 1991), 97-98.

[9]Harmon, *Beneath the Image*, 238-268; Stone, *Regime Politics*, 77, 79.

Wesley Dobbs, founder of the Georgia Voters League, into politics. At the age of thirty-one, after practicing law for only three years, Jackson ran for public office.[10] His grandfather provided Jackson with political links to the past, but many white leaders considered the young man "touchy" and "arrogant". Nor did established black leaders feel entirely at ease with Jackson, thinking him a political maverick, especially in light of the fact that Jackson's sudden rise meant that he was "not beholden to [any of them]." But in the long run, as Atlanta's first black mayor, Jackson's devotion to African Americans, as well as his aggressive, outspoken style, would prove a greater threat to the city's white business interests.[11]

Now firmly in the hands of African Americans, Atlanta's municipal government attracted a great deal of national publicity. Its reputation as a city of racial moderation seemed cemented. White businessmen and local media, however, despite their previous rhetoric in praise of racial harmony, expressed discomfort with this new arrangement.[12] Local business leaders were concerned about their access to City Hall. "In the old days," recalled one white businessman, "you could pick up the phone and dial the Mayor at his office or his home or his club—your club, or his friend's house—your friend's house, and you could get your business done, right there, first name basis."[13]

---

[10]In 1968, with little planning, Jackson challenged and lost the U.S. Senate race to the incumbent Herman Talmadge. No one believed a first time candidate running for the Senate could win, but this race gave Jackson experience and exposure, enabling him to fare better in his second race, that of Vice Mayor of Atlanta. Fonts, interview.

[11]Fonts, interview; Stone, *Regime Politics*, 78; Harmon, *Beneath the Image*, 278.

[12]Surveys show that after Jackson's election the level of trust in city government remained relatively stable among African Americans, but dropped severely among whites. See F. Glenn Abney and John D. Hutcheson Jr., "Race Representation and Trust: Changes in Attitude After the Election of a Black Mayor," *Public Opinion Quarterly* 45 (Spring 1981): 91-101.

[13]Eisinger, *The Politics of Displacement*, 73. The change in leadership threatened the white business interests who in the past shared with the city's administration "the badges of honor . . . of the white elite establishment." This included graduation from Boys High School or Tech High School, followed by college at Georgia Tech or Georgia, and later, membership in Piedmont Drive Club or Capital City Club. Fonts, interview.

Prior to Jackson's administration, City Hall functioned through strong departmental chairs—career bureaucrats to whom the business community felt they could turn and get results when needed: "When nothing else would work you could go to them and something would happen, and you knew that, that's how the city worked." Jackson changed the administrative structure by "cleaning out the whites through . . . resignations and forced resignations." He brought in African Americans who had previously never been given the opportunity to assume such administrative roles. But problems arose not merely because Jackson replaced career bureaucrats with less experienced people, but because he was replacing white bureaucrats with African American bureaucrats.[14]

The resulting criticisms, expressed by business interests, found their way into Atlanta's papers. In 1975, the *Atlanta Constitution* ran a seven-part series entitled "City in Crisis" chronicling the rising crime rate, white flight, racial problems, and the failures of inexperienced city leadership. While the Chamber of Commerce criticized the paper for overstating the case, it became painfully apparent that relations between the Mayor and the city's business elite would not be as friendly as they had been under Ivan Allen Jr.[15]

Reform of the police department produced another source of tension between the Mayor and white Atlantans. White residents were concerned about the high crime rate, especially among African Americans. The latter, on the other hand, were concerned about the shooting of twenty-three blacks by police officers between 1973 and

---

[14]Fonts, interview. Although the first serious efforts toward affirmative action began during Sam Massell's term, Jackson's efforts were both more systematic and resulted in greater numbers of women and minority hiring. Sharon Michelle Watson, "Mayoral Leadership Changes and Public Policy: Exploring the Influence of Black Urban Government," (Ph.D. diss., Northwestern University, 1982), 103-111.

[15]This newspaper article was prompted in part by a survey conducted by Central Atlanta Progress (CAP). The survey essentially listed the business elite's many grievances with the mayor, including the charge that the mayor was perceived as anti-white. The letter was sent from CAP chair Harold Brockey to Mayor Jackson. Gary M. Pomerantz, *Where Peachtree Meets Sweet Auburn* (New York: Scribner, 1996), 437-438; Fonts, interview; Stone, *Regime Politics*, 89-91.

1974. Police Chief John Inman, with whom Jackson had long been at odds, was known as a racist who condoned the use of excessive force by his officers. Jackson fired Inman as one of his first acts as Mayor. Inman responded by barricading himself in his office, surrounded by a phalanx of SWAT team officers. The Chief still had six years left on his contract, and he insisted that he was not going anywhere.[16]

Although a state court upheld the validity of Inman's contract, Jackson had another trick up his sleeve. The Mayor reorganized the city government based on authority granted him in the city charter. He created a Public Safety Department with a Commissioner to supervise police, fire, and emergency medical services. Under this new system, the Police Chief was subordinate to the Commissioner. In 1978, Mayor Jackson appointed Lee P. Brown as Commissioner. A former police officer and university professor with a Ph.D. in criminology, Brown assumed office in time to witness Atlanta's already high crime rate soar.[17]

Since 1965, Atlanta's crime rate for major crimes had risen three hundred percent. In 1974, the Federal Bureau of Investigation ranked Atlanta as "the worst city in the country for per capita violent crime." The city experienced the largest annual crime increase in the country in 1978, including more crimes per capita of any of the forty largest cities in the nation. Suddenly, Atlanta found its carefully crafted image of a city of progress and racial harmony exploding on the national stage. Mayor Jackson had by this time begun to position

---

[16]Stone, *Regime Politics*, 88; Bayor, *Race and the Shaping of Twentieth Century Atlanta*, 182-184. The high number of African Americans killed by police officers is attributed to Chief Inman's plan to combat convenience store robberies. Police officers would secret themselves in the back room of these stores armed with shotguns. During a robbery attempt, the hidden officer would burst forth, and violence would often ensue. As Commissioner Lee Brown later noted: "It was a condition that forced police officers to shoot somebody." More to the point, as Larry Fonts recalled, it was "one hell of a shooting rampage." Upon election, Maynard Jackson immediately put a stop to this policy. Fonts, interview; Lee P. Brown, interview by author, tape recording, Houston, Texas, March 12, 1997.

[17]Lee Brown was the second individual to occupy the position of Commissioner of the Department of Public Safety, replacing Reginald Eaves. Fonts, interview; Brown, interview.

himself for another run against Senator Herman Talmadge. Instead he found himself publicly unable to control his own city.[18]

The Mayor's explanations for the soaring crime rate were inflation, unemployment, drug trafficking, and a lack of gun control. But a manpower shortage caused by a discrimination suit filed in 1973 was the biggest factor causing crime to spiral upward. Brought by the Afro-American Patrolmen's League, this suit asserted that while fifty-one percent of Atlanta's population was black, blacks comprised only twenty-two percent of its police force. The issue was unresolved a year later when the Fraternal Order of the Police brought a reverse discrimination claim. The end result was a five-year hiring and promotions freeze—while the courts sorted out the mess—that left Atlanta's police force undermanned by 200 officers.[19]

In addition to the ongoing hiring freeze, poor pay and the crackdown on brutality created a morale problem among the rank and file. Officers were resigning at a rate of ten per month. By this time, Inman had been demoted to Director of the Bureau of Police Services. His replacement, George Napper, was black. Many white officers felt that the ascendancy of African Americans impeded effective police enforcement because the Mayor, to avoid offending his core constituency, was soft on crime. The racial lines in this dispute were clearly marked. One white officer, waxing nostalgic for the days of Chief Inman, commented that "no nonsense law enforce-

---

[18]Howell Raines, "Atlanta, Fearing for National Reputation, Mounts Urgent Fight on Crime," *New York Times*, August 18, 1979, 7; "Atlanta: Bad for Business," *Newsweek*, August 27, 1979, 27.

[19]Brown, interview; Bayor, *Race and the Shaping of Twentieth Century Atlanta*, 182-183; Pomerantz, *Where Peachtree Street Meets Sweet Auburn*, 435. In 1973, the city personnel board recommended that two-thirds of all new police hires be African American. Chief Inman, however, supported by local newspapers and the city council, refused to implement the plan. When Reginald Eaves was appointed Commissioner, he quickly moved to adjust the racial imbalance. By 1976, the number of black police officers had risen to thirty-five percent. The lawsuits continued, however, until Eaves's successor, Commissioner Brown requested the Community Relations Services of the U.S. Department of Justice to assess the situation, mediate between the groups involved in the litigation, and offer an agreement which was accepted by the courts, enabling hiring to begin again. Brown, interview; see also Harmon, *Beneath the Image*, 295-297.

ment" was needed to curb the rising crime rate: "That's something that the Atlanta Police Department has gotten away from in recent years and therefore we've got a crime problem."[20]

By August 1979, the crime situation in Atlanta had further deteriorated and negative national publicity intensified. The number of reported rapes rose fifty-three percent while overall crime increased twenty-nine percent. By the summer of 1979, the homicide rate had already surpassed by eight deaths the number of murders for all of 1978.[21] With the annual homicide count at 151, several murders in the summer and fall of 1979, captured the city's attention. As a symbol of the lawlessness that reigned in Atlanta, the killing of two white adults riveted the city. An Ohio doctor, visiting Atlanta for a convention of the Society of Nuclear Medicine, was robbed and killed on a downtown street. As if to underscore the danger in the downtown business district, that fall, the legal secretary of former governor Carl Sanders was shot and killed during her lunch hour. Fearing for the future of Atlanta's tourism and convention industry, these two murders were taken very seriously by the city administration and the business elite.[22]

---

[20]Reginald Stuart, "Atlanta's Murder Inquiry is Focus of Much Criticism," *New York Times*, February 2, 1981, 13; Raines, "Atlanta, Fearing for National Reputation," *New York Times*, August 15, 1979, 7; M. A. Farber, "The Investigator: Leading the Hunt in Atlanta's Murders," *New York Times Magazine*, May 3, 1981, 62-90.

[21]In an effort to regain control of the city's image, Mayor Jackson hired former United States Attorney General Griffin Bell to advise him on crime, and a public relations firm to reverse the city's crumbling reputation. Governor George Busbee offered Mayor Jackson the services of fifty state troopers which he reluctantly accepted. This "flying squad" was to help restore order to the city. But the damage had already been done. The violent images were difficult to dispel given the assertions that the downtown business district was a "war zone." Mayor Jackson and Commissioner Brown both believed the media unfairly exploited the story for political reasons. Raines, "Atlanta, Fearing for National Reputation," *New York Times*, August 18, 1979, 7; Wendell Rawls Jr., "Atlanta Acts to Fight Crime After Spate of Slayings," *New York Times*, October 23, 1979, 16; "Atlanta: Bad for Business," *Newsweek*, August 27, 1979, 27; Brown, interview.

[22]Fonts, interview; "Atlanta: Bad for Business," *Newsweek*. August 27, 1979, 27; "Atlanta Acts to Fight Crime After Spate of Slayings," *New York Times*, October 23, 1979, 16.

Compared to the outcry over the two white adults, little public attention was paid when the bodies of black children began to turn up among Atlanta's many homicides. The first two bodies were discovered on the same day, July 28, 1979, within 150 feet of one another. Fourteen-year-old Edward Hope Smith was last seen on July 20, 1979, leaving a skating rink near his home. He had been shot to death. The second victim was Alfred James Evans, also fourteen, who had last been seen on July 25, 1979, while waiting for a bus. Unlike Smith, however, Evans had been strangled. Police recovered the body of fourteen-year-old Milton Harvey on November 5, 1979, two months after he disappeared while riding his bike near his home. This time the body was so badly decomposed the cause of death could not be determined. Three days later, the strangled corpse of nine-year-old Yusef Bell, last seen running an errand for a neighbor, was found in a maintenance shaft in an abandoned school.[23]

An early criticism frequently leveled at the Atlanta Police Department regarding the investigation into the child murders was that additional deaths might have been prevented had the investigators immediately linked the killings and examined them as though they were connected. The chief proponent of this position was Camille Bell, mother of Yusef Bell and founder of Committee to Stop Children's Murders (STOP), an organization comprised of the parents of the victims. Bell relentlessly pursued the police department, the Mayor's office, and the media, claiming that authorities were indifferent to the child victims because they were poor, black, and from the public housing projects of Atlanta's south side.[24] This was a

---

[23]Transcript of Proceedings Before the Honorable Clarence Cooper, Judge, in the Superior Court of Fulton County, State of Georgia v. Wayne Bertram Williams, Criminal Action File No. A-56186 (Hereafter Transcript), Testimony of Gary M. Lloyd, 2398-2416; Testimony of Dr. John Feegal, 2433; FBI Report, Special Agent Harold Deadman, June 11, 1981, Book 2963, 437; James Baldwin, *The Evidence of Things Not Seen* (New York: Holt, Rinehart and Winston, 1985), 39; Reginald Stuart, "Atlanta's Murder Inquiry is Focus of Much Criticism," *New York Times*, February 2, 1981, 13.

[24]Transcript, Testimony of Angelo Fuster, 6679-6681. Marked by ramshackle houses, outdoor toilets, unpaved streets, trash strewn vacant lots, and a large transient population, South Atlanta was the location of most of the city's public housing units. Attempts at urban

sentiment soon expressed by other African Americans and the subject of much media commentary. Given her fondness for referring to Mayor Jackson as "the fat boy," Bell was at times unpopular at City Hall. But she would not desist, convinced that apathy on the part of the police, as well as the racial climate in Atlanta, "caused this tragedy to continue until there were fourteen victims instead of ending after the first."[25]

Mayor Jackson and Commissioner Brown now found themselves in an unenviable position. Police rank and file generally believed the administration coddled the lawless black community while STOP accused them of indifference in the deaths of the children. Lee Brown, however, denies the accusation that the police failed to connect the killings until forced to by the publicity generating activities of STOP. While acknowledging that "as is always the case, you don't know you have a problem until you have a problem," Brown insists that finding two bodies in the same area and knowing a third child had disappeared during the same period immediately prompted the police to investigate the killings in connection with one another. Juvenile and homicide officers quickly began looking at other killings and reports of missing children in the area. The police department conducted its investigation quietly, however, and by the time the

---

renewal served only to worsen conditions. The city ordered the destruction of older substandard tenements without making living arrangements for displaced persons waiting for new housing to be built. Harmon, *Beneath the Image*, 177-179; Christopher Silver and John V. Moeser, *The Separate City* (Lexington: University Press of Kentucky, 1995), 152.

[25]Baldwin, *The Evidence of Things Not Seen*, 54-55; "Killing of 6 Black Children in a Year Baffles Atlanta," *New York Times*, August 24, 1980, 59; Nathaniel Sheppard Jr., "Atlanta Marking Halloween Carefully," *New York Times*, November 1, 1980, 12. Although STOP was critical of the efforts of the Atlanta Police Department, Commissioner Brown remained sympathetic to its efforts. "If you could just put yourself in their position, here's a mother that lost her child," he explained, "You want to be as supportive as you can of them individually and collectively." To that end two officers were assigned to STOP to act as liaisons to APD. As to the criticism, Brown maintained, "It's our responsibility to accept that—understanding why it's being done." Brown, interview.

media picked up the story, it appeared as if the police had been complacent.[26]

With the body count rising and a multiplicity of law enforcement jurisdictions becoming involved in the investigation, Commissioner Brown formed the Missing and Murdered Children Task Force on July 7, 1980. Originally consisting of one sergeant and four officers, the new organization could do nothing to stop the killing. By August 1980, six children were dead and four were missing. Two months later the count had risen to nine dead with none of the missing children having been located.[27]

When the task force was formed in July, Atlanta's police had just begun to recover from the problems that plagued the department in 1978 and 1979. The discrimination lawsuit had been settled and the hiring freeze ended. The department was finally up to full capacity and the racial imbalance had been ameliorated with blacks now comprising forty-two percent of the police force. Moreover, Commissioner Brown instituted a community-relations program to improve the strained relationship between the department and Atlanta's residents. The city even seemed to have gained the upper hand in its battle with crime. Whereas crime in the nation rose an average of ten percent, in Atlanta, it rose just one percent. As Commissioner Brown noted in 1980, "if it weren't for the deaths of these children, we would have a success story." But unfortunately, Atlanta did have an individual (or several individuals) killing its children with impunity. The negative media exposure the city received during the crisis of

---

[26]Brown, interview. Brown's version of events is supported by Larry Fonts who was told that the police "thought they had a serial killer" on their hands after the first few murders. Fonts recalls that the investigation was conducted quietly to prevent "unnecessary fear." Fonts, interview.

[27]The various jurisdictions involved in the investigation included, the City of Atlanta, DeKalb County, Cobb County, Fulton County, and the Georgia Bureau of Investigation. Commissioner Brown created the Task Force, consisting of eleven different organizations, to avoid duplication of work by the various jurisdictions and provide a central depository for all of the information. As the number of victims grew, the Task Force grew, numbering over one hundred officers at its peak. Transcript, Testimony of Lee P. Brown, 939; Brown, interview.

1978 and 1979 would appear mild compared to what was now headed its way.[28]

It is one of the tragic ironies of the child murders crisis that the administration of Maynard Jackson should be accused of indifference to the plight of poor black children. Since the Hartsfield administration, the civic-business alliance pursued policies of racial moderation hoping to attract new enterprise to the city. The efforts succeeded as business flourished and blacks became a political force. The economic benefits primarily benefited the white community, however, and it was demographic change resulting from white flight that swept the black political power structure into office. Add to this mix the lingering ill will toward the police department left in the wake of John Inman's reign as police chief, and the result is that Atlanta's new black political elite sat atop decades worth of repressed racial tensions. Now that someone seemed to be hunting the city's black children, those tensions could no longer be contained. The public outcry over the downtown murders of the two white adults, compared to the relatively quiet response to the deaths of the first black children, seemed to offer an insight into the true attitudes of Atlanta's residents. Finally, there were those in Atlanta who refused to be placated by the presence of a black power structure. In *The Evidence of Things Not Seen*, author James Baldwin gave voice to these doubts when, in discussing the concept of "the Black Mayor," he charged:

> This phenomenon is, on the part of the Republic, cynical. It is a concession masking the face of power, which remains White. The presence of these beleaguered Black men—some of whom, after all, putting it brutally, may or may not be for sale—threatens the power of the Republic far less than would their absence.[29]

---

[28]M. A. Farber, "The Investigator," 88.

[29]Baldwin, *The Evidence of Things Not Seen*, 26-27.

Regardless of the presence of an African American mayor, police chief, public safety commissioner, and an improving police department, the continuing dominance of a white economic elite gave credence to such sentiments.

Despite the accusations of Camille Bell and the suspicions expressed by Baldwin, it was, nevertheless, probably the presence of blacks in positions of responsibility that prevented the city from exploding. Lee Brown had a "game plan" for Atlanta that was disrupted by the two-year search for the child killer. The plan revolved around community policing, which involves assigning a police officer to a given geographical territory and assigning to him the responsibility for everything that happens within the area. Through the assignments of a regular beat, this program attempts to create a partnership between the police and the community. It was, Brown believes, the rapport created by this program that prevented the city from erupting in violence during the course of the investigation.[30]

In the fall of 1980, however, that the city would avoid an explosion was not a foregone conclusion. Tensions came to a head October 16, after a boiler explosion killed four children and one adult at a day care center in the Bowen Homes, a public housing project. African American residents were frightened and outraged. Rumors immediately circulated that a Ku Klux Klan conspiracy was afoot. It was said that just prior to the explosion three white men ran from the building and sped away in a pickup truck adorned with a Confederate flag. The residents of Bowen Homes were convinced that the Klan had planted a bomb.[31]

---

[30]Brown, interview.

[31]Brown, interview; Fonts, interview. Fears of Ku Klux Klan had been heightened by a series a local Atlanta television station ran as an extension of the "City in Crisis" series in the newspaper. This story, shown on the evening news, documented the activities of a white supremacist paramilitary unit operating just across the state line in the woods of Alabama. Using hidden cameras, the station filmed the group performing military maneuvers and making wild threats: "It was highly suggestive that maybe the killings were being done by the Klan." Fonts, interview.

Mayor Jackson and other civic leaders met with the residents the night of the explosion. The crowd was volatile. Commissioner Brown later recalled: "We had a tough time with that group . . . they were all mad—scared, angry—there were rumors that some whites had gone into the housing projects and killed some babies." Hosea Williams, a leader in Martin Luther King Jr.'s Southern Christian Leadership Conference and a fixture on Atlanta's political scene, is credited with calming the angry crowd. Williams took over the microphone and urged the residents to march to City Hall. Taking up the call, the residents walked the twelve miles into downtown, by the end of which the crowd had tired and its anger diffused. Mayor Jackson later commented that had it not been for Hosea Williams, city officials might have lost control of the residents that night.[32]

As the body count increased, the level of fear and frustration within the city kept pace. Every weekend volunteers wearing orange vests and red armbands, armed with walking sticks and flashlights, combed the vacant lots, abandoned buiidings, old cars, and wooded areas where bodies had been discovered or might be discovered. The crowds of volunteers grew each week until they numbered over a thousand. After volunteer search parties discovered the remains of two more victims, police and firefighters began canvassing South Atlanta, going door to door searching for any information that might prove helpful. They handed out photographs of the missing children and pamphlets providing safety tips. The Fraternal Order of the Police distributed 100,000 bumper stickers warning, "Kids, Don't Go With Strangers." The City Council unanimously approved a citywide curfew for children under the age of fifteen, and as Halloween approached, Mayor Jackson urged parents to forego trick-or-treating. By October, the city had established a $100,000 reward fund.[33]

---

[32]Fonts, interview; Brown, interview.

[33]"Atlanta Volunteers Find Bones in Their Search for Missing Child," *New York Times*, October 19, 1980, 26; "Officials Hunt for Clues to 10 Slayings as Atlanta Imposes Partial Curfew," *New York Times*, October 21, 1980, 16; Wendell Rawls Jr., "Atlantans Worry and Pray Over Slayings of 10 Children," *New York Times*, October 22, 1980, 19; Nathaniel Sheppard Jr., "Atlanta and Miami Curbing Halloween," *New York Times*, October 31, 1980,

October was a particularly rough month for the city's administration. The child murders were just beginning to pierce the national consciousness, and as the volunteer search parties multiplied in number each weekend, the media coverage grew with it. Racial fears did, however, ease somewhat as it was confirmed that the boiler explosion was caused by poor maintenance. More significantly, heartened by the swelling ranks of the multiracial search parties as the city rallied in support, many blacks began to temper the frequently stated opinion that had the victims been white a greater effort to find the killer would have been launched sooner. A feeling of unity began to build as the community pulled together in a common effort. "I was one who thought the white community really didn't care about what was going on here," said William McClendon, a black postal worker, "But I must say, the white community has been out here searching and working right alongside blacks. . . . We're all in this together."[34]

Not only were individuals volunteering their time for the grim work of searching for bodies, but Central Atlanta Progress (CAP), a private non-profit corporation comprised of the CEO's of the leading corporate entities of downtown Atlanta, organized the rebuilding of the day care center. Two contractors—one white-owned and one black-owned—offered their services.[35] Playground and playschool items were donated. Contributions came in from across the country, and CAP convinced HUD to rush through the insurance check so rebuilding might begin immediately. "If any such thing is possible," CAP president Dan Sweatt hopefully offered, "maybe something

---

A14; Wendell Rawls Jr., "4 Children Hunted By 1,000 in Atlanta," *New York Times*, November 2, 1980, 28. Atlanta residents were anxious and wanted to help, but "there was not much they could do," observed Lee Brown, "except get in the way in many instances." The searches, organized by city councilmen Arthur Langford, gave people a sense of purpose by providing a means through which to assist. The searches also eased racial tension by allowing the white community the opportunity to outwardly show its concern. Brown, interview.

[34]Wendell Rawls Jr., "4 Children Hunted By 1,000 in Atlanta," *New York Times*, November 2, 1980, 28.

[35]These contractors, Herman Russell and Larry Gellerstadt, were both members of CAP's Board of Director and had previously worked in a joint venture together under Maynard Jackson. Fonts, interview.

positive has come out of the tragedies if it has brought the community together again."[36]

The earlier claims of indifference faded as the city united in the searches, but a related criticism rose in its stead. After decades of claiming an essentially segregated city as the quintessence of the New South, the city's business elite felt the brunt of a backlash. Critics were quick to note that the Atlanta corporate establishment rushed to aid in the rebuilding of the Bowen Homes for the same reason Coca Cola and the Chamber of Commerce spent $15,000 on an advertising campaign with the theme "Let's Keep Pulling Together Atlanta!"—because they realized that Atlanta's troubles were bad for business.[37] The media and business interests stood accused of glossing over the truth—that the same urban ills and problems of race present in other southern cities also plagued Atlanta—in the name of attracting business and tourists to the city. This new theme possessed a greater staying power than the accusation of indifference, and in it lay the seeds of future conspiracy theories.

Certainly no member of the business elite denied that the child murders were damaging to the city's reputation and therefore its business interests. Chamber of Commerce Executive Director, Tom Hamall, later recalled feeling concern over the fact that although businesses were still interested in coming to Atlanta, they were moving to DeKalb County rather than within the city limits. Nevertheless, it was Maynard Jackson who requested CAP's assistance, and, Larry Fonts later recalled, CAP gladly responded, eager to

---

[36]Fonts, interview. Dan Sweatt quoted in Wendell Rawls Jr., "4 Children Hunted By 1,000 in Atlanta," *New York Times*, November 2, 1980, 28.

[37]Glen Headley, "The 'Atlanta Tragedy' and the Rule of Official Ideology," *Journal of Black Studies*, 18 (June 1988): 458-459. Headley contends that the city's elite were less interested in solving the murders than in damage control and preserving the city's image. Headley also charges that the major media outlets, the *Atlanta Journal* and the *Atlanta Constitution* were owned by Atlanta based Cox Enterprises and therefore had a vested interest in protecting the Atlanta business interests. As such, the papers ignored reports of whites hanging around the housing projects prior to the disappearance of some of the victims, leaving all such claims to be investigated by a local black-owned paper, the *Atlanta Voice* and an underground paper, the *Revolutionary Worker*. Headley, "The 'Atlanta Tragedy,' " 464-466.

do something to aid the city in this time of crisis. CAP had been frustrated and previously unable to come up with a means of assisting during the crisis. Here at last was a way in which they could help—building was one thing they knew how to do.[38]

Although these small signs of unity offered some hope, the investigation continued to run into brick walls. By the end of February the number of dead soared to twenty. A distinct pattern to the killings, however, was still lacking. All of the victims were poor, young black children from the south side of Atlanta. But among the victims were two girls, one of whom had been sexually assaulted. While strangulation was the most common cause of death, other victims had been shot, stabbed, and beaten to death. Nor did any discernible pattern exist in the location or manner in which the bodies were discarded. The Task Force sought any help it could find.

Now numbering over thirty men, with assistance from the Georgia Bureau of Investigation, two FBI agents, and a psychic, the Task Force nevertheless failed to turn up any clues or evidence.[39] Commissioner Brown sent letters to every police department in the country

---

[38]Pomerantz, *Where Peachtree Meets Sweet Auburn*, 477; Fonts, interview. The business community helped in other less well-publicized ways. This investigation was one of the earliest police efforts to use computers on a wide scale. IBM donated all of the computer equipment, but did so anonymously. Local businesses arranged for complimentary hotel accommodations for officers and their spouses for weekend getaways as part of an effort to boost officer morale. Brown, interview.

[39]The size of the Task Force increased as the number of jurisdictions involved in the investigation increased. At its peak the Task Force numbered over one hundred individuals. This number included officers from Fulton, DeKalb, and Cobb Counties, the Georgia Bureau of Investigation, and the FBI. The FBI coordinated its activities with the Task Force, but essentially worked its own investigation and was not subordinate to the Task Force Commander. Transcript, Testimony of Lee P. Brown, 953, 959.

Despite the repeated pleas for assistance from Mayor Jackson and Commissioner Brown, since all of the murders were within the state of Georgia and there was no evidence that the killings were racially motivated, the FBI could not intervene. On November 6, 1980, United States Attorney General Benjamin R. Civiletti directed the FBI to initiate a preliminary investigation to determine whether any of the victims in Atlanta had been held in violation of the Federal Kidnaping Law, Title 18, U.S.C. sec. 1201. Using this claim of jurisdiction, the Atlanta office of the FBI entered the investigation on November 17, 1980. FBI Prosecutive Report of Investigation Concerning ATKID, Major Case Number 30, Report of Special Agent James T. Procopio, June 17, 1981, Book 2963, 299.

seeking advice or assistance. The Task Force consulted every investigator or psychiatrist it could locate with experience in serial murder cases. Noting that most police departments would not seek outside help in this manner, Brown reasoned: "What I wanted to do was to stop those killings—and I wanted the best minds any place in the country to work with us."[40]

Among those who came to Atlanta to offer advice were five detectives from across the country with experience in solving difficult or multiple homicides. A year later, one of the consultants, speaking to the *New York Times* on the condition of anonymity, lent credence to the assertion that racial conflicts impeded progress in the investigation. The consultant noted that individuals working the case had very little experience in homicides. While this defect was likely due to the high turnover rate during 1979, the consultant went on to level a more serious charge: "Another thing the five of us discussed," he remarked, "was that the people in homicide were not enthusiastic about pursuing the cases. Homicide was headed by whites at the time, and I think there was some rivalry."[41]

As the investigation intensified, racial fears continued to swirl around the periphery. A group of residents at the Techwood-Clark Howell Homes housing project, claiming police response time to emergency calls was too slow, took matters into their own hands. Calling themselves the "Hank Aaron Crime Stoppers, the residents patrolled the housing project at night armed with baseball bats.[42] Still angry over the perceived battle to force the police to take the killings

---

[40]Brown, interview.

[41]Reginald Stuart, "Atlanta's Murder Inquiry Is Focus of Much Criticism," *New York Times*, February 2, 1981, 13. As to the claim that racial problems still existed, Brown denied having heard this assertion or being aware that tensions still existed. Brown, interview.

[42]Transcript, Testimony of Israel Green, 5121-5129; "Activists in Atlanta Vow To Begin Armed Patrols," *New York Times*, March 19, 1981, 14. Once again, Commissioner Brown believes the situation with the bat patrol never got out of hand because of the rapport developed between police and the citizens through his community policing program: "Absent having established that good relationship with the citizens, that city would have undoubtedly exploded. It did not explode because the citizens did not lose confidence in their police department." Brown, interview.

seriously, many blacks in Atlanta worried that the murders were related to a spate of racial violence occurring across the nation. Miami, Florida and Flint, Michigan had recently experienced rioting. A busing controversy provoked violence in Staten Island. In Buffalo, six black men were murdered, two of whom had their hearts cut out, and the FBI was presently looking for the individual who shot National Urban League President Vernon Jordan. Given the national picture, African Americans were hardly reassured when FBI Director William Webster publicly stated he did not believe a connection existed between the deaths of the children in Atlanta and the men in Buffalo. In Atlanta, passions were so high that the Department of Justice Community Relations Service sponsored a meeting among black leaders to calm conspiracy fears and warn against retaliatory racial violence.[43]

Although fears that the killings were race related haunted black Atlantans, the Task Force profile posited that the murderer was black. Many African Americans were slow to join in this conclusion because, as Maynard Jackson stated, "most black people could not believe that somebody black would do this. There was no history of a black serial killer. Everybody assumed right off the bat that it had to be somebody white." Special Agent John Douglas of the FBI Serial Crimes Unit, however, accepted neither the notion that the Klan was behind the murders, nor that the killer was white. Douglas quickly discounted Klan involvement because hate crimes "tend to be public, highly symbolic acts. . . . Such crime or other racial murder is an act of terrorism, and for it to have an effect it must be highly visible." "Ku Klux Klansmen," he added, "don't wear white sheets to fade into the woodwork."[44]

---

[43]Pomerantz, *Where Peachtree Meets Sweet Auburn*, 483; Bennett H. Beach, "Terror on Atlanta's South Side," *Time*, November 3, 1980, 67; Dennis A. Williams, "Worry Time For Blacks," *Newsweek*, December 1, 1980, 39; Nathaniel Sheppard Jr., "US Officials Work to Calm Racial Fears in Atlanta," *New York Times*, October 30, 1980, 21; Robert Pear, "FBI Chief Foresees Little Change Under Reagan," *New York Times*, November 21, 1980, 23.

[44]Pomerantz, *Where Peachtree Street Meets Sweet Auburn*, 476; John Douglas and Mark Olshaker, *Mindhunter* (New York: Pocket Books, 1995), 202.

Moreover, not only was it not true that there were no black serial killers, but serial killers almost always kill within their own race. Based on the foregoing information, as well as the fact that a white serial killer would have difficulty moving about unnoticed on Atlanta's south side, Mayor Jackson eventually agreed with the opinion that the killer was likely to be black. When the Atlanta Police Department requested Harvard Medical School psychiatrist Dr. Alvin Poussaint to study the impact of the killings on Atlanta's black youth, he found, to his surprise, that many of the victims' parents had also come to believe the serial killer was black. As Camille Bell observed: "We've got somebody in this city who can charm children away." Many of Atlanta's blacks, however, refused to consider the possibility.[45]

It was near the end of May 1981, that the Task Force finally got the break its members had been waiting for. Newspapers reported the discovery of fibers on some of the victims. Previously the bodies had been found clothed and on land, but after publication of this information, every new corpse was stripped to its underwear and thrown in the Chatahoochee River.[46] The Task Force quickly placed stakeouts on twenty-four different bridges crossing the river. On May 22, one Atlanta police officer, two recruits, and an FBI agent were assigned surveillance of the Jackson Parkway bridge.[47] One of the recruits was located in a pup tent on the bank below the bridge, the second recruit crouched behind the underbrush near the guardrail on

---

[45]Douglas and Olshaker, *Mindhunter*, 201, 205; Pomerantz, *Where Peachtree Street Meets Sweet Auburn*, 476; Jerry Adler and Vern E. Smith, "The Terror in Atlanta," *Newsweek*, March 2, 1981, 36.

[46]Commissioner Brown was careful about the information he released to the press. He was, therefore, distressed when an individual in the Georgia State Crime Laboratory leaked the information on the fiber evidence to the *Atlanta Constitution*. Now, however, he views the leak as a "blessing in disguise." Transcript, Testimony of Lee P. Brown, 946; FBI Prosecutive Report of Investigation concerning ATKID, Major Case Number 30, Report of Special Agent James T. Procopio, Book 2963, 299; Brown, interview.

[47]Recruits still attending the police academy were utilized in the bridge surveillance because such a large number of bridges were being watched the city would not have otherwise possessed the manpower. Transcript, Testimony of Lee P. Brown, 938; FBI Report, Special Agent Gregg D. Gilliland, May 22, 1981, Book 2967, 496-499.

the opposite side of the river, and the third officer and the FBI agent were each in unmarked chase cars on opposite sides of the bridge.[48]

At 2:30 a.m., according to the police account of events, in the pup tent on the bank beside the river, the recruit heard a loud splash. Looking up at the bridge, he saw headlights and radioed the man crouching in the underbrush. Hiding behind the guardrail, the second recruit observed a car appear to pull out of a parked position and slowly approach. None of the officers had either heard or seen the car drive onto the bridge. The recruits then radioed the chase car on the south side of the river. As the car, a green station wagon, came across the bridge, both chase cars fell in behind it. The officers pulled the car over after following it for a time. Behind the wheel sat Wayne Williams, a twenty-three-year-old African American who worked as a freelance photographer, television cameraman, and self-styled music promoter. When questioned by the officer, Williams explained he had thrown trash off the bridge. He would later assert that he never even stopped on the bridge, much less thrown anything over the side—he had merely slowed while searching for a telephone number on a sheet of paper, lost in his car. Two days later, however, the body of twenty-seven year old Nathanial Cater surfaced downstream.[49]

The son of two retired school teachers, Homer and Faye Williams, Wayne Williams had been considered something of a prodigy. Fascinated by electronics, by the time he was eleven, Wayne and a friend had earned the money to purchase an oscillator or radio frequency generator. Soon they were operating WRAP, a radio station broadcasting to the houses within a block of Williams's home. By 1973, WRAP had become WRAZ and Williams expanded his

---

[48]Transcript, Testimony of Freddie Jacobs, 1076-1132; Testimony of Robert Campbell, 1136-1190; Testimony of Carl Holden, 1197-1225; Testimony of Gregg Gilliland, 1260-1292.

[49]Transcript, Testimony of Freddie Jacobs, 1076-1132; Testimony of Robert Campbell, 1136-1190; Testimony of Carl Holden, 1197-1225; Testimony of Gregg Gilliland, 1260-1292; Atlanta Bureau of Police Services, Statement of C.L. Holden, June 5, 1981, Book 2967, 528-529; Atlanta Bureau of Police Services, Statement of Recruit R.E. Campbell, June 5, 1981, Book 2967, 530-531; FBI Report, Special Agent William McGrath, John R. Benesh, May 29, 1981, Book 2967, 533-539; FBI Report, Special Agent Charles Mathews, William McGrath, June 3-4, 1981, Book 2963, 398-403.

audience by placing transmitting equipment in high population areas such as the Dixie Hills public housing project.[50] Those who remembered Williams's accomplishments as a teenager—interviewing from his homemade radio station former Mayor Sam Massell, State Representative Tyrone Brooks, Congressman and future mayor Andrew Young, and posing for a 1974 *Jet* magazine photo spread with NAACP leader Benjamin Hooks—were stunned when he emerged as the primary suspect.[51]

Homer and Faye Williams tended to indulge their "miracle child." Proud of his success, they invested their life savings to finance the expansion of Wayne's radio station into a profit-generating venture. Wayne moved the station out of his parent's house and into a small office. Although he was only sixteen, Wayne managed the operation. The station lasted less than a year—in 1976, the station, and Homer and Faye Williams, declared bankruptcy.[52]

Wayne graduated from high school the year the station collapsed. After a failed attempt at college, he began an unsuccessful series of career moves, hopping from one interest to the next. Working as a news stringer selling stories to WSB-TV, the local ABC affiliate, he

---

[50]Transcript, Testimony of Homer Williams, 5718-5723; Testimony of Faye Williams, 6037-6042; Testimony of Wayne Williams, 6182-6192, 6231; Testimony of Keith Knox, 5469-5488.

[51]Transcript, Testimony of Faye Williams, 6037-6043; Testimony of Wayne Williams, 6189-6192. Not all of the individuals questioned by the Task Force and the FBI recalled Williams in glowing terms. Almost all remembered Williams as extremely bright, describing him as a "whiz kid," "boy genius," "highly intelligent," and "brilliant." But Williams was also described as "skitchy," "weird," suffering from "delusions of grandeur," "obsessed with doing something noteworthy," and as someone who dwelled on his early successes. Most of these comments came from individuals whom Williams had listed on his resume, none of whom had given Williams permission to do so. Atlanta Bureau of Police Services (ABPS), Interview with Felicia Geter, August 25, 1981, Book 2971, 653; ABPS, Interview with Doug Candis, August 26, 1981, Book 2971, 656-658; ABPS, Interview with Zenas Sears, August 26, 1981, Book 2971, 663; ABPS, Interview with Joycelyn Dorsey, August 27, 1981, Book 2971, 679; Memo to Deputy Chief M.G. Redding, From Lee P. Brown, Regarding Statement of David Franklin, June 9, 1981, Book 2967, 697; Statement, East point Police Department— Detective Division, Sergeant E. A. Lowery interview with Bobby Toland, June 4, 1981, Book 2967, 896.

[52]Transcript, Testimony of Faye Williams, 6037-6043; Testimony of Homer Williams, 5723-5728; Testimony of Wayne Williams, 6192.

would monitor a police radio scanner late at night looking for fires or car accidents to report.[53] Unable to secure work steady work as a stringer, Williams again turned to the music industry. Calling himself a music promoter, he attempted to organize a Jackson 5-style pop group named Gemini. Wayne would tour Atlanta's school yards and shopping malls looking for boys and girls to audition. He distributed leaflets promising the opportunity to become a "professional entertainer," but insisting "no experience is necessary" and "all interviews are private and free." By Williams's own estimate, he auditioned thousands of children between November 1980 and May 1981.[54]

Despite his efforts to solicit teenagers for his pop group, Williams's name never surfaced during the investigation. The Task Force sifted through thousands of tips and placed thousands of names into its database, but Williams was not one of them. Moreover, although teachers by the dozen would emerge after Williams's arrest claiming he had notified them, wanting to audition their students, not one had mentioned him when the Task Force was busy knocking on the door of every classroom in Atlanta looking for suspicious characters. No one noticed him. Commissioner Brown recalled, "He just fitted into the community."[55]

On June 21, 1981, Williams was arrested and charged with the murders of Jimmy Ray Payne and Nathanial Cater, the last two of the twenty-eight victims. Williams's trial lasted nine weeks, and the jury heard testimony from almost two hundred witnesses. The jury consisted of nine women and three men, eight of whom were black

---

[53]Transcript, Testimony of Wayne Williams at 6192-6194; 6216-6218; Testimony of Homer Williams at 5728; Testimony of Faye Williams at 6043.

[54]Defendant's Exhibit 163, Letter from Williams to community leaders regarding formation of Gemini, November 12, 1980, 8135; Defendant's Exhibit 164, Letter From Williams to parents regarding formation of Gemini, March 6, 1981, 8138; Defendant's Exhibit 165, flyer distributed by Williams regarding auditions for Gemini, 8143; Transcript, Testimony of Wayne Williams at 6204, 6341-6348.

[55]Brown, interview; Tip #9558, Book 2967, 794; Police Report, reference Wayne Williams, J. B. Wilhoit, June 11, 1981, Book 2967, 820-823; ABPS, statement of Gloria Washington, Book 2971, 690-691.

and three of whom were white.[56] The prosecution attempted to portray Williams as a person who had experienced tremendous success as a child followed by a series of crushing failures as an adult. The publicity surrounding the investigation and Williams's subsequent arrest, the argument continued, provided him with the attention he craved but had not received since childhood. The defense countered that Williams was a nice boy from a good family and incapable of murder.[57]

When the trial started, District Attorney Lewis Slaton told the jury that this case would prove to be like "a jigsaw puzzle with a whole lot of little pieces fitting in." The pieces quickly fell into place. To begin with, Williams never offered a credible explanation for his presence on the bridge that morning. He claimed he was on his way to the apartment of a woman he was planning to promote, when he slowed his car on the bridge to search for her phone number. Neither the phone number nor the address he provided yielded the woman in question. Next, analysts matched the dog hairs and fibers recovered from the victims to those found on Williams's German shepherd and in his home and car.[58] Finally although Williams claimed to have

---

[56]The makeup of the jury was believed to favor the defense, although the defense hoped to avoid impaneling black mothers with young sons. "9 Women and 3 Men Are Chosen For Jury in Atlanta Murders Trial," *New York Times*, January 5, 1982, 11.

[57]This argument was compelling given Williams's behavior when he emerged as the primary suspect. The day the police questioned him for twelve hours he was discovered secreted away in the police station watching live coverage of his detainment on a secretary's television. After the questioning ended he lingered on asking investigators about the case until he had to be asked to leave. The next day, Williams held his own press conference at his parents' home, during which he handed out copies of his resume. He also played cat and mouse games with the officers assigned to watch him. Williams led police cars on wild chases through the city, at one point ending the chase in front of Commissioner Brown's house where he pulled into the driveway and honked his horn. Transcript, Testimony of William McGrath, 1690-91; State's Exhibit 604, unedited transcript of news conference, June 4, 1981, 7418; City of Atlanta Police Offense Report, June 10, 1981, Book 2967, 789-791; Brown, interview.

[58]The use of scientific evidence in the courtroom is the subject of an ongoing legal debate. Jurors who are incompetent to judge scientific evidence for themselves are reliant upon the conclusions of experts who are paid for their opinions. Moreover, studies show a high percentage of crime laboratory results to be inaccurate. See generally Irving C. Stone, "Capabilities of Modern Forensic Laboratories," *William and Mary Law Review* 25 (1984):

never met any of the victims, the prosecution offered witnesses claiming to have seen Williams with Cater the day he disappeared and with Payne shortly before his disappearance. The defense team failed in its efforts to cast doubt on the prosecution's evidence. In explaining Williams's presence on the bridge that morning, the defense asserted that the officers were asleep when awakened by the splash. By the time they responded, they found Williams crossing the bridge while the real murderer had already escaped.[59] Moreover, the defense had virtually no response to the fiber evidence and their efforts to impeach the witnesses claiming to have seen Williams with the victims failed. After deliberating twelve hours the jury returned a guilty verdict. Williams received a sentence of two life terms in prison.[60]

659-674; Edward J. Imwinkelreid, "The Standard for Admitting Scientific Evidence: A Critique from the Perspective of Juror Psychology," *Military Law Review* 100 (1983): 99-118; Michael S. Jacobs, "Testing the Assumptions Underlying the Debate About Scientific Evidence," *Connecticut Law Review* 25 (1993): 1083-1115. For a detailed examination of the evidence used to convict Wayne Williams, see Harold Deadman, "Scientific Evidence and the Wayne Williams Trial," *FBI Law Enforcement Bulletin*, March 1984, 12-20, and May 1984, 10-19.

[59]From the time he was first questioned, Williams claimed to have crossed the bridge several times that morning, during which he witnessed three other cars crossing the bridge. The claim that the officers were sleeping would explain the fact that not one of them heard or saw Williams drive onto the bridge prior to the splash. Transcript, February 5, 1982, Testimony of Ken Lawson at 17-21, 29; Transcript, Testimony of Mark Oviatt, 5937-6007; FBI interview with Wayne Williams, June 3-4, 1981, Special Agent Charles Mathews and William McGrath, Book 2963, 398-403.

[60]Transcript, Opening Statement, 802; Testimony of Diane McCook, 1411; Testimony of Betty Sellers, 1444; Testimony of Harold Deadman, 2279-2339; Testimony of Larry Peterson, 2105-2198. A little less than a month into the trial, the judge, Clarence Cooper, agreed to allow the prosecution to admit evidence of prior uncharged bad acts. Usually inadmissible, evidence of prior bad acts may be heard if they show a "plan, scheme, pattern, bent of mind, and identity." The use of uncharged prior misconduct is quite controversial. Because the misconduct is not charged, the defendant is not allowed discovery on the evidence and may not be aware such evidence exists until presented with the prospect of defending himself against it at the trial. This decision sealed Williams's fate. Prosecutors now offered fiber evidence and a parade of witnesses linking Williams to ten of the remaining twenty-six murders. See generally Edward J. Imwinkelreid, "The Worst Surprise of All: No Right to Pretrial Discovery of the Prosecution's Uncharged Misconduct Evidence," *Fordham Law Review* 56 (December 1987): 247-275.

Homer and Faye Williams naturally believed their son had been "railroaded," but they were joined by others. Calling the proceedings a "kangaroo court" and commenting that Judge Clarence Cooper was "obviously part of the prosecution team," STOP founder Camille Bell proclaimed Williams's innocence. "I've been doing my own investigation," Bell avowed, "and there are other people who need to be looked at." Comedian and activist, Dick Gregory added to the controversy when he charged that the government actually committed several of the murders. After being pressed on the matter, however, he admitted that he had no actual proof of such a plot. Jimmy Ray Payne's sister, Evelyn and Nathanial Cater's father, Alonzo, both expressed the hope that Williams was the killer, although neither was completely convinced. Finally, the mother of Alfred Evans articulated a commonly held opinion when she expressed dissatisfaction with a conviction based on fiber evidence.[61]

The murders in Atlanta galvanized the nation partially in reaction to the tragedy of the killings, but also as a metaphor for lingering problems of race in America. STOP founder Camille Bell captured the essence of the fears of African Americans when she observed, "Whoever is doing this to our children is indicating how vulnerable we really are." This profound feeling of vulnerability existed on many levels. Specifically, Bell was responding to the vulnerability created by the knowledge that "[t]here are actually people who can walk into your neighborhood in broad daylight, steal your children, murder them, and throw them back in your face."[62]

But the circumstances of the Atlanta murders pointed to the greater vulnerability of being black and poor. All but two of the victims came from single-parent households, foster homes, or extended families, and most of them lived in public or low-income housing. Sociologist Anna Grant of Morehouse College noted that

---

[61]"Atlanta," UPI, February 27, 1982, Saturday, AM cycle; Claude Lewis, "Spike Lee's Conspiracy Theory," *Dallas Morning News*, November 12, 1992, 29A; "Victim's Relatives Unsure of Guilt," UPI, February 28, 1982, Sunday, AM cycle.

[62]Camille Bell quoted in Jerry Adler and Vern E. Smith, "The Terror in Atlanta," *Newsweek*, March 2, 1981, 36.

the victims lived a "very public life on the street" because of over-crowding within the public housing projects. Moreover, most of the Atlanta victims increased their vulnerability by running errands to earn extra money. Middle-class children, by contrast, are less at risk because they come from single-family dwellings with closer supervision. The circumstances into which the victims were born presented a microcosm of the larger national picture. The Children's Defense Fund reported that a black child has "almost a one in two chance of being born into poverty, is more than two and a half times as likely as a white child to live in substandard housing and is twice as likely to live on welfare." In addition, a black child stands a much greater chance of living with neither parent, being born to a teenage mother, experiencing the separation of his parents and more is likely to see his father die.[63]

A feeling of vulnerability extended to frustrations felt by African American leadership over the direction in which race relations seemed to be headed in the early 1980s. In a March 1981 speech in Washington, D.C., the Reverend Jesse Jackson stated that the Atlanta murders could only be understood in a broader context. Challenges to affirmative action in the DeFunis and Bakke decisions,[64] violence against blacks in Philadelphia, Miami, and Buffalo, and a rising tide of conservatism represented by the election of Ronald Reagan meant, he concluded, "It is open season on blacks." Washington, D.C. Mayor Marion Barry agreed with Jackson, making the frequent charge that had the Atlanta victims been white, federal authorities would have offered more assistance to the investigation. Jackson and Barry were heavily criticized for their comments, but they claimed merely to be repeating what they heard other blacks saying

---

[63]Wendell Rawls Jr., "Experts Find Environment a Factor in Vulnerability of Slain Atlanta Children," New York Times, March 18, 1981, A 24. See also Douglas S. Massey and Shawn M. Kanaiaupuni, "Public Housing and the Concentration of Poverty," Social Science Quarterly 74 (March 1993): 109-122; Harrell R. Rogers Jr., Poor Women, Poor Families (New York: M.E. Sharpe, Inc., 1990).

[64]DeFunis v. Odegaard, 416 U.S. 312 (1974); University of California Regents v. Bakke, 438 U.S. 265 (1978).

in stronger language. "The blatant racism that we suffer in America is just another level of the killing of black children in Atlanta," claimed one man quoted by the *Washington Post*. "Ronald Reagan himself is a sign of that racism—his whole diversion of funds from social programs to the military budget. I don't think Reagan had any concern in seeing that racial violence be stopped."[65]

Those searching for the hand of racism at work in the investigation of the missing and murdered children did not have far to look. When FBI agent Michael Twibell announced to the press that four of the murders had been solved, he claimed the children had been killed by members of their own families because they had been considered "nuisances." While it was true that the Task Force believed several of the killings were committed by family members, Twibell's "nuisance" comment exhibited a stunning lack of sensitivity in an explosive environment. Moreover, parents of the victims expressed alarm upon the immediate withdrawal of the FBI after Williams's arrest. They believed officials had given up on attempting to solve the remaining cases. Their fears were confirmed when ten days after his conviction the remaining twenty-two cases were tied to Williams and closed. Police Chief Lewis Graham insisted, "Closing a case on paper doesn't mean anything. It doesn't mean we won't look further. And by no stretch of the imagination will we forget." But the parents knew better. Mayor Jackson commented years later that although he encouraged people to go along with this decision, he himself never agreed with it. It simply fueled the fires of the conspiracy theorists. Those who wanted to believe a cover-up was at work claimed the closing of these cases was evidence of a whitewash.[66]

---

[65]Ellie McGrath, "Exploiting Atlanta's Grief," *Time*, April 6, 1981, 18; "Grief and Exploitation," *The New Republic*, March 28, 1981, 5-6. On black mayors and the rising conservatism of the Reagan years see Michael Stewart Bailey, "The Role of Black Mayors in the Agenda Politics of American Cities," (Ph.D. diss., Ohio State University, 1990), 10-11.

[66]Wendell Rawls Jr., "FBI Agent's Remarks on Murders Strain Bureau's Ties With Atlanta," *New York Times*, April 16, 1981, 24; Pomerantz, *Where Peachtree Meets Sweet Auburn*, 490; "FBI starts to Withdraw Agents Assigned in Atlanta," *New York Times*, June 25, 1981, 14; "Atlanta Killer: A Life of Isolation," *Newsweek*, September 20, 1982, 18.

For many observers, the fact that a black man was convicted of the murders simply offered further confirmation that a larger racial construct was at work. Author James Baldwin, in *The Evidence of Things Not Seen*, argued against what he perceived as the many inconsistencies in the case against Williams. His greatest concern, however, was revealed in a conversation he related between two African American men in Atlanta. Upon noticing the lack of blacks at the trial, Baldwin quoted one individual as stating, "We just weren't there. It was as though we didn't want to believe that this was happening, that one of us could do this." But more to the point, the other replied, "Oh, yes. It means we in the White shit, now! They got us. They win—when a Black person can do this!"[67]

Three years after the trial ended, Baldwin repeated the claims that the concern of Atlanta's power structure was less about the threat to the children or to Atlanta's blacks than "stifling an incipient scandal in order to protect the magic of the marketplace." This, Baldwin asserted, was the reason why the body count rose so high before the authorities took note:

> Authority can only scent danger to itself. It demands a crisis of whatever proportions before the private danger can be perceived as menacing the public safety. For you, or for me, for example, the missing child distorts, totally, the universe, but, for Authority, it is a statistic and, for bureaucracy, a detail. Only when these details and statistics begin to multiply is a public danger perceived.[68]

Wayne Williams maintains his innocence to this day. He has many supporters. The conspiracy theory positing Williams's innocence is based on Baldwin's notion of protecting "the magic of the marketplace." The murders, the theory runs, were committed by the Klan. Atlanta authorities suspected and investigated the possibility of

---

[67]Baldwin, *The Evidence of Things Not Seen*, 9.
[68]Baldwin, *The Evidence of Things Not Seen*, 60, 49.

Klan involvement. But fearing the negative publicity that a "race war" would generate, after stumbling onto an odd character like Wayne Williams, they knew they had a patsy they could plausibly blame. This theory was born of suspicions, as expressed by Baldwin, of "the Black Mayor" co-opted by the system. But it was also a mistrust based on a frank recognition that for decades the city's business elite under-played, if not ignored, the real racial and social divisions in Atlanta, hoping to present the city as a model of racial peace. But for the conspiracy theory to work, of course, its proponents must be able to point to actual evidence of Klan involvement. They can.

Much of the continuing controversy is centered on the alleged confession to the killing of Lubie Geter by Klan member Charles Sanders. Sanders was apparently angry after Geter ran into his car with a go-kart. "I'm going to kill the little black bastard," a witness reported Sanders to have said. After Geter's picture appeared in the paper as one of the missing and murdered children, the same witness asked Sanders if he killed the boy. "[Y]eah, I damn sure did," Sanders allegedly responded, "We killed a lot of those fucking niggers." The larger motivation was to spark a race war. After killing twenty black children, these same Klan members claimed they would begin killing black women.[69]

In 1985, Williams filed a Petition for a Writ of Habeas Corpus seeking to overturn the verdict of the jury and the affirmation of that verdict by the Georgia Supreme Court. Alan Dershowitz and William Kunstler joined the Williams defense team in 1991, at which time a hearing was held and testimony heard in Butts County, Georgia. The primary claim in the petition was that the prosecution withheld exculpatory evidence from the defense in violation of Williams's Fourteenth Amendment due process rights. In particular, they claimed that the prosecution failed to disclose the evidence gathered

---

[69]In the Superior Court of Butts County, State of Georgia, *Williams v. Zant*, File # 85-CV-410, Proposed Order of the Court Findings of Fact and Conclusions of Law, July 15, 1997, 53, 54, 58; Mark Curriden, "New Questions in Atlanta Murders: Did Prosecutors Withhold Evidence of Klan Involvement in Children's Deaths?" *ABA Journal* 78 (May 1992): 36; Headley, "The 'Atlanta Tragedy' and the Rule of Official Ideology," 44.

by the Georgia Bureau of Investigation regarding Charles Sanders. But the petition alleges much more than simply "the Klan did it."[70]

Wayne Williams's conviction was based on the trace evidence of fibers and blood matches; witness accounts asserting Williams, who claimed to know none of the victims, was seen with or knew many of them; witness accounts that Williams made disparaging remarks about poor blacks; witness accounts that shortly before they were murdered, several of the victims were seen entering a green station wagon similar to the one that Williams drove; and a trail of circumstantial evidence including the fact that he had come into contact with thousands of young boys during the course of his "talent search," and his unexplained presence on the Jackson Parkway Bridge the night of the "loud splash." The petition questions each of the above elements with the exception of his "talent search" and his presence on the Jackson Parkway Bridge. In each instance, Williams's attorneys claim that the prosecution withheld information that might have been used at trial to impeach the witnesses or call the trace evidence into question. Moreover, the confession of Charles Sanders is troubling, because since fiber matches connected Williams to Lubie Geter, if it can be proved that Sanders killed Geter, every other fiber match would, of necessity, also be found suspect.[71]

Adding to the controversy surrounding Williams's conviction, the FBI crime lab, long considered to be the best in the country, has recently come under attack after a chemist in the Bureau's explosives unit loudly complained about sloppy scientific procedures and problems with the handling of evidence. This whistle blowing led to an investigation by the Justice Department that subsequently confirmed the existence of problems in a January 1997 report. A recent book by two journalists underscores the weaknesses of the FBI

---

[70]In the Superior Court of Butts County, State of Georgia, *Williams v. Zant*, File # 85-CV-410, Proposed Order of the Court Findings of Fact and Conclusions of Law, July 15, 1997, 1.

[71]See generally In the Superior Court of Butts County, State of Georgia, *Williams v. Zant*, File # 85-CV-410, Proposed Order of the Court Findings of Fact and Conclusions of Law, July 15, 1997.

lab, stating that the problems are systemic—such as scientific testing being conducted by FBI agents rather than scientists and a failure to implement and follow scientific protocols. But the most serious claim is that the FBI lab suffers from a pro-prosecution bias. The lab works to secure convictions, which means in practical terms that the Bureau is beginning with a presumption of guilt and looking for evidence to prove the assumption. This has led in practice to FBI agents overstating conclusions when testifying in courtrooms and even to the withholding of exculpatory information from defendants. Although the authors do not examine the evidence in the Williams case, they unequivocally state that this pro-prosecution bias has led to the conviction of innocent individuals.[72]

In a series of cases beginning with Brady v. Maryland, the Supreme Court has held that the prosecution in a criminal trial is obligated to seek out any exculpatory evidence and provide the defense with the information. The withholding of such information amounts to an unconstitutional denial of due process. The standard to be applied in determining whether a due process violation has occurred is "if there is a reasonable probability that, had the evidence been disclosed to the defense, the result of the proceeding would have been different." The obvious policy behind this rule is to avoid imprisoning innocent individuals, and such a finding by Butts County Superior Court Judge Hal Craig would result in the ordering of a new trial.[73]

Described by Georgia Assistant Attorney General Mary Beth Westmoreland as "the longest running petition for habeas corpus in Georgia history," Judge Craig finally denied the motion in July 1998.

---

[72]David Johnston and Andrew C. Revkin, "Report Finds FBI Lab Slipping From Pinnacle of Crime Fighting," *New York Times*, January 29, 1997, 1; David Johnston, "FBI Lab Practices Faulted In Oklahoma Bomb Inquiry," *New York Times*, January 31, 1997, 1; John F. Kelley and Phillip K. Wearne, *Tainting Evidence: Inside the Scandals at the FBI Crime Lab* (New York: Free Press, 1998).

[73]In the Superior Court of Butts County, State of Georgia, *Williams v. Zant*, File # 85-CV-410, Proposed Order of the Court Findings of Fact and Conclusions of Law, July 15, 1997; *Brady v. Maryland*, 373 U.S. 83 (1963); *United States v. Bagley*, 473 U.S. 667 (1985); *Kyles v. Whitley*, 514 U.S. 419 (1995).

The judge dismissed the claims that potentially exculpatory informa-tion was withheld as irrelevant when considered in light of the witness testimony and scientific evidence used to convict Williams. It may be impossible to ever state with absolute certainty that Wayne Williams is guilty. Some of the assertions made by the press arguing that Williams is innocent are preposterous on their face, but the argu-ments put forward in the Petition for Habeas Corpus must be taken seriously. In the case of Wayne Williams, as so often occurs in the messy world of criminal law, the finders of fact do not have the benefit of a "smoking gun," forced to pass judgment instead on a "loud splash." There will be no easy answers in this case and the refusal of the court to grant the Petition for Habeas Corpus has not yet ended the matter—Williams's attorneys plan to appeal the ruling to the Georgia Supreme Court.[74]

After decades of attempting to distance Atlanta from other southern cities, the business elite, often in collusion with the city's political elite, succeeded in creating a culture of appearances. The child murders crisis cut through the artifice by exposing the true nature of Atlanta's social problems. Although Atlanta ranked as the thirtieth largest city in the nation, its concentration of public housing was the third highest. In addition, a large income gap existed between whites and blacks. Despite possessing a sizable and growing black middle class, most black Atlantans lived in impoverished areas. "[P]overty in our city," lamented Mayor Jackson, "poses a grave, persisting and escalating problem if not confronted by systematic, coordinated efforts." Atlanta's poverty level, at twenty-three percent, was double the national average. In 1980, the white unemployment rate in Atlanta stood at three and a half percent, but for blacks the number was 9.4 percent. Unemployed blacks were also more likely to spend a greater amount of time jobless than were unemployed whites. Moreover, because Atlanta experienced a loss of industrial jobs as it moved toward a white-collar economy, the unemployment rate for

[74]Mary Beth Westmoreland, telephone conversation with author, September 12, 1997; Rick Bragg, "Convictions Are Upheld in Atlanta," *New York Times*, July 11, 1998, A6.

blacks showed little potential for improvement. Finally, white flight meant an eroding tax-base for the city and despite the best efforts of organizations such as CAP, downtown businesses followed white residents into the suburbs.[75]

If the child murders revealed anything, it was that "the city too busy to hate" had not yet escaped the problems of race. As the James Baldwin essay and continuing conspiracy arguments reveal, the notion that Atlanta's leaders would go to any extent, including covering up evidence of Klan murders and sending an innocent man to prison to prevent a race war that would prove devastating to the city's economy, retains a strong appeal. In response, some business leaders such as CAP president Dan Sweat expressed dismay that the murders were "driving a wedge into what has been great progress in the city involving all segments of the community." But Michael Trotter of the Atlanta Action Forum, a group of thirty powerful business and political elites, noted a growing "white backlash" by those who believed they had helped in every way they could but received only criticism in return. "If you express concern about the problem you may be viewed as criticizing black leadership," Trotter noted, "But if you don't speak out, you're considered not caring." Trotter's comments exhibited a continuing level of discomfort that white business leaders felt with Atlanta's African American power structure.[76]

The city of Atlanta spent decades scrambling to position itself as the hub of the southeast. Image conscious at all times, through its policy of racial moderation, the city hoped to distinguish itself from the remainder of the South and as a result grow and prosper. It was a remarkably successful strategy. Atlanta projected an image of a progressive city, and business boomed. Growth brought with it,

---

[75]Reginald Stuart, "Tension Over Atlanta Killings Tests Racial Harmony," *New York Times*, March 24, 1981, 16; Harmon, *Beneath the Image*, 310-311; Charles Jaret, "Black Migration and Socioeconomic Inequality in Atlanta and the Urban South," *Humboldt Journal of Social Relations* 14 (1987): 68-71, 80-97.

[76]Reginald Stuart, "Tension Over Atlanta Killings Tests Racial Harmony," *New York Times*, March 24, 1981, 16.

however, a corresponding array of urban social problems. With the ascension of a black political power structure, moreover, the response of the white elite demonstrated that the issue of race had not yet been resolved. Despite the city's best efforts to continue the illusion of prosperity and racial peace, Atlanta was revealed as possessing all the problems of a large metropolis after the child murders brought the city's social and racial problems into sharp relief. "I wonder," mused Georgia state senator Julian Bond, "if in its own way this means that Atlanta is finally becoming the city it's always wanted to be."[77]

---

[77]Julian Bond, quoted in Reginald Stuart, "Tension Over Atlanta Killings Tests Racial Harmony," *New York Times*, March 24, 1981, 16.

8

ASA/FORREST CARTER AND REGIONAL/POLITICAL IDENTITY[1]

Jeff Roche

In May 1974, lifelong white supremacist and southern terrorist Asa "Ace" Carter strode into the Anniston, Alabama, office of the Federal Bureau of Investigation and asked the agent in charge for an audience. Though shocked, the agent agreed. The FBI had been monitoring Carter, a former Klansman, speech writer for George Wallace, bombing suspect, and, at the time, the leader of a paramilitary white supremacist group called the Southerners, for almost twenty years. FBI officers had questioned Carter on numerous occasions since the 1950s usually concerning the bombings of African Americans' homes in the Birmingham area.

Apparently, however, Carter was ready to leave his past behind him. The previous fall he had self-published his first novel, and was at that moment writing two other books. Carter explained to the

[1]I would like to thank Margaret Connell-Szasz, Catherine Kleiner, and Rex Renk for their many helpful suggestions, along with John Boles for his insightful critique of and helpful recommendations when this essay was in its early stages. I owe a great debt to David Farber for helping me to place Asa/Forrest Carter in the context of postwar regional political cultures. Ferenc Szasz not only offered penetrating analysis and superb editorial suggestions, but taught the graduate seminar in biography that produced the original draft of this essay. Lastly, I would like to thank the late Howard N. Rabinowitz not only for his contributions to this essay, but also for his guidance while I attended the University of New Mexico.

agent that he had a potential movie offer for his first book, had acquired the services of a literary agent, and that his new career would require frequent travel outside Alabama. He promised the agent that the FBI could reach him anytime and provided two telephone numbers of people who would always know his whereabouts. Carter made clear that he would find it embarrassing if the FBI contacted his agent or publishing firm in an effort to find him. The skeptical FBI agent asked Carter if there was a particular reason that the FBI might need to reach him. Carter answered no, but it had been two years since his last interview and he wanted to make sure that he was accessible. For the first time in his life, he explained, he was going to make some money, and he did not want anything to go wrong. Then, Ace Carter walked out of the FBI office and ceased to exist.[2]

Twenty-six months later, Asa Carter, now calling himself Forrest Carter, was the toast of the Dallas, Texas, literary scene. His first novel, *Gone To Texas*, (originally published as *The Rebel Outlaw Josey Wales*) had been made into a major motion picture directed by and starring actor Clint Eastwood. Carter had moved to Abilene in summer 1974 and had told everyone that his name was Forrest. To explain his past, he declared that he had been a wandering cowboy since being orphaned at ten. He also claimed a Native American heritage and that he was one-half Cherokee. As Forrest, Carter published four books, and although rumors of his Alabama past dogged him until his death in 1979, he never abandoned his facade. When asked about "Ace," Forrest changed the subject or mumbled something about a no account brother or cousin. Amazingly, neither his agent nor anyone affiliated with Dell Books (his publisher) pressed him for details even after a 1976 *New York Times* article claimed that novelist Forrest and white supremacist Asa shared an identity. In a conversation with his agent Eleanor Friede, Carter offered to take a fingerprint test. She refused to call his bluff.

---

[2]U.S. Department of Justice. Federal Bureau of Investigation Files and Records. Asa Earl Carter File. File Number 157-4634 and 100-4651 (Carter FBI File).

Forrest seemed to be exactly what people wanted—a larger-than-life cowboy and sensitive Native American. He cried at the mention of Wounded Knee or the Trail of Tears; he danced Cherokee "war dances" or jumped on stage to sing "cowboy" tunes when out on the town; he disappeared for weeks at time to "fast" and get in touch with nature; and, on his return, he regaled his friends with fabulous tales from Hollywood, the reservation, the ranch, or the mountains. Forrest Carter represented a piece of frontier America that many believed had been lost. He was, simply, a mythological character from the Old West, charming, witty, and never at a loss for some piece of homespun philosophy or Native American wisdom. As a folksy raconteur and as a novelist, he offered simple solutions to complex problems. Moreover, his guise of cowboy/Indian enabled Carter to appropriate and exploit two seemingly contradictory halves of American frontier mythology—the rugged individualism of the cowboy/pioneer who had carved an existence from the harsh landscape and the wisdom of the noble savage who was able to coexist with nature.

The strange tale of the transformation of Asa Carter, professional white supremacist into Forrest Carter, mythological figure come to life, is interesting for its own sake. It is perhaps more powerful, however, as an example of how social and political conservatives have appropriated frontier mythology and symbolism to promote a particular agenda. Since the sixties, politicians from the far right wing have incorporated the myth of "rugged individualism" to promote libertarianism and social conservatism. Throughout his 1964 presidential campaign, Barry Goldwater played to his western background and cowboy image. In his campaigns, Ronald Reagan not only relied upon his own past portrayals of western characters in film and on television to hearken back to some nineteenth–century ideal, but also received political endorsements from "Rifleman" Chuck Connors and perennial western actor John Wayne.[3]

As a right-wing political zealot, Asa Carter lurked at the fringes of normative political culture. His career exemplified the most radical strains of right-wing ideology: an intense paranoia over Communism and Communist plots, a reactionary backlash against the civil rights movement, and employing Protestant religious fervor as a political tool. Moreover, Ace Carter consistently packaged his message as a modern version of mythic Confederate ideology, tying his political philosophy to the symbols and figures of the Lost Cause. Like many conservatives, he looked backward for models of political structure and behavior. If, as Dan T. Carter has suggested, modern conservatism has its roots in postwar racist politics, Ace Carter played an important role among the grass roots advocates of this neo-Confederate conservatism. I would argue, however, that although southern conservatives are certainly principal constituents of the New Right and have helped to carve out its agenda, western symbolism and appeals to frontier mythology have provided the New Right with a language understood by Americans from all regions. As both Ace and Forrest, Carter demonstrates the regional political idioms that postwar conservatives have used to achieve power.[4]

Born in 1925 in Anniston, Carter spent most of his life in northern Alabama. He graduated from Oxford High School in 1943 and enlisted in the Navy, where he served three years, part of that time in the Pacific Theater. After his discharge, Carter attended the

---

[3]For more on Goldwater and Reagan and their use of western symbolism see Kurt Schuparra, *Triumph of the Right: The Rise of the California Conservative Movement, 1945-1966* (Armonk, New York, 1998), 83-84, 89-91,127-128, 142; Robert Goldberg, *Barry Goldwater* (New Haven, Connecticut: Yale University Press, 1995) 133-134; Peter Iverson's, *Barry Goldwater: Native Arizonan* (Norman: University of Oklahoma Press, 1997) focuses on Goldwater's career as a western political figure. Richard Slotkin, *Gunfighter Nation: The Myth of the Frontier in Twentieth-Century America* (New York: HarperPerennial, 1993), 643-654.

[4]Dan T. Carter, *The Politics of Rage: George Wallace, The Origins of the New Conservatism, and the Transformation of American Politics* (New York: Simon and Schuster, 1995); *From George Wallace to Newt Gingrich: Race in the Conservative Counterrevolution* (Baton Rouge: Louisiana State University Press, 1996.

University of Colorado, became a radio announcer, and worked in Denver and Mississippi before returning to Alabama in 1953. The next year, the American States' Rights Association, a white supremacy group, sponsored a radio program hosted by Carter on WILD in Birmingham. Carter broadcast white supremacist ideology and anti-Communist rhetoric on a twenty-station network for over a year. When his anti-Semitic remarks caused advertisers to boycott the station, WILD fired Carter. By that time, however, he had become a leader in the statewide organization of White Citizens' Councils.[5]

Seeking respectability and a constitutional (non-racist) basis for rejecting the *Brown* edict, the business-like council leaders continually clashed with Carter over his anti-Semitism and violent rhetoric.[6] For his part, Carter tired quickly of the chamber of commerce atmosphere of the Alabama councils and founded his own North Alabama Citizens Council (NACC) drawing his membership from the white working-class residents in and around Birmingham. Carter also helped found the Original Ku Klux Klan of the Confederacy (OKKKC), a paramilitary "branch" of the NACC. Carter's NACC-OKKKC members established a reputation for extreme violence. They incited riots when Autherine Lucy attempted to integrate the University of Alabama in 1956. Four members of Carter's Klan group were sentenced to twenty years in prison for castrating a randomly chosen black handyman in their clubhouse as an "initiation" ceremony. (George Wallace later paroled the perpetrators during his first administration.) On another occasion, several of Carter's colleagues

---

[5]After the 1954 *Brown v. Board of Education* decision, businessmen throughout the South organized county-based councils to combat desegregation through economic intimidation rather than violence. Largely due to Carter, Alabama boasted one of the strongest state council organizations. For more on the Citizen Council movement see Neil A. McMillen, *The Citizens' Councils: Organized Resistance to the Second Reconstruction, 1954-1964* (Urbana: University of Illinois Press, 1971); and Numan V. Bartley, *The Rise of Massive Resistance: Race and Politics in the South During the 1950s* (Baton Rouge: Louisiana State University Press, 1969).

[6]For more on the competing strands of thought prevalent among massive resistance leaders see David L. Chappell, "The Divided Mind of Southern Segregationists," *Georgia Historical Quarterly* 82 (Spring 1998): 45-72.

jumped on a Birmingham stage during a Nat "King" Cole concert and beat the black singer. When told of the attack on the man that Carter once had called "a vicious agitator for integration," he defended the men and said, "I've swung on niggers myself."[7]

After being arrested and later released for shooting two members of his Klan group after they questioned him about the group's finances, Carter faded from the public scene and opened a dry cleaning business and a gas station. The FBI, however, suspected that Carter went underground and was behind several bombings of African American homes and churches across the South. Carter occasionally resurfaced to run for public office. He ran against Eugene "Bull" Conner for police commissioner in 1957 and lost. And, in 1958, he finished a distant fifth in the Democratic primary for Lieutenant Governor, but gained the attention of George Wallace, who hired Carter as a speech writer for his 1962 gubernatorial campaign.[8]

From 1962 until 1970, Wallace and Carter enjoyed a symbiotic relationship. Wallace provided Carter with a powerful tool to express his ideas, and Carter provided Wallace with the rhetoric needed to make him the most powerful man in the history of Alabama politics. Carter's speeches were widely credited for Wallace's successful 1962 gubernatorial campaign. Carter also penned Wallace's 1963 inauguration speech that brought Wallace national attention. Just when it seemed that massive resistance had gasped its last breath and that white southerners were resigned to at least token integration of public schools, Wallace stood on the statehouse steps in Montgomery and trumpeted Carter's words: "I draw a line in the dust and toss the

---

[7]Dana Rubin, "The Real Education of Little Tree," *Texas Monthly*, February 1992; Carter quoted in John Leland with Mark Peyser, "New Age Fable From an Old School Bigot?" *Newsweek*, 14 October 1991. For more on Carter's career as a white supremacist in Birmingham see Glenn T. Eskew, *But for Birmingham: The Local and National Movements in the Civil Rights Struggle* (Chapel Hill: University of North Carolina Press, 1997), 114-118. See also William A. Nunnelley, *Bull Connor*, (Tuscaloosa: University of Alabama Press 1991), 51; and Jim Auchmutey, "The Man Who Lived Twice" *Atlanta Journal and Constitution*, 27 October 1991.

[8]Carter FBI file. Eskew, *But for Birmingham* 114-118.

gauntlet before the feet of tyranny. And I say 'Segregation now, segregation tomorrow, segregation forever.' " Carter continued to work for both George and Lurleen Wallace during their respective terms as governor, writing speeches, and speaking on their behalf to extremist groups.[9]

By the 1968 presidential campaign, candidate George Wallace and Carter had apparently come to disagree on the usefulness of racial politics on a national scale. Carter urged the governor to use racially charged phrases like "race-mixing." Wallace, however, while preaching the same message, used code words like "busing" and "law and order" to make a racist appeal.[10] The two men officially parted company during the 1970 gubernatorial campaign. That year Asa Carter ran for governor against George Wallace.

Buying air time on local television and radio stations to broadcast his speeches, Carter, whose campaign slogan was "Save the Children," promised that, if elected, he would personally pull all white children out of integrated schools. He urged voters to "get rid of the professional politicians who are building their selfish careers off the broken spirits, destroyed minds, and degenerated morals of our children." Garnering only 15,000 votes, he finished last in the Democratic Primary. Even worse, his financial losses in the campaign forced him back into the Wallace camp. Facing a runoff against a popular incumbent (Albert Brewer, who had been elected Lieutenant Governor in 1966, and had taken office upon the death of Lurleen Wallace in May 1968), Wallace conducted a vicious, underhanded, racist campaign perhaps unparalleled in the annals of modern American politics.[11]

---

[9]See Dan T. Carter, "The Transformation of a Klansman," *New York Times* , 4 October 1991.

[10]Dana Rubin, "The Real Education of Little Tree"; Auchmuty "The Man Who Lived Twice." For an excellent explication of Wallace's campaigns reflecting changes in American political culture, see Carter, *The Politics of Rage.*

[11]Carter, *The Politics of Rage*, 348, 391-395. See also *Montgomery Advertiser*, 5 and 19 February 1970.

Although his ignominious election defeat certainly doomed any aspirations Carter might have harbored for public office, he quickly seized on the possibilities of marshaling the power of the 15,000 voters who had supported him. Carter formed a new organization—the Southerners—from the ashes of his defeat. Leading a large group of members devoted to the tenets of white supremacy could yield Carter considerable political power without exposing him to the vagaries of the electoral process. Carter also hoped to take advantage of the vacuum left by the decline of the Klan and Citizens' Councils. The councils had proven ineffective in preventing integration, and its middle-class membership largely accepted the inevitability of token school desegregation by enrolling their children in the exploding number of new private schools opening across Alabama and the South. Thoroughly discredited in almost every circle by 1970, the Klan was under almost constant surveillance by the FBI. Carter focused his energies on recruiting working-class whites who lived in cities undergoing the initial stages of desegregation.[12]

The first public act of the Southerners was to picket and protest the inauguration of the new "liberal" governor of Alabama—George Wallace. A reporter covering the event asked Carter about the protest. He responded,

> George Wallace has changed in the last eight years. . . . I think he has found himself getting too close to the White House, and he can't cope with the idea of being a racist who failed to win the presidency. I am a racist. I understand that. I fight for a cause I hope to win. If we keep going the way we're going, with the mixing of the races, destroying God's plan, there won't be an earth on which to live in five years.[13]

---

[12]Several of the FBI's informants shared in their reports that they believed that Carter's primary goal in founding the Southerners was to further his own career. See Carter FBI file.
[13]Carter quoted in Wayne Greenhaw, *Watch Out for George Wallace* (Englewood Cliffs, New Jersey, 1976), 158-160.

Over the next few months Carter gathered his followers around him and promised an organization that would eventually become an independent community. The group leased a parcel of land outside Mobile and built three steel structures to serve as a grocery store, a church (for tax purposes), and a school. Carter planned to achieve independence from local, state, and national governments and economies. He expected members to patronize the businesses of other members and to place the needs of the group above their own. Certainly aware of FBI and state police surveillance (there were usually FBI informants at each meeting), Carter continually stressed the nonviolent nature of the organization. He remarked in July 1971 that violence had disrupted or destroyed every white supremacy organization that he had ever joined.[14]

Carter continually reminded the members that they were preparing for a racial Armageddon. He warned that black militants throughout the South were stockpiling weapons (using money provided by the federal government) and were conducting military maneuvers. He predicted that these black revolutionaries would target and destroy southern cities and towns. At a summer 1971 meeting, Carter promised that the Southerners would stand aside and permit the cities' destruction. A murmur rippled through the crowd, Carter explained further, that accompanying the devastation would be the obliteration of urban power structures. "Just think about it," he smiled eerily, "just you and a Nigger and nothing in between." The Red Neck, he assured his constituents, would no longer be the tool of the Chamber of Commerce to prevent integration; the Red Neck would protect only his own and leave the businessmen, to the mercy of the Black Panthers, Communists, the FBI, and the federal government.[15]

The first step toward economic independence, the Southerners' grocery store, opened with great fanfare in August 1971. The proceeds from grocery sales would subsidize tuition at the all-white

---

[14]Carter FBI file.
[15]Ibid.

school, Carter explained at the gala opening. The store, with no shelves and featuring mostly off-brands still in their cardboard cases, failed to catch on with the membership. In September, Carter ordered every member to spend at least twenty dollars a month at the enterprise. The next month, the organization was broke, the store closed, and the canned goods repossessed. The school, which had finally opened that month (after three months of delays), survived for a few months and closed after the spring semester.[16]

Carter grew despondent, militant, and paranoid. He recruited new members from the state prison population and urged existing members to strike up friendships with white prisoners, especially those convicted of racially motivated crimes. FBI agents heard rumors that the group was stockpiling weapons and conducting close order drills in the north Alabama mountains. Carter surrounded himself by bodyguards. He told the Southerners that state police were harassing him and that his house and car had been "bugged" by the FBI. Asa began missing meetings. He told the others that he was working for several Texas politicians writing a "straight conservative line" and hinted that he might take the job permanently.[17]

There was no job in Texas. Carter had begun writing a novel. He rarely left his home in Oxford, spending his days in his pajamas, smoking Pall Mall cigarettes and writing longhand on yellow legal tablets. (Carter also spent many hours in the local hospital caring for his son, who had accidentally shot himself in the leg while cleaning his shotgun.) At least twice in 1972, Carter drove his ten-year-old Pontiac Catalina west to Sweetwater, Texas, to research his book. There he told the local librarian his name was Forrest Carter and began to weave the elaborate tale that would serve as his autobiography.[18]

In Carter's absence, interest in the Southerners waned. Membership plummeted. Only the hard core remained. One second-tier

---

[16]Ibid.
[17]Ibid.
[18]Ibid.

leader explained that he and Asa had decided that a smaller elite force would be better prepared to fight the coming race war. Finances remained a constant worry. Some members suggested selling Amway or Mary Kay products to raise money. On the rare instances in spring and summer 1972 when Carter attended meetings, his rhetoric grew more shrill and strident. He warned that the Communists had already taken over the federal government and would reveal themselves after violence broke out in the wake of the November elections. The group openly discussed how best to prepare for a guerrilla warfare campaign. Carter predicted that the government would begin to confiscate weapons and urged the members to hide their guns underground or in trees.[19] Members were urged to drop subscriptions to newspapers published by "states rights" groups, who had "sold out to the liberals," and instead purchase the newspaper published by the American Nazi Party. Carter claimed that the constant harassment by state policemen led him to always carry a sawed-off shotgun in his coat pocket. The group sought recruits familiar with explosives. Carter cautioned the members that one of their own had been waylaid and beaten by a "coalition of drug using hippies and sheriff's deputies." Late in 1973, Carter claimed to have spoken with God, who allegedly promised to help the group. Carter warned them that the only way to leave the Southerners was by assassination.[20]

Carter, however, found another way out. Claiming that buying a printing press and then printing campaign materials for acceptable candidates could fill the coffers of the organization, he offered the men hope. Carter then, most assuredly, began using the printing press to self-publish his novel, *The Rebel Outlaw Josey Wales*. Throughout fall 1973, Carter brought copies of the book to sell at Southerners meetings. He cautioned members not to confuse the Whippoorwill printing company (the Southerners' money-raising scheme) with the Whippoorwill Publishing Company that had published his novel. Carter, who had published the book under the name Bedford Forrest

---

[19]Ibid.
[20]Ibid.

Carter, sought to sell it through the Johnny Reb Book Club. (At an earlier meeting, Carter had announced his belief in reincarnation and predicted that Confederate general and founder of the Ku Klux Klan, Nathan Bedford Forrest, a man with only a third-grade education, would reappear in the body of an intellectual.) In December, he promised that he would share any proceeds from the book with the Southerners after taking a "small commission for himself to live on."[21]

The next month Asa attended his last meeting as a Southerner. Anti-Semitism dominated the meeting. The men discussed favorably "Hitler's final solution." Carter described Caucasians as the true Israelites and "the Jews as the Sons of the Devil." By summer, the group had faded into obscurity while its founder and leader moved to an island in the Gulf of Mexico, grew a moustache, lost thirty pounds, and became Forrest Carter.[22]

It did not take long for Asa Carter to adopt the characteristics of his new persona. In May 1974, the same month he met with the FBI for the last time, he assured his new literary agent, Rhoda Weyr of the William Morris Agency that he had several Indian friends ready to help promote *The Rebel Outlaw Josey Wales*. Furthermore, he told her that certain members of the Texas Legislature were prepared to introduce a resolution that would fine "any non-Texan $100 who is caught with the book in the state of Texas. A tongue in cheek kind of thing."

The next month he debated Native American philosophy with his publisher, Eleanor Friede, and offered her advice on how to deal with her father. "You can only reach sweetness through bitterness . . . light through dark . . . happiness through sorrow . . . laughter through tears." He signed his letter by circling the smallest of three trees drawn at the bottom of the page, surely chuckling to himself at the new uses he had found for his writing skills and gifts for aggrandizement. His publisher and his agent—smart, sophisticated members of

---

[21]Ibid. Carter had also named his son Bedford Forrest Carter.
[22]Ibid. See also Dana Rubin, "The Real Education of Little Tree," 94.

the literary establishment—apparently bought his charade with no reservations.[23]

Over the course of the next few years, Carter honed his fictional autobiography through constant repetition. In many ways, Forrest Carter's new life emerged as an anachronism, a story from the nineteenth century, better told by novelist Zane Gray or film maker John Ford. Carter's claims to be a half-Cherokee orphan from the mountains of Tennessee went unquestioned. The literary Horatio Alger life he claimed to have led charmed his fans and the literary world. Early in life, he said, the grandparents who had raised him, instilled within him a love of learning and reading that had lasted throughout his life. He later told reporters that thanks to his grand-mother's fireside readings of Shakespeare, he could recite from memory any scene from the Bard's plays. When his grandparents both died during Carter's tenth year, he said, he set out alone for the West and worked when and where he could as a cowboy, dishwasher, wood chopper, and at other odd jobs. But, he said, he never lost his love of knowledge and reading.[24] Carter once told a reporter, "everywhere I went, I would hunt the bookstores and the libraries . . . [they] are full of good people. It's kind of a world all its own. And they like to get hold of someone like me. They kind of educated me."[25]

A large part of Forrest Carter's image involved his experiences as a cowboy. He claimed to have had a "steel pin in [his] busted knee, [a] busted shoulder, [and to have been] tickled by a cow horn on the back." Wearing a black cowboy hat, bolo tie, and jeans on a much leaner frame, plus brandishing his dark moustache, Carter resembled

---

[23]Forrest Carter to Rhoda Weyr, 16 May 1974, Forrest Carter to Eleanor Friede, 6 June 1974. UNM Press, Forrest Carter, Josey Wales file (Josey Wales file.)

[24]Apparently, Carter was working on a sequel to *The Education of Little Tree* when he died. *The Wanderings of Little Tree* would describe the next ten years of this life.

[25]Forrest Carter's standard biography can be found in Hal May, ed., *Contemporary Authors* (Vol. 107); Geoff Sadler, ed., *Twentieth Century Western Writers*; Carter quoted in Leonard Sanders, *Fort Worth Star-Telegram*, undated clipping. Josey Wales file.

something from the imaginary West of the movies or western novels. He looked like Josey Wales.[26]

In letters to his agent Eleanor Friede, Carter polished his cowboy image. He described poker games, cutting and hauling "hosses," and other experiences "on the ranch." In one letter, a fifty- year-old Carter told Friede that he

> rode a race horse at the Anadarko [Oklahoma] Indian Fair ... but lost ... a Kiowa on a bay coming in first. ... It might near stripped me and the Comanches as we bet pretty heavy. ... The horse had no bottom when it come to the stretch ... being from Dalhart, Texas in the Panhandle ... and I have never trusted Panhandle bred horses to start with.[27]

To further his image as a wandering cowboy, Carter left return addresses from all over the South and West in his letters to Friede, often enlisting the aid of friends to mail the letters for him so that they would have the proper postmark. He told her that he could only write in solitude, after a period of fasting and getting in touch with nature. To Friede, Carter represented a larger-than-life character, and he carefully cultivated his charade.[28]

Once described as a man who "looked like Clark Gable and talked like Will Rogers," Carter practiced his flamboyant cowboy image at

---

[26]*Contemporary Authors*, 79. The description of Wales in Carter's first novel describes him as medium height and build, dark, with a medium moustache.

[27]Carter's use of ellipses in place of commas, semi-colons, and often periods is one of the hallmarks of his particular writing style. It is perhaps a lingering result of writing speeches in which ellipses might signify a dramatic pause. Carter's remarks about "Panhandle bred" horses make little sense (that particular region in Texas is world-renowned for its breeding of quarter-horses), and is more than likely a throwaway comment meant to make him sound more legitimate. Forrest Carter to Eleanor Friede (undated, probably spring of 1975), Josey Wales file. Other letters from Carter to Friede that include his "cowboy" comments include: 17 June 1974, 1 August 1974, (Undated letter, 1976), 23 July 1974. Josey Wales file.

[28]Rubin, "The Real Education of Little Tree"; Carter's return addresses from 1974, 1975, and 1976 include: Sweetwater, Texas, Ducktown, Tennessee, Abilene, Texas, and East Point, Florida. Josey Wales file.

every opportunity. Appearing on a Dallas, Texas, television program to promote his books, Carter walked in, decked out in his boots and jeans looking the part of a working-class cowpoke. Glancing up from under the brim of his hat, he told the host that he had just flown in on an airplane. Before the crowd came to the obvious conclusion that he was a hopeless bumpkin, however, he looked up, smiled, and said, "It was *my* airplane." Afterwards, he had the Texans in the palm of his hand. One Texas bookstore owner described the writer's charm: "Forrest had set up two of his sons in a Texaco station in town. He'd go down there sometimes and pump gas and clean windshields. He'd get to talking to a customer, and the next thing you know they'd be coming into the bookstore saying this guy was so interesting they wanted his book."[29]

Asa Carter rarely slipped in his portrayal of Forrest Carter. Western literature authority and friend of Carter's, Lawrence Clayton, described him as a "master of his material and master of his identity as Forrest Carter." He claimed that although the writer told different people slightly modified versions of his life, "there was rarely, if ever, a slip in the facade that he maintained." Perhaps, Clayton offered, Carter "just turned his back on his earlier life."[30]

The most unusual aspect of the creation of the Forrest Carter character was his Indian identity. Asa Carter might have had traces of Cherokee blood, but he certainly was not raised as a cultural Native American.[31] Well aware of this, Carter continually sought ways to prove his legitimacy. He dedicated each of his books to a

---

[29]Carter quoted in "Moccasin Telegraph," *Miami* (Oklahoma) *News-Record,* 29 June 1986; Carter's unnamed acquaintances, quoted in Jim Auchmutey, "The Man Who Lived Twice." Apparently, Carter had actually set up his sons in business in Abilene while he was still in Alabama and the leader of the Southerners. Carter FBI file.

[30]Lawrence Clayton, "Forrest Carter/Asa Carter and Politics"; *Seattle Times,* 5 October 1991.

[31]The truth about Carter's Cherokee heritage is still a point of contention, and part of the debate swirls around whether he can (or should) be classified a Native American writer. Carter's brother Doug claims that any Cherokee blood in his family is very distant. Eleanor Friede maintains that his great-grandmother was a full Cherokee, which would make him one-eighth Cherokee. Dan T. Carter maintains that Asa Carter was one-sixteenth Cherokee at the most.

different Indian tribe and claimed to share the profits with them. Carter also maintained that he was the "official storyteller- in-residence to the Cherokee Nation in Oklahoma" (no such position exists).[32] In a brilliant piece of self-promotion, Carter once had someone named Nevaquaya (whom he claimed was a Comanche flute player) send a telegram to the NBC *Today* program asking that they interview Carter about his book *Gone To Texas*. The telegram described it as "the first major book which accurately shows the character, the spirit and the moral of the Comanche." Nevaquaya (who was possibly Carter) asserted that the Comanche were "impressed" with the book and its message and wanted to "share" it with America." The scheme worked. Barbara Walters interviewed Carter live on the *Today* show in summer 1976.[33]

Carter once told a Newsday magazine reporter that he owed the origin and success of *Gone To Texas* to the guidance and the good medicine of his Comanche sage, Nevaquaya. His Comanche friend had assured him that he could write the book and that the spirits were behind his efforts. Further straining credulity, Carter then described a ritual that he and Nevaquaya conducted in which they revived the spirits of the famous Comanche chief Ten Bears (who appears in *Gone To Texas*) and the Chiricahua Apache leader Geronimo (who would later appear as the subject of the Carter novel *Cry Geronimo*). Carter claimed that the two legendary Indians "were pleased that [he], as a gesture of loyalty towards his own heritage, had pledged that his friends the Comanches, are going to share in the profits of the book."[34]

---

[32]Ross Swimmer, the principal chief of the Cherokee nation in Oklahoma from 1975 to 1985, said that Carter held no position with the Cherokee, honorary or otherwise. Jim Auchmutey, "The Man Who Lived Twice."

[33]Telegram from Nevaquaya to *Today Show*, Forrest Carter, Josey Wales file.

[34]*Newsday*, 10 August 1975. The unnamed reporter, although skeptical, kept a straight face because "along with the courtliness of manner, Carter carries an air which suggests that it would be good for your health to treat him politely in return. So one hesitates to ask him point blank how much of the Indian mysticism which he uses as a constant reference point is the baloney of showmanship and how much he really believes."

In addition to his efforts to establish his Native American mysticism as the touchstone of his personal philosophy, Carter also showed a compelling need to establish his legitimacy as a member of the Native American community. When Carter first sought an agent, he offered Rhoda Weyr testimonials for his *Josey Wales* book from a "full Chief of all the Creeks, [a] sub-chief of the Cherokee [and an] Apache and Comanche [who] are just Indians." Responding to a remark by one of Eleanor Friede's colleagues that in his photograph he did not appear to be a Native American, Carter wrote, "Tell your folks in the next picture, I will be a blanket head with a feather in my hair (Hollywood style) and write 'How!' on the picture."[35] After sending his book to Delacorte Press in 1974, Carter sent Eleanor Friede a copy of his "genealogy." He explained that although she could have a copy of the document "with seal," he could not part with the original "as it proves I am legitimate."

Carter's fictional family tree interestingly demonstrates Carter's racism by incorporating what Sioux scholar Vine Deloria Jr. has called the "Indian grandmother complex." According to Deloria, when whites seek to claim Indian ancestry they most often claim Cherokee and always claim that their Indian blood came from their grandmother's side of the family. He notes, "Somehow the white was linked with a noble house of gentility and culture if his grandmother was an Indian princess who ran away with an intrepid pioneer."[36] Forrest Carter's "family tree" lists five distinct interracial marriages over four generations, and, in every case, the women partners are at least half "Cherokee." Moreover, each of the men involved has exactly one-half more white blood than their wives—an all white man marries a one-half Cherokee woman, a one-quarter Cherokee man marries a three-quarter Cherokee woman and so on. Even in his own creation of a family tree, Carter could not fathom an instance where a "white" woman might be attracted to and marry a "Cherokee" man.

---

[35]Forrest Carter to Rhoda Weyr, 16 May 1974; Forrest Carter to Eleanor Friede 31 December 1974, Josey Wales file.

[36]Vine Deloria Jr., *Custer Died for Your Sins: An Indian Manifesto* (1970; reprint, Norman: University of Oklahoma Press, 1988), 2-5, quote on p. 3.

Even after his elaborate attempts at establishing himself as a legitimate Native American author, Carter still feared being exposed as a fraud. When asked by a friend why he had never enrolled with the Cherokee nation in Oklahoma, Carter brushed off the question by responding that he was a "little scared of the spirits of my outlaw Indian forbears. Maybe hanging around Apaches and Comanches so much has got me superstitious." In the months before Delacorte Press published *Little Tree*, Carter (perhaps after doing more research) wrote to Eleanor Friede and asked her to change some of the Cherokee words in the book, because, as he explained, he had used "breed words . . . which are kind of pidgin Cherokee. Maybe it would be in better taste if I substituted the pure Lsa-la-gi," he offered.[37] Before Delacorte Press published *Gone To Texas*, he wrote to Friede to express his hope that he would not cause her or the Press any embarrassment. "Eight or ten thousand Carters through that neck of the woods . . . bound to be some objections; maybe we ought to have just used the Indian name," he suggested. He also told her that he hoped that "the high Sheriff in Polk County, Tennessee doesn't recognize me . . . as I once left my watch, inscribed with my name, hanging on a persimmon bush, while running from a still."

In the same letter, he expressed doubts as to whether he should continue writing or go back to "making whiskey." He explained that the moonshining business was simple and that "any mess that you make is entirely your own without causing one for anybody else." He asked Friede if she thought he should use a pen name for the *Josey Wales* books to prevent western novel buyers from becoming confused. "I care little or nothing for notoriety or recognition," he explained, adding:

> In fact, it is contrary to my beliefs of the spirit. . . . I know Ira Houston's [Ira Hayes] family well. . . . What it did to him . . . and to other Indians. I want to help you sell the book . . . but

---

[37]Rebecca Chandler Prunkard, "Moccasin Telegraph," *Miami* [Oklahoma] *News-Record*, 29 June 1986; Forrest Carter to Eleanor Friede (Undated letter 1976). Josey Wales file.

use me or my name . . . ONLY if it helps you. I do not want any consideration of author . . . or personality building."[38]

Despite Forrest Carter's public and private denials that he and Asa Carter were the same man, his true colors shone often enough. While under the influence of alcohol, his personality often resembled the white supremacist "Ace," rather than the compassionate cowboy "Forrest." One night at an Abilene, Texas, steakhouse, a drunken Carter flew into a "racist rage," according to one of his dinner companions. On another occasion, Carter appeared drunk at a luncheon given by the Wellesley College Club in Dallas. Addressing the gathering, he stressed the need for everyone to love one another regardless of race or creed. Displaying his "benevolence," he turned across the dais and pointed to historian Barbara Tuchman, who was also being honored that day, and said "Now, she's a good ol' Jew girl." Then Carter pointed out into the audience toward Stanley Marcus and said "Now, Stanley, there's a good ol' Jew boy."[39]

For Carter, alcohol was part of his persona. When he went drinking with his friends, he often ended the evening doing what he claimed were Cherokee war chants and dances or jumped uninvited upon a stage to sing old western ballads. He understood his image and he played the part with relish. In a letter to Eleanor Friede, after hearing she was not feeling well, Carter (jokingly?) prescribed "whiskey [as] the best medicine. If you will measure out three fingers in a water glass and drink this every half-hour, and continue this until

---

[38]Forrest Carter to Eleanor Friede (undated, probably spring of 1975); Forrest Carter to Eleanor Friede (undated, probably fall of 1975), Josey Wales file. Ira Hamilton Hayes was a Native American soldier during World War II who became famous for helping to raise the American flag at Iwo Jima. Hayes, who died penniless and alone, was later portrayed in a movie by Tony Curtis. Carter's reference to Hayes as Ira *Houston* marked a rare slip in Carter's portrayal.

[39]Kent Biffle, "Texana," *Dallas Morning News*, 13 October 1991; Dana Rubin, "The Real Education of Little Tree."

you're well rid of it [the cold not the whiskey], you will feel much better."[40]

Shades of Carter's personal philosophy also appeared in his letters to Friede. He once described the problems inherent in writing western fiction and attempting to portray Native Americans as real people: "The liberal idiota builds a noble redman without human qualities, that['s] why the L-idiota gets disgusted when he discovers his cardboard idol has all the imperfections. The conservative idiota builds his "pioneer," white man the same way, and each one spends the rest of their days poking at the weaknesses of the other." Here we see Carter conscious of his incorporation of western myth and the ways that political activists have used frontier symbols to promote their agendas. He is claiming, however, to present a version of the past closer to reality. In another instance he expressed to Friede his feelings on the problems with American youth, who:

> feel no purpose, no future, [they are] children of disillusion-ment [who] try to hype their body minds with drugs [and] rebel against the hypocrisy of the body-minds who·run the world [and] to indulge in phony humanitarianisms, "civil" rights, four letter words, any thing to spit at the body-mind masters. So it is indicative they pick up the ecology kick, but they don't know what it is, or why, so they only play with it; and never enter the separate reality; for they grow older, and as cynical as their parents, and join the Junior Chamber or the Rotary, and they adopt the body-mind of materialism like a harness to strap their mind and a yoke to subdue the urge of spirit.[41]

---

[40]For a good example of Carter's antics while under the influence of alcohol, see Bob St. John's column in the *Dallas Morning News*, 17 September 1991; Forrest Carter to Eleanor Friede, undated letter (1976), Josey Wales file.

[41]Carter to Friede, 5 August 1974, 17 June 1974, Josey Wales file. The quotations in this passage have been altered somewhat. Carter had a literary habit of using ellipses more frequently that any other punctuation mark, and I have substituted them with commas when appropriate.

In this letter, many of "Ace" Carter's enemies reappear: the civil rights movement, youth culture, liberalism, and business elites, all wrapped up in "Forrest" Carter's phony Native American mysticism and cowboy conservatism. The Forrest character enabled Carter to express himself in ways that the Ace character never could. Critical of contemporary America, however, his message remained the same.

In the last months of his life, Carter dabbled at a number of projects: a sequel to *The Education of Little Tree*, another installment in his *Josey Wales* series, a screen adaptation of his fourth novel, *Cry Geronimo* (the story of the years before Geronimo's capture), and a book of poetry. He continued to drink heavily, and those who knew him feared that he would never be sober enough to write again. Their fears were confirmed when he died in June 1979. He was fifty-three years old. The ambulance driver dispatched to the scene claimed that Carter had fallen against a countertop in the kitchen and choked to death. The official cause of death was aspiration of food and blood. Carter reportedly had sunk into a drunken rage, fought with his son, and during the altercation slipped and hit his throat. His family told everyone that he had died of a heart attack while visiting his sons on his way to California. Forrest Carter continued to misrepresent himself even from the grave.[42]

Even today Carter continues to create controversy. His novels, especially *The Education of Little Tree*, remain popular and for many years, Carter's widow, family, agent, and publisher, continued to deny rumors that he and Asa shared an identity. A careful reading of each of his four books, however, illustrates consistent aspects of Carter's ideology. In *Gone To Texas*, Carter described the escape from his own past. The protagonist, Josey Wales, an unreconstructed Confederate, escapes to Texas after the Civil War. A peaceful farmer at the beginning of the novel, Wales is drawn into the war when soldiers from Kansas cross the Missouri border, murder his wife and son, and burn his house; Asa Carter believed that he too had been pulled into

---

[42]Lawrence Clayton, "Forrest Carter/Asa Carter and Politics," 20.

a "war" when northern communists brought the civil rights movement to the South. Wales joins "Bloody" Bill Anderson and fights
with a band of Missouri guerrillas known for their ruthlessness;
throughout his career, Carter associated with the most ruthless and
violent white supremacist organizations in the South. After the Civil
War, Wales refuses to surrender and slowly fights his way to Texas;
after resistance to civil rights weakened, with even George Wallace
making overtures toward African Americans, Carter refused to
surrender and slowly made his figurative and literal way to Texas.
Wales makes his new home within the physical boundaries of Indian
country and begins life anew; Carter made his new home within the
ethnic boundaries of a self-proclaimed Native American identity and
began his life anew. When people from his Wales's past began looking
for him around his new home, his friends lie and tell them that he was
killed in Mexico; when a reporter threatened to reveal his true
identity, Carter pleaded with him not to do anything that might "hurt
old Forrest."[43] While this is hardly a subtle reading of Carter's first
novel, it is important to remember that while he was writing the book,
he was still the leader of the Southerners—an organization dedicated
to promoting white supremacist and anti-Semitic ideology. Perhaps
Wales's escape to Texas was simply fantasy when Carter wrote the
novel, but from the time of its initial success in spring 1974, it became
a metaphorical blueprint for Carter's future.

Perhaps feeling brazen more confident after living as Forrest for
three years, or perhaps because of the success of his first novel, in his
next two books Carter became more explicit in revealing his worldview. In *The Vengeance Trail of Josey Wales*, Carter seemingly transfers
his southern racism onto a western setting. Rather than attacks upon
African Americans, Carter describes most of the Mexicans in the
book as violent, corrupt, and ignorant people. After a renegade band
of Mexican soldiers kills two of his friends and kidnaps another (the
same people who had protected his identity in the first novel), Wales
follows them into Mexico. Whereas in the first novel, Wales kills

---

[43]Wayne Greenhaw, Letter to the Editor, *Los Angeles Times*, 11 October 1991.

reluctantly, and usually only when cornered, in *Vengeance Trail*, he goes out of his way to kill as many people as possible. Carter justifies Wales's actions when he describes "The Mountain Code":

> Marrowed in the bone, singing in the blood, the Code was brought to the mountains of Virginia and Tennessee and the Ozarks of Missouri. Instantaneously it could change a shy farm boy into a vicious killer. . . . Josey Wales was conceived of the Highland Code, born of the Tennessee mountain feud, and washed in the blood of Missouri. It was puzzling to those who lived within a government cut from cloth to fit their comfort. Only those forced outside the pale could understand. The Indian—Cherokee, Comanche, Apache. The Jew. . . . The unspoken nature of Josey Wales was the clannish code. No common interests of business, politics, land or profit bound his people to him. It was unseen and therefore stronger than any of these. Rooted in human beings' most powerful urge—preservation. The unyielding, binding thong was loyalty. The trigger was obligation.[44]

With the exception of the inclusion of Jews with those Carter admired, this passage might have been lifted from any one of Ace Carter's speeches to the Southerners. Consider the core tenets of the code: clannish loyalty, blood oaths, an outsider mentality, self-preservation, and violent retribution. Compare the Mountain code with Carter's earlier description of the ideal white southerner:

> Through his veins flow the fire, the initiative, the stalwartness of the Anglo Saxon. Proof of his enviable reputation is the attack upon him. For such has been coined the words "red neck" and "wool hatter" . . . "cracker," and "hillbilly." He has accepted the words rather than fought them . . . accepted them for what they are: For "red neck," takes mind of the toil

---

[44]Forrest Carter, *The Vengeance Trail of Josey Wales* (Albuquerque, 1990), 247-248.

beneath God's Sun and with His good earth, of that he feels no shame; the "wool hat" has been his way, with little money, of wearing something "special" to God's house on Sunday morning: the "cracker" he adopts as his calling card of delicate cocksureness; and if "hillbilly" he be, then he exults in the high whine of the fiddle's bow that calls up the sound of the fierce Scotch blood that sounded the bagpipe of battle and lamented in the ballads of yore.[45]

Here we see again the clannish Highland ancestry, the confident swagger of the outsider and the code of violence seemingly contained within the "fierce" Scottish blood.

When Carter takes Wales, his ideal southerner, west he is no longer an outsider; Mountain Code and Frontier Code merge. In the process, neo-Confederate ideology and western myth melt into one—a criticism of centralizing forces, hatred and distrust of non-whites (except Native Americans who are seemingly the ultimate in clannish self-segregated societies), and seeking refuge from an all-powerful government. According to Carter's "code," protecting their distance from "illegitimate" authority (whether the Reconstruction government in *Gone To Texas*, the New Deal government in *Little Tree*, or the federal government of the 1970s) fosters a loyalty among western/southern men.

In *Cry Geronimo*, originally published as *Watch for Me on the Mountain*, Carter lambastes the federal government through its Indian policy and capture of Geronimo. Carter describes most U.S. Army officials as lazy, corrupt, self-serving egotists who only wanted to catch the Chiricahua war leader for their personal glory. Carter also continues to portray Mexicans in a bad light. In cooperation with the Catholic church, Mexican colonel Luis Gomez creates a program to provide workers for gold mines in Northern Mexico by capturing Indian women and forcing them to breed workers. Carter sums up

---

[45]From Carter's newsletter, "The Southerner," March 1956, quoted in McMillen, *Citizen's Councils*, 54.

Geronimo's personal philosophy as a perfect blend of Cherokee philosophy from *Little Tree* and "the mountain code" of Josey Wales.

It is in *The Education of Little Tree* that Carter most fully expresses his blend of southern and western ideology through hatred of the federal government and centralized authority. Meddling government is the chief antagonist for *Little Tree* and his family. His Granpa's "trade" was whiskey making, and he and *Little Tree* were always on the lookout for federal agents that who sought to "bust up" their still, and that, Granpa assures; "would be as bad as the Chircargo fire to the people in Chircargo."[46] The government also takes *Little Tree* away from home and places him in a state-sponsored, church orphanage, where he is unloved and unwanted.

Describing *Little Tree*, Carter once said, "I got in some good licks in this one."[47] *Little Tree* finally brought Carter the fame that he sought—twelve years after his death. In one of the strangest stories in modern publishing, *Little Tree* reached the number one position on the *New York Times* bestseller list fifteen years after its original publication. Then, at the height of the book's popularity, Forrest Carter was finally and permanently exposed as the racist hatemonger Asa Carter.

The story of *The Education of Little Tree* began in 1976. That year, Delacorte Press, a division of Dell books, originally published the book.[48] Carter had approached Eleanor Friede, an editor for the press with her own line of signature books (she served as the editor for Jonathan Livingston Seagull and had been Richard Bach's agent), with the idea of publishing a book tentatively titled "Me and Granpa." This was to be Carter's childhood memories of living with his Cherokee grandparents in rural Tennessee during the nineteen thirties. The manuscript, however, proved more than a simple reminiscence; it was filled with a Native American philosophy that

---

[46]Forrest Carter, *The Education of Little Tree* (Albuquerque, 1991), 71.

[47]Lawrence Clayton, "The Enigma of Forrest Carter," *Texas Books in Review*, Vol. 5, 1983.

[48]Carter originally self-published *The Rebel Outlaw: Josey Wales* and sold his copyright to Delacorte. The publishing house changed the name to *Gone To Texas*.

stressed spirituality, respect for humanity, and an environmental awareness—a message that found increasing popularity after the late 1970s. This was also when Carter sent Friede the manuscript for *The Vengeance Trail of Josey Wales*, the sequel to his popular first novel. Delacorte Press agreed to publish each of Carter's new works, but it published *Vengeance Trail* first. Friede explained that it was better to publish "two strong books, each with a good Indian background, before launching the very special, personal childhood autobiography of "Me And Grandpa" [later, *The Education of Little Tree*]." It was also likely that Friede and Delacorte wanted to capitalize on the success of the popular Josey Wales movie then playing in theaters. *Little Tree* sold a respectable 20,000 copies during the next nine years before Delacorte allowed it to go out of print.[49]

The Education of Little Tree tells the story of a recently orphaned five-year-old boy who goes to live with his grandparents. Using a breezy anecdotal style, Carter describes his learning both the modern and ancient ways of living. The universal messages contained in the stories allow a reader to recapture the wonder of a child as he discovers himself and his surroundings. His Granpa teaches Little Tree the ways of the contemporary world; he describes untrustworthy politicians, "if'n ye taken a knife and cut fer half a day into that politician's gizzard, ye'd have a hard time finding a kernel of truth." Later, he told Little Tree that many times someone could have "a half a dozen more words that could discolor the meaning of the same thing." This, Granpa explains, "was why politicians could git away with slickr'n folks and always claiming they didn't say this 'er that—or that they did."[50] He also warned Little Tree about college professors, "for he had heard that more of them was crazy than not." Granpa explained that organized religions fought too much over minor details in worship and that "if God was as narrer-headed as them idjits that

---

[49]Forrest Carter to Eleanor Friede (undated spring of 1975); Eleanor Friede to Forrest Carter, 25 April 1975, Josey Wales file. *Little Tree* sales figures from The University of New Mexico Press, Forrest Carter, Little Tree file.

[50]Carter, *The Education of Little Tree*, 79, 90.

done the arguin' about piddlin' such, then Heaven wouldn't be a fit place to live anyhow."

Nestled in a hollow in the Tennessee mountains, Granpa reflected on the problems in the larger world and its obsession with materialism:

> People who store and fat themselves with more than their share [will] have it taken from them. And there will be wars over it . . . and they will make long talks, trying to hold more than their share. They will say a flag stands for their right to do this . . . and men will die because of the words and the flag . . . but they will not change the rules of The Way.

The Way is, according to Carter, the proper way a Cherokee should live his life. "Take only what ye need," Granpa told Little Tree. "When ye take the deer, do not take the best. Take the smaller and the slower and then the deer will grow stronger and always give you meat." An Indian, Granpa said, "never fishes or hunts for sport, only for food [because] it was the silliest damn thing in the world to go around killing for sport." *Little Tree* seemed to offer its readers a simple, Native American philosophy, as well as a gentle criticism of modern society.[51]

Perhaps the book's biggest fan was Eleanor Friede. In her role as agent, she continued to represent the Carter estate after his death, and in 1985 she searched for a press to continue publishing *Little Tree* after Delacorte had dropped it. Friede approached the University of New Mexico Press about a possible reprinting because she had heard that it published books by and about Native Americans. Elizabeth Hadas, an acquisitions editor at the time, took Friede's call and agreed to read the manuscript. Hadas then recommended the book to the managing editor, who agreed to purchase the paperback publishing rights.[52]

---

[51]Carter, *The Education of Little Tree*, 85, 19, 153, 10, 9, 107.
[52]Beth Hadas, interview with author, 11 September 1996.

In the year between the UNM Press's purchase of *Little Tree* and its publication, Hadas and others glimpsed hints of the intensity of the book's following. Friede and Delacorte forwarded numerous letters to them from the book's fans to congratulate the press for republishing it and asking when they could expect the new printing. The initial printing of two thousand copies in March 1986, sold out very quickly, and the press continued to double the printing twice a year. Within a few years, *Little Tree* had turned from a pleasant surprise to the UNM Press's biggest seller. By 1994, the book had sold almost one million copies. It was translated into several languages as well as issued in Braille, large print, and audio versions.[53]

Almost every level of educational institution across the country responded favorably. Colleges and universities utilized *Little Tree* for classes on parenting, Native American history, literature, and philosophy. English departments assigned the book in literature and writing classes. Primary and secondary schools drew on it as well, declaring it an excellent example of introducing diversity to classrooms. Children and adults formed *Little Tree* clubs and discussed its philosophy and message. The Washington State court system used the book to help rehabilitate juvenile offenders. Broadway director Tommy Tune gave the cast, crew, and audience copies of the book at the opening night of his musical "The Will Rogers Follies."

Little Tree was a "must read" in book circles, and several public radio stations read the book on the air. Many people bought multiple copies to give as gifts to friends and relatives. In early 1991, *The Education of Little Tree* received the inaugural ABBY award from the American Booksellers Association as the book that booksellers enjoyed selling the most. The publicity created by the ABBY award

---

[53]The book was translated into German, French, Spanish, Japanese, Finnish, Dutch, Swedish, Norwegian, Portuguese, Thai, Chinese, Korean, and Czechoslovakian. Beth Hadas interview; the first printing of the book was 2,000 copies in March 1986, the second 3,000 copies in September that same year. The following spring UNM Press printed 5,000 copies and another 7,000 that fall. In 1988, it printed 20,000 copies, the next year 40,000, in 1990 60,000, and, in 1991, almost 300,000 copies. Little Tree file.

caught the attention of the *New York Times*, which began to track the book's sales for its bestseller list.[54]

The book's popularity is difficult to explain. Part of its charm lies in its wealth of literary devices that evoke laughter, sadness, nostalgia, or empathy. Many critics have called it "the Indian Huck Finn." Perhaps *Little Tree* provided the right story at the right time—a simple message in a confusing era. One reviewer pointed to its "utter simplicity—as if the boy *Little Tree* were the narrator of the beauty, power, and majesty of the earth as God gave it." A Native American reviewer described the book "as a Cherokee basket, woven out of the materials given by nature, simple and strong in its design, capable of carrying a great deal." *Venture Inward* magazine called it "a glimpse beneath the surface to the magic and wonder of communication and closeness to the Earth."[55]

The Education of Little Tree made its debut at number ten on the *New York Times* best seller list on 23 June 1991. By July 7, it had moved into the number two spot.[56] The book took over the number one position on the nonfiction paperback list on September 22 and remained there until reclassified on November 10. On that day, for the first time in its history, the *New York Times* moved a book from its nonfiction list to its fiction category. [57]

During 1991, the literary world was agog at the success of the little book that had become so popular, largely through word of mouth advertising. That fall, as *Little Tree's* sales figures grew, the story of the book itself gathered increased publicity. On 17 Septem-

---

[54]Several reports on book's progress and letters to the press describing its popularity with schools, reading clubs, libraries, and individuals can be found in the Little Tree file; *People*, 28 October 1991; Jim Auchmutey, "The Man Who Lived Twice" *Atlanta Journal and Constitution*, 27 October 1991.

[55]Grady Long, *Chattanooga Times*, 5 December 1976; Joseph Bruchac, *Parabola*, March 1989; Ruth White, *Venture Inward*, March/April 1991.

[56]The list also included Robert Fulghum's *All I Needed to Know I Learned in Kindergarten* and *It Was on Fire When I Lay Down on It*.

[57]*Little Tree* entered the "fiction" list at number six and fell off the list on 24 November. Little Tree file; *USA Today*, 11 October 1991; *New York Times*, 23 June, 7 July, 22 September, 10 and 24 November 1991.

ber, a member of the University of New Mexico's Public Affairs staff issued a press release relating the achievement of the UNM Press in making an out-of-print book the top selling, non-fiction paperback. The Associated Press published a story about *Little Tree*'s sales and other newspapers and magazines picked up the story.[58] Then, a page one article about the book that appeared in the 1 October edition of *USA Today* caught the attention of historian Dan T. Carter.

Then writing a biography of George Wallace, Dan Carter was quite familiar with the Asa/Forrest tale. He felt it was time to expose the hoax that Carter continued to play on unsuspecting readers. In an October 4 op-ed piece for the *New York Times* the Emory university historian revealed that Forrest Carter was really Asa Carter. Dan Carter briefly considered writing a journal or magazine-length article about the ties between the white supremacist propagandist and the bestselling author, when an editor of the *New York Times* convinced him to write an op-ed piece for the newspaper. In his piece he revealed that "between 1946 and 1973, the Alabama native [Asa Carter] carved out a violent career in southern politics as a Ku Klux Klan terrorist, right-wing radio announcer, home-grown American fascist and anti-Semite, rabble-rousing demagogue and secret author of the famous 1963 *inaugural* speech by Governor George Wallace of Alabama in which the governor trumpeted 'Segregation, segregation tomorrow, segregation forever.' "[59]

The allegations of Asa/Forrest Carter's career as a violent white supremacist created an immediate media sensation. Calls to the University of New Mexico Press began early the morning that Dan T. Carter's op-ed piece appeared in the *New York Times*.[60] Although the

---

[58]See for example: Angeline Goreau, "A 'Tree' Grows," *Entertainment Weekly*, 13 September 1991; "Little Tree Grows into Bestseller" *USA Today*, 1 October 1991. *Publishers Weekly* had closely followed the story of the book's rising popularity, beginning with an article on 19 May 1989.

[59]Dan T. Carter, "The Transformation of a Klansman," *New York Times*, 4 October 1991; Conversation with author, November 1995.

[60]A partial list of the news agencies that called the press that day include: the *Albuquerque Tribune*, the Associated Press, the *Chicago Tribune* (twice), National Public Radio, U.S. News and Features (U.K.), the *Steinberg Journal*, *Entertainment Weekly* (twice),

Press's director, Beth Hadas (who had been promoted from acquisitions editor), was not in the office that day, Peter Moulson, the marketing director quickly established the official stance of the University of New Mexico Press.[61] All questions about the truth of the allegations against Forrest Carter were forwarded to his agent, Eleanor Friede.

Since Carter had died in 1979—seven years before the UNM Press had published *Little Tree*—their only connection to him had been through his agent. The Press continued to defend the authenticity of the book, attempting to separate the work from its author. Peter Moulson called the evidence against Forrest Carter "circumstantial" and "pretty dramatic." "If it is true he [Asa] is *Little Tree*, he grew up to be a rather unpleasant old man, but it doesn't detract from the book. It's a beautiful book." Upon returning to Albuquerque, Beth Hadas agreed with Moulson's assessment. "People who read it love the book itself. Simply calling it a 'hoax' [a word several reporters had used in describing *Little Tree*] doesn't really tell the story. Carter must have undergone a personality change: it's hard to believe that those stories were faked. If he was a bad man he took on a new identity and became a good man." For several months, Hadas continued to defend the author, but only as a writer. She said that she would "like to see Forrest Carter considered in terms of confused identity and mixed blood." She continued, "It's my understanding that a lot of people in the Native American writing community have known this stuff about him for a long time, and while they considered him an unsavory, mixed-up guy, they didn't reject him as an Indian writer."[62]

Eleanor Friede, on the other hand, defended Forrest Carter in her responses to media inquiries. She categorically denied that the two

---

USA Today, the Atlanta Journal and Constitution, Montgomery Advertiser, the Daily Lobo (the University of New Mexico's student newspaper), the Los Angeles Times, Newsday, and Newsweek. These are the only documented calls found in the Press's files. Little Tree file.
[61]Beth Hadas interview.
[62]Albuquerque Journal, 5 August 1991; Little Tree file; Reid Calvin, "Widow of Little Tree Author Admits He Changed Identity," Publisher's Weekly 25 November 1991; Lingua Franca, December 1991.

men shared an identity. "It's the same old story," she said. "Forrest denied it when he was alive; his family has denied it. . . . [A]nyone who wrote *Little Tree* could not have worked for George Wallace. To me, it's just a very sad bore. I just don't believe it. I know it's not true." Carter's widow, India, and their children initially refused comment.[63]

Three weeks later, however, India Carter ended her silence. In a facsimile transmission to Eleanor Friede (India refused to use the telephone), she confessed that Asa and Forrest were indeed the same man, adding, "I thought you knew." However, she vehemently denied that Asa had ever been a member of the Klan, admitting only that he "was for segregation." Friede flew to Abilene, Texas, to speak with India Carter and to reconfirm that much of the *Little Tree* story was true. After the meeting, Friede told reporters that Forrest's childhood had been identical to that described in *Little Tree*, but that he had taken certain "narrative license" in some of his descriptions. She continued to assert that Carter's grandparents were Cherokee Indians and that the stories he related in his book were both true and well known to his family.[64] A diligent agent, Friede continued, "He always said he was a white man with Indian blood. I do not feel betrayed or hurt. I feel sad he didn't make it clear to me. I think he felt ashamed and guilty about his past so he tried to pretend it would go away. He was always unsophisticated and uncomfortable in society. I forgive him. He wanted to protect me and protect his publisher. I do forgive him."[65]

After the confirmation of Dan T. Carter's findings by India Carter, the UNM Press changed its official position only moderately. Beth Hadas explained,

I think that *Little Tree* is a wonderful book, but it always read like a novel to me. I read novels and I read autobiographies,

---

[63]Felicia R. Lee, "Best Seller Is a Fake, Professor Asserts," *New York Times*, 4 October 1991; Dana Rubin, "The Real Education of Little Tree."
[64]Reid Calvin, "Widow of Little Tree Author Admits He Changed Identity."
[65]Ibid.

and for somebody to come along and say "Gee, you know, this is really a novel" is not surprising if you read it. People don't write memoirs where they recount the level of memory that kid is supposed to have when he is that young. That's not the way memoirs are. The literary evidence always seemed to me to be very much on the side of being fiction rather than being nonfiction.[66]

As the controversy surrounding Asa/Forrest Carter, *Little Tree*, and the UNM Press grew, Beth Hadas and Eleanor Friede drafted a letter to the American Booksellers (the organization that had awarded the book the ABBY prize) to serve as a statement. It outlined their thoughts on the seeming duality of Carter's work and his previous life. Addressing her remarks to the "readers of *The Education of Little Tree*," Friede explained that although Asa had changed his name to Forrest the biographical information and stories in the book actually were a part of his past. Understanding this, she argued, was necessary to give his work "a fair chance." Friede further tied the individual stories and characters from the book to events and people in Carter's life.[67] She hoped to convince readers that Carter's earlier political activism did not represent his fully developed philosophy. Moreover, reflecting the perspective of Carter's wife, Friede asserted that he had written speeches for Wallace and other groups "to support his family." She claimed that the real tragedy of the accusations about Forrest Carter was the attempt "to focus public sentiment on sensationalized alleged aspects of the author's early life [that] denies his inalienable right to go back to his roots and adapt to a more

---

[66]Ibid.

[67]She specifically describes Carter's relationship with his grandfather, who had owned a country store on his farm, and some of the character from *Little Tree* that he met there. She claimed that he learned the lessons expressed in the book from his grandfather. Carter's brother Doug, however, told a reporter from the *Anniston Star*, that their grandfather had died when Asa was five, and it was unlikely that Asa ever really knew him. *Anniston (Alabama) Star*, 21 April 1992.

world-conscious order."[68] The UNM Press removed the words "A True Story" from the covers of all subsequent printings of the book, and in the 1998 printing added the words "a novel" to the cover.[69]

Perhaps Carter's widow, India Carter, offered the most peculiar insight into the seeming incongruity of her husband's two lives. She claimed that the Asa Carter of the 1950s and 1960s was a "fabrication" of the news media of that day. She said her husband was not an anti-Semite, nor was he ever a member of the Ku Klux Klan. He wrote speeches for Wallace solely to make enough money for his family, not out of any sense of hate, "and yet biographical details of an author no longer alive to defend himself are being brutalized by an investigator [Dan T. Carter] who is comparing past political activities to some form of contemporary political correctness." India told the readers of Little Tree that the book's philosophy "was so much a part of Forrest's being . . . he did not write Little Tree to make a fool of anyone. . . . He didn't have to change, to write this book."[70] In India Carter's defense, it should be pointed out that during the time when Asa Carter was most active in Alabama politics and in the Klan, he lived in either Birmingham or Montgomery and traveled home to Oxford [?] on the weekends. Several of his contemporaries suggested that he wanted to shield his wife from his activities.

Public responses to the revelations about Forrest Carter were mixed. People who loved the book wrote to the Press to describe their shock at finding out about Forrest Carter's former life. Many believed that the author had undergone a radical change in his personality and worldview. A Wisconsin man refused to believe that Forrest and Asa were the same man. "Something doesn't add up," he said. Another woman described her total confusion that a book that had played

[68]Eleanor Friede to the American Booksellers Association, 1 November 1991, Little Tree file.

[69]Beth Hadas to the American Booksellers Association, 1 November 1991; Official Press Release of the University of New Mexico Press, 1 November 1991. Both documents can be found in Little Tree file.

[70]India Carter to American Booksellers Association, 1 November 1991; Reid Calvin, "Widow of Little Tree Author Admits He Changed Identity."

such an important part of her life and personal philosophy could have been written by a man as evil as Asa Carter. "I am shocked that Forrest Carter is a racist, but I do not know what that means, and it only proves that 'the Lord works in mysterious ways!' I want to give copies of the book to people who will understand, but I do want them to know the real truth. Please help," she wrote.[71]

Other fans of the book condemned both Carter and the UNM Press. One woman returned her copy of Little Tree with a letter that expressed her "total and complete sense of disillusionment, frustration and anger that . . . you, the publisher, did not more thoroughly research the background of this author when apparently information about him was available." She continued, "once again white America has taken a piece of the Native American's sense of being and abused it by, of all things, the words of a white supremacist. I feel dirty and cheap for having been taken in by this author. There is no place in my life, or my bookshelf, for the words of a bigot and racist."[72] A bookstore chain in California (as well as other bookstores scattered across the nation) pulled Carter's books from their shelves after they heard rumors that the book's royalties went to white supremacy groups, including the Ku Klux Klan. (Considering Carter's earlier promise to the Southerners, this rumor contained a kernel of truth). In some communities, people demanded that libraries cease lending Little Tree because it contained hidden, segregationist messages.[73]

The University of New Mexico Press also received dozens of letters from university professors and teachers requesting more information about Carter and the authenticity of his work. Many pledged to continue using Little Tree in the classroom, but questioned whether it was a true example of bringing multiculturalism onto

---

[71]John Ebert to the UNM Press (undated letter), Cindy Gray to the UNM Press, 26 August 1992, Little Tree file. I have changed all the names of people corresponding with the Press to protect their anonymity.

[72]Laura Walters to UNM Press, 23 January 1992, Little Tree file.

[73]Various memos and letters relating to rumors, Little Tree File.

campus.[74] One bookstore owner identified the extreme irony in the fact that a book "that fit everyone's definition of multiculturalism [and a] politically correct book to read" was written by a man affiliated with the Ku Klux Klan. This irony was not lost on many critics who pointed to the book as an example of the limitations of political correctness and multiculturalism.[75]

Although Carter had little, if any, Cherokee blood and was most certainly not raised as a Native American, secondary schools, colleges and universities continue to use *Little Tree* in Native American literature classes and as an example of multiculturalism in the classroom.[76] Requests for the film, stage, and reprinting rights still flood into the University of New Mexico Press offices. One inquirer even asked for the rights to turn the book into a ballet. The film version of *The Education of Little Tree* was released in 1997, and although praised by many critics, did poorly in theaters."

Arguments over what role *The Education of Little Tree* might play in a curriculum continue to rage. One school of thought suggests that the book stands apart from its author—audience appeal is what matters, not the background of the author. Book critic Kate Seago argued that a distinction should be drawn "between the writer and his work." Historian Dee Brown agreed, "It's the book that counts, not

---

[74]Among those who wrote to the Press requesting information were professors from the University of Hawaii at Manoa (Education Department), California State University, Chico (History Department), Colorado State University (Native American Literature), and San Bernadino Valley College (English Department). Little Tree file.

[75]Doug Dutton quoted in the *New York Times*, 18 October 1991; "Native Cunning" *The Independent Magazine* (London), 6 June 1992.

[76]The Native English Curriculum Guidelines from the Province of British Columbia, (The province endorses the book as Native literature, even though it denies that Carter was native because the Cherokee nation has called the book "essentially accurate"; California State University, Fresno uses the book for a class on Multicultural Education, 26 August 1994, the University of Michigan for a class on Sociocultural Issues, 28 August 1995, Concordia College for a freshman education class, 20 May 1996, Riverside (CA) County School District for an unknown class 2 May 1995, Little Tree file, Permissions request.

the author." He asked, "If people like the book, what does it matter who the author is."[77]

Others have strongly defended Carter's "right to write." A British journal once chided Americans for their "suggestion that only a representative of a particular social group can properly create a character who belongs in that constituency" and called the *Little Tree* case "an extreme expression of a common modern literary dilemma." "Ventriloquism," the article states, "has always been part of what a novelist does. Now, however, there seems to be a requirement that the dummy on their knee should contain at least eighty percent of their own flesh." Writing in the *New York Times Book Review*, critic Henry Louis Gates Jr. argued against what he called the "as a" syndrome that one must preface every comment, critique, or observation by calling attention to one's gender, race, creed, sexual orientation, or nationality. As Gates pointed out, "segregation of these barriers . . . is hard to maintain in art, where the reader provides at least half of the relationship."[78] These arguments, however, gloss over the fact that the book was purported to be an autobiography and that Carter continued to present himself as a Native American until he died.

There are those who argue that portraying *Little Tree* as the work of a Native American author detracts from both "real" Indian authors, as well as the value of genuine multiculturalism. As critic Robert Allen Warrior put it, the interesting thing about the book "is the extent to which U.S. culture in general prefers a fraud like Asa Carter to tell them about Indians to going to the trouble of searching out reliable material, even if that material does not cater to their desire to hear about power animals and medicinal crystals." Geneva Jackson of the Cherokee Eastern Band in North Carolina once called the book "The closest thing to a farce that has ever been published in

---

[77]Kate Seago, "Bookmarks," *Los Angeles Times*, 13 October 1991; Brown quoted in *Entertainment Weekly*, 3 April 1992.

[78]"Native Cunning," *The Independent Magazine* (London), 6 June 1992; Henry Louis Gates, "'Authenticity,' or the Lesson of Little Tree," *New York Times Book Review*, 24 November 1991.

the Cherokee name."[79] And Geary Hobson, a Cherokee and professor of English at the University of Oklahoma, ridicules the book for its unrealistic portrayal of Indians, describing them as "sweet little creatures who can't do any wrong."[80]

Educator Michael Marker pointed out the most important problem with Little Tree's success. He argued that using Little Tree to teach about Native American culture is wrong, not because of the author's past, but because the book does not address the modern-day problems that Native Americans face. He avers that books that feature different cultures as slightly different versions of white America will not teach anyone the value of a multicultural education. He warned that "a continued diet of feel-good New Age pseudo-cultural pap will only produce a generation of ethnocentric ignoramuses ill-prepared to deal with the complexities of a bewildering modern world [and] it should be the school's job to expose, not to promote, the Forrest Carters of this world."[81]

Fittingly, it was historian Dan T. Carter who finally exposed the tale of Asa Carter. History, after all, will determine Asa/Forrest Carter's final legacy within the context of southern, western, and literary history. Asa/Forrest Carter offers an extreme example of how white southerners, deeply committed to the principles of white supremacy, have been forced to confront the malevolence inherent in their worldview. Times change. Before his death, George Wallace offered many public apologies for his segregationist past. Former Georgia governor and senator Herman Talmadge, a principal leader

---

[79]Robert Allen Warrior, "Selling Indians: Make It Painless, Make It Up," *Christianity and Crisis*, 13 January 1992; Jackson quoted in *People*, 28 October 1991.

[80]Another professor (and Cherokee) at the University of Oklahoma disagrees. Rennard Strickland believes that "the book captures the experiences of isolated pockets of Indians in the South. In fact, it shows that there's a common thread running through the lives of both Indians and non-Indian 'outsider' communities, which explains its universal popularity." Quoted in Calvin Reid, "Widow of Little Tree Author Admits He Changed His Identity." Hobson quoted in Dana Rubin, "The Real Education of Little Tree."

[81]Michael Marker, "*The Education of Little Tree*: What It Really Reveals About the Public Schools," *Phi Delta Kappan*, November 1992, 227.

of massive resistance, claimed to have been secretly working behind the scenes to help the civil rights movement. In his final years, former Arkansas governor Orval Faubus, who initiated the trend of "standing in the schoolhouse door," maintained that his efforts had been misunderstood.

On the other hand, Asa Carter retreated into the mythology of the West to escape his former life and promote his enduring message. When being a white supremacist ceased to popular or profitable, Carter became *both* a cowboy and an Indian. The public's acceptance of his western persona and his popularity as "Forrest" offer startling insight into the powerful grip that the western past still has on Americans. Perhaps what Carter's story reveals, however, is the similarity of the philosophy *behind* the myths of West and those of the South.

Public reactions to revelations about Carter's past, especially those that defend his work or claim for him some personal or ideological transformation, highlight the confusion over the Convergence of racism and politics in America. Many commentators have addressed politicians' use of code words to promote racist agendas—from more recent calls for school vouchers, to Newt Gingrich's attacks on "welfare queens," to George Bush's ads featuring Willie Horton, to Richard Nixon's use of the phrases "law and order" and "busing," to Ronald Reagan's support of "freedom of association" when promoting racist housing restrictions in his 1966 gubernatorial campaign. Little has been written, however, about the merger of the neo-Confederate ideology of men like Asa Carter and the symbolism of western "frontier" mythology. Beyond the libertarianism expressed in frontier code words like "maverick entrepreneur," "Sagebrush Rebellion," "pioneer spirit," "rugged" or "frontier" individualism, lies a blinding white vision of America. The frontier success story promoted for so long in American history textbooks and classrooms, as well as novels, television programs, and movies, simply does not include people of color.

Therefore, when post-sixties politicians hearken back to the simpler times of a glorious frontier past, they are doing more than celebrating individualism at the expense of the federal government. They are also romanticizing America's white past at the expense of African Americans and others whose fortunes advanced since mid-century. The image of a frontier past held a certain allure for Americans who were horrified over urban rioting, school busing, increases in crime, the growth of the welfare state, and the media's portrayal of the "excess" of the 1960s.

The same confusion, frustration, and anger that helped many right-wing politicians come to power in the 1970s and '80s can be found in Carter's books: a longing for simpler times, a deep mistrust of centralized authority and bureaucracy, anti-intellectualism, resistance to change, resegregation, and a hyper-reliance upon some form of spiritualism to provide guidance. Although some modern commentators have suggested that Carter's novels were nothing more than thinly-veiled defenses of segregation, this is a misreading. His books actually reflect a deeply-held core ideology, shared by many Americans, that went largely unarticulated until the nationalization of regional political symbolism and ideology. The careers of Asa/Forrest Carter provide an alarming example of how Americans' cherished myths and symbols can be appropriated for vulgar ends. Perhaps it is time more closely to examine the role of both western and southern myth in our current political culture.

9

EPILOGUE

Donald G. Mathews

Whether they are historians or not, people explain themselves and others through myth and simplified generalizations perhaps understood as types. If we transform "type" into "stereotype" we emphasize the pejorative connotations of a manifestly human propensity for generalizing about different kinds of people in order to tell meaningful stories. Myths are basically narratives we tell each other within our various communities about our common origins and how we came to be the people we are today. Inherent in the telling is a conceded collective identity, a "we-ness" that is not so much proved as assumed. Although those not sharing our collective identity inhabit our myths too, their difference from "us" is moralized so that they become antagonists whose existence reminds us who we are not, even as we conjure images to define whom we insist that we are.

These images and types—which are never subjected to critical scrutiny save perhaps by scholars and opponents—which populate our myths are not the conscious constructions of individuals. Rather, images, types, and myths are spun collectively by imaginative people from popular belief, common values, and consensually authenticated certainty that somehow create credible stories. These images, types, and myths are absorbed into collective consciousness as authentic expressions of what has happened, what is true about what has happened, and what is likely to happen in the future. Myth clarifies morality in self-justifying drama that recounts stories of "America," the "South," "Christianity," "Atlanta" and even *Little Tree* in such ways that we may find ourselves strangely included in the narrative.

The stories in this collection are *histories* in that they have been fabricated by the critical, perhaps even the skeptical, scrutiny of the sources and the narratives. But these stories also implicitly and in some cases explicitly deal with the pervasiveness of myth, type, and image—that is, with popular belief that seems to hide or at least to confound the historical. In the first essay, we may find that our own mythic understanding of civilians and soldiers caught up in such dramas as the Seminole Wars, is challenged by critical scrutiny. Yet the actors in the Seminole wars—as in all wars—encountered the reality of difficult times through myth; myths of Manifest Destiny, white supremacy, Native American degeneracy, and "the vagabond white man" were melded with the myths of Christianity and Republicanism in such ways as to belie belief that myth unites conflicted parties or resolves contested issues.

In another essay, the beliefs that have justified male power within the family from time immemorial are seen through the pain we infer from court documents that reveal the capacity of juries to provide partial relief when patriarchal reality belies the benefits to all of the patriarchal myth. Perception of brutality as the sad exception to the rule of benign patriarchy allowed the myth to continue unexamined save perhaps by its victims until the later, more politicized and realistic scrutiny of feminists. How the mythic aura of married life affected people moving from formal slavery to "freedom" after the Civil War may be inferred from the determination of freed people to establish respectable lives in the reconstruction of the South. The harsh realities that afflicted freedpeople in Wake County, North Carolina, immediately after the war were alleviated in part by valiant attempts to make real in their own lives the imagined opportunities of "freedom" and "family." To belong to one's own family in a brand-new status that began with the myth of human autonomy was—despite the cruel realities of poverty and hunger—liberating and the basis for renovation within a developing African American community.

The myth of Black Solidarity—never believed by African Americans themselves—is scrutinized here in post-Civil War Louisiana in such a way as to clarify the ways in which divisions among black people as well as whites' power precluded the ideal. Indeed, "free persons of color" had seemed to be an effective buffer between whites and slaves to such an extent that such persons could join a Confederate militia during the war to protect their interests. When slavery was ended, white power made all blacks equal, but even then, divisions among African Americans persisted and were sharpened by jockeying for political position to benefit certain elite persons of color rather than "the race." Aloofness from the slaves that characterized free persons of color persisted in decisions that continued to distance these people from the freedpeople. Mutual antagonism sustained by differences in religion, taste, behavior, and self-consciousness as well as politics meant that no myth of Black Solidarity could develop against the realities of class distinction and historical alienation.

The mysterious connections between popular belief, public discourse, and private reality are inherent in Asa/Forrest Carter's stories. The South of Klansmen, Confederacy, Nathan Bedford Forrest, and segregation was as much the imaginative fabrication of Asa Carter as were the artful creations of Forrest Carter—cowboy, Indian, novelist, and folk-philosopher. Asa's production did more damage than Forrest's; its hold on the popular imagination was made possible because so many others joined Asa in producing the same romantic story of valiant white men fending off those who would befoul Eden. This story Asa found difficult to sustain in the discourse and politics of the 1970s. Indeed, the man who had articulated Carter's vision—George Wallace—himself rejected the story that sustained it; so Carter repackaged the story, retelling it in the language of a West that resulted from the same kind of artifice as the Confederate myth. As if to emphasize that a once-confessed racist could understand the credulity, illusions, conventions, and pretense of liberal middle-class Americans—even multicultural partisans—Forrest dispensed a philosophy sifted through his own fertile imagination and his capacity for understanding what many Euro-Americans wanted to believe was Indian folk wisdom.

The debate about the *Education of Little Tree* suggests that Americans are more concerned about believing an appropriate myth than engaging historical reality with no illusions. Forrest Carter understood illusions, and, like Asa Carter, he created a reality from them. Forrest's illusions were made palatable in the "memory" of Little Tree; but they were essential to those of the fictional outlaw Josey Wales as well as to the all-too-real Militia who disturb our reality through attachment to their own myths.

Myths can be dangerous; myth and imagination killed Leo Frank. Scholars have puzzled over a white jury's accepting a black man's word over that of a white man in convicting Leo Frank. But it is clear that James Conley, a black janitor who, as much as anyone, secured Franks's conviction for the rape and murder of Mary Phagan, helped transform Frank into a black man. Frank conversed intimately with Conley; he was explained by those who thought him guilty in highly sexualized terms as if he were black; he was a Yankee; and he was a boss. His "whiteness" was obliterated by these "facts" and a mythic invention that imagined the worse possible inference from them. After all, Frank was a Jew; he was the ultimate outsider—even African Americans were Christian. Frank had not been baptized in the name of the Father and the Son and the Holy Spirit and was therefore impervious to the self-discipline to be expected of one who knew the saving grace of Jesus Christ! That Frank should have been helped by New York Jews seemed to seal his fate for those who believed that wealthy Jews thought they could always buy their way out of trouble. That religion and popular imagination combined to lynch Leo Frank is not surprising when popular convictions of right and wrong were so vividly dramatized in the morality play that white Georgians could imagine as they read or heard what the jury had decided and then—horrified—heard or read that his just sentence was to be commuted. Firm conviction in absolute right associated in the popular mind with a murdered girl and the mythic marginalization of an innocent man fit easily into the lynching mentalité that had been nourished in Georgia for over a generation. The fusion of patriarchal, sexual, Christian and tribal myths when mixed with the morality of absolute good and evil did not serve Leo Frank well as it could not serve any marginalized person who had been made black as the devil—that is, black as an African American. Such fusion justified a punishment of mythic proportions.

The child murders in Atlanta continue to be enshrouded in myths that arose as the old myth of progressive Atlanta slipped into the abyss of historical reality. The transition from a business-oriented, white dominated power structure to one capped by a new African American mayor was accompanied by racial tension and a rapidly escalating crime rate that was itself the source of new and dangerous myths. When black children became the object of a serial killer and when nothing seemed to be happening to stop the slaughter, myth birthed African American belief in a Klan conspiracy that had the logic of African American experience, if not empirical evidence, to support it. When a jury found Wayne Williams—a black man—guilty of two of the murders, myth prevented his conviction from demythologizing race relations, suspicion of government, official explanations of Williams's complicity in twenty-two remaining cases, and a pervasive belief in Williams's innocence.

The myth of Klan complicity continues to make sense in light of questions raised by Williams's lawyers, but empirical evidence still awaits the scrutiny of jury and judge. And if the myth of FBI infallibility has been punctured recently, the myth of business-dominated Atlanta still shapes the views of the historian as well as many Atlantans. That business leaders should want investors, consumers, politicians, and historians to believe the progressive myth is understandable; that those who benefit from it least should scoff is equally understandable. That resentment on the part of black Atlantans should target actions by influential whites on behalf of racial reconciliation is also credible. Myths of white perfidy, violence, and hypocrisy hundred years. Perhaps those who live by myth also perish by it.

CONTRIBUTORS

Angela Boswell is an assistant professor of history at Henderson State University in Arkadelphia, Arkansas. She is currently working on a legal and social history of women in Colorado County, Texas, 1837-1873.

Stephen A. Brown received his doctorate in American history from the University of Illinois at Chicago in 1999. He teaches at Roosevelt University in Chicago.

David Dillard is an assistant professor of history at James Madison University where he teaches courses on the Civil War and the Old South. He is currently completing a study of the Confederate debate over arming the slaves.

Randal L. Hall received his Ph.D. from Rice University and currently serves as assistant director of admissions at Wake Forest University. His biography of William Louis Poteat is forthcoming in Spring 2000.

Clayton E. Jewett received his Ph.D. from the Catholic University of America in 1998 and currently teaches at Austin Community College. He has published articles dealing with Confederate politics and is currently finishing a monograph titled "On Its Own: Texas in the Confederacy," an in-depth investigation of political and economic relationships in Texas during the American Civil War.

Nancy Lopez is a Ph.D. candidate in history at Rice University. Her dissertation is a study of the procedures, form, and function of two congressional investigating committees, the Special House Committee on Un-American Activities under chairman Martin Dies (1938-1944) and the Senate Civil Liberties Committee under chairman Robert M. LaFollette, Jr. (1936-1941).

Donald G. Mathews is professor of history at the University of North Carolina at Chapel Hill. He is the author of *Religion in the Old South* and *Slavery and Methodism: A Chapter in American Morality 1780-1845*. Currently he is at work on two books on religion and the American South.

David H. McGee is an instructor of history at the University of Georgia, where he recently completed his Ph.D. His dissertation is a community study of Raleigh, North Carolina, during the Civil War. He has published articles in the *North Carolina Historical Review* and the *Georgia Historical Quarterly*.

Jeff Roche is a Ph.D. candidate in history at the University of New Mexico. He is the author of *Restructured Resistance: The Sibley Commission and the Politics of Desegregation in Georgia*. He is currently writing his dissertation, "Origins of the New Right: High Plains Political Culture."

Samuel Watson is an assistant professor at the U.S. Military Academy. He received his Ph.D. from Rice University in 1996. He has published a number of articles and essays on the U.S. Army officer corps in the borderlands of the early republic and is preparing a book on the subject.

James D. Wilson Jr., currently a graduate student at Cornell University, received a B.A. in history and political economy from the Tulane University of Louisiana in 1995 and a M.A. in history from the University of Southwestern Louisiana in 1997. He has published several works in the journal *Louisiana History* and is co-editor of *A Dictionary of Louisiana Biography: Ten Year Supplement, 1988-1998*.